THE
DISASTER
PROFITEERS

THE
DISASTER PROFITEERS

HOW NATURAL DISASTERS
MAKE THE RICH RICHER AND
THE POOR EVEN POORER

JOHN C. MUTTER

St. Martin's Press
New York

www.stmartins.com

Library of Congress Cataloging-in-Publication Data

Mutter, John C.
   Disaster profiteers : how natural disasters make the rich richer and the poor even poorer / John C. Mutter.
      pages   cm
   ISBN 978-1-137-27898-2 (hardcover)
   ISBN 978-1-4668-7941-6 (e-book)
   1. Natural disasters—Economic aspects. 2. Natural disasters—Social aspects. 3. Profiteering. 4. Equality. I. Title.
HC79.D45M87   2015
363.34'4—dc23

2015001251

St. Martin's Press books may be purchased for educational, business, or promotional use. For information on bulk purchases, please contact the Macmillan Corporate and Premium Sales Department at 1-800-221-7945, extension 5442, or write to specialmarkets@macmillan.com.

First Edition: August 2015

10 9 8 7 6 5 4 3 2 1

CONTENTS

INTRODUCTION

CROSSING THE FEYNMAN LINE

AS NEW ORLEANS REELED FROM THE BLOW DELIVERED BY HURRICANE KA-trina in late 2005, many scholars described how the disaster revealed hidden social ills[1] that most people who lived outside the city did not know existed. I was one of those awakened to the difficulties of everyday life in New Orleans made visible by Katrina. I had been to New Orleans a few times, but, having stuck to the French Quarter and other tourist spots, I had no idea that it was home to one of the poorest communities in the country, that its crime rates broke national records, and that its public officials were routinely under indictment for corruption. But soon the academic literature, as well as the local and international media, pointed to these factors to explain the tragedy that Katrina—not an especially intense storm—had visited on that city.

Disasters can conceal as much as they reveal. What was concealed was the way a powerful few were able to use the "fog of disaster" that lingered for many years after the storm for personal gain and social reordering. This book is more about what is concealed than what is revealed.

BEFORE KATRINA, most of my work as a natural scientist had little to do with natural disasters and nothing at all to do with any subjects outside my field, such as economics or political science—areas of inquiry that are needed to see what is concealed by disasters. For the last several years, I have spent almost as much time feeling my way around the social sciences landscape as I have working in the natural sciences. And I have found that any serious attempt to understand natural disasters demands entry into the world of social science.

This book is about the way we should, but don't, think about natural disasters and about how we should consider the social consequences that result from them. It is hardly the first book to be written on the subject of disasters, but I believe it is the first book by a scientist that approaches the subject from both sides of the line between the natural and the social sciences. I like to call this the Feynman line, after Richard Feynman, a famous and tremendously influential nuclear physicist who wrote popular books and gave many interviews in which he was often asked questions like "Is God real?" He typically answered by saying such questions were outside the scope of science: you can't prove that God does or does not exist through scientific methods, so the question is not one for science.

I can't think of a better example of a subject that cannot be understood from natural science alone than natural disasters. Nor can we gain understanding of disasters by staying only on the social side of the Feynman line. Having studied seismology for many years, I know how seismologists think about earthquake disasters. They think, in a completely appropriate and entirely defensible way, that their task is to understand the mechanics of earthquake generation and the way seismic energy propagates away from a quake. We *do* need to know this. But in the past, seismologists also looked for—hoped for—ways to predict earthquakes; however, they essentially threw in the towel on that quest quite a few years ago. Seismologists learned that the prediction problem can't be solved if the objective is to say exactly when, where, and how large the next earthquake will be, even though many think that is what society wants. Earthquake prediction has moved to a mode in which probabilistic statements are more the norm, like weather forecasts. A prediction might suggest that there is a 50 percent chance of an earthquake of magnitude 6.0 in a prescribed area in the next 20 years. Seismologists now know that the nature of earthquake mechanics is such that probabilistic predictions can be made, but event prediction—where, when, and how large—is not possible.

I HAVE GRADUALLY COME to understand that the largest, most difficult, and most important problems we face in the world today cannot be solved by natural science alone, no matter what natural scientists might think or, frankly, what I myself used to think. While natural science contributes to solving social problems, it cannot be the only solution. The most important issues we face today come broadly under the subject of sustainable development: how to address climate change; the need to provide electric power to everyone on the planet without making climate change worse; how to feed an estimated 9 billion or more people by 2060; how to (and if we should) use genetically modified organisms; how to preserve the environment for our own good and for the good of future generations; how to improve the conditions of the poorest; and how we can counter the trend toward massive inequality in the world.

These issues cannot be solved by natural scientists who believe that their role is to work in splendid isolation, ignoring everyone and everything else, and then publish their results in scientific journals, where a crowd of social scientists will eagerly grab the work and use it for the good of society. But that's what most natural scientists think they should do.

IN THE DISCUSSION OF natural disasters (and, more broadly, of climate change), the words *risk, probability,* and/or *uncertainty* are center stage. A major endeavor in one branch of natural disaster studies is called disaster risk reduction (DRR to the cognoscenti). Daniel Kahneman, author of *Thinking, Fast and Slow,*[2] along with Amos Tversky, originated "Prospect Theory,"[3] which describes how people use probabilities to make decisions about risk. This idea is crucial to understanding how we all think about risk, probability, and uncertainty.

One of Kahneman's central ideas is that all of us have two quite different ways of thinking. System 1 thinking is fast, instinctive, and emotional. It is used for tasks like driving a car (if you have a lot of experience behind the wheel). System 2 thinking is slower, more deliberative, and logical. It is needed for solving crossword puzzles and math problems or using maps to get from one place to another. A well-trained professional mathematician would be able to get much further on a math problem with pure instinct—System 1 thinking—than most of us, but eventually System 2 thinking will be needed. It is System 2 thinking, whether in the social or the natural sciences, that is needed to fully understand natural disasters, but I fear that System 1 thinking has dominated most discussions.

In the discussion of disasters, the word *prediction* is a major actor, too, and often takes the lead, at least for those in the natural sciences. One of the most important roles that natural scientists (who I am sure would universally regard themselves as System 2 thinkers) have assigned themselves is the role of predictors—not predictors of disasters, exactly, but predictors of the natural disturbances that are associated with these disasters. As noted, prediction is very closely associated with concepts of risk, probability, and uncertainty, and sometimes it is the only actor on the stage.

Natural scientists tie their thinking to the physical events—hurricanes and earthquakes. But to understand disasters and what they conceal, we need to use the System 2 thinking of prediction, probability, and uncertainty from both the natural and the social sciences to see what happens before and after the events themselves. Those are the areas that we can affect.

Stating the probability of a physical event does not predict its social and economic consequences very well at all. Large physical events can give rise to trivial consequences while quite small events can have large consequences. What is particularly revealing are those instances when disasters have been more socially consequential than you would expect, given their geophysical magnitude. The 2010 earthquake in Haiti is a leading example. It was not what seismologists call a great earthquake in physical magnitude, but it was catastrophic in mortalities, injuries, and property loss.

And why did so many people die in Hurricane Katrina? Why were those who died mostly poor? Why were so many victims elderly? Why were most of the sad, distressed faces in the Superdome black? Why was the area so quickly militarized? Why did controlling the survivors take priority over helping them? What was inescapable about Katrina was how unjust it all seemed. Why did so many die in Haiti? These injustices had nothing at all to do with Nature; they were our own doing. We ourselves victimized the victims, not Nature.

NATURAL DISASTERS ARE LIKE a two-headed coin: They exist on both sides of the Feynman line at once. On one side is some sort of natural extreme—earthquake, hurricane, volcano. Natural science can tell us a lot about these natural extremes. On the other side, the result of Nature's tantrums—how many people are killed, how badly an economy is impacted and for how long—is entirely a social construct.

Natural and social systems are so conjoined that it is not useful to try to separate cause from consequence—do earthquakes cause earthquake disasters, or do people cause earthquake disasters? The answer is both. Natural disasters occur when Nature meets human nature under conditions of great duress.

Each time a disaster happens, the same questions arise, questions that simply have no natural science answer. Why do disasters seem so unjust? Is the world they stab at an unjust place, or is it that the poor shield the rich from the harshest effects of disaster? *Natural* science has no answer to this, but *social* science does.

This book does not try to catalog disaster after disaster, citing statistics and moralizing about how people should have been prepared but were not. If you are looking for image after image of destruction and death, you will be disappointed. Disasters are written about endlessly. After the 1912 *Titanic* disaster, there was an immediate avalanche of grief, including a vast number of poems that eulogized the sinking of the unsinkable ship. So many were sent to the *New York Times*, in fact, that the paper printed advice to authors: "To write about the *Titanic* a poem worth printing requires that the author have something more than paper, pencil, and a strong feeling that the disaster was a terrible one."[4]

Disasters are not terrible for the reasons we are told they are.

To understand this, we need first to understand the full scope of disasters. I will describe their phases, reveal their "evil" and "good" long-term outcomes, and discuss how such very different outcomes can arise from physically similar natural phenomena. We can then examine how these natural and social processes convolve, fast and slow, in disasters from Haiti to Chile and Japan to New Orleans. And once we've taken that journey, we will be able to see how disasters are manipulated for profit, both personal and political.

There is something more about disasters that I find quite troubling, something more than the spectacle that the news media feed on so gluttonously. This book is about the tragedy of natural disasters. It asks uncomfortable questions about death. It examines human nature as much as Nature. It interrogates to find injustice. It comes to harsh conclusions: it is human nature more than Nature that makes disasters so terrible. I hope that revealing what has been concealed will help us all understand the true harm that disasters bring.

CHAPTER 1

NATURAL DISASTERS

AGENTS OF SOCIAL GOOD AND EVIL

ARE NATURAL DISASTERS GOOD OR EVIL? THAT QUESTION, YOU MIGHT THINK, hardly merits asking since we all think we know the answer. Surely their effects have been relentlessly harsh and endlessly destructive. How could they have anything but a bad effect? People who live in disaster-prone regions of the world must have a tougher time making social progress because they constantly use their financial resources to rebuild rather than to invest in new institutions and structures like schools, public health systems, and judicial systems that bring about social progress. Even if help for rebuilding comes from donor funds or the World Bank, people still are only restoring everything to the way it was, with perhaps a bit of a face-lift, rather than promoting social progress.

This chapter shows that disasters are not as well-understood as we might think and that the good and the evil that result from natural disasters are not doled out equally.

DESPITE MASSIVE AND HEROIC EFFORTS by the United Nations (UN) and a huge number of country-based agencies, as well as uncountable nongovernmental organizations (NGOs), all aimed at reducing the risk of disasters, they *will* still happen. There is no evidence at all that people want to avoid settling in disaster-prone places, no matter how well aware they are of the risks. If anything, the evidence is to the contrary. In some small countries, such as small island states, the entire country may be disaster prone. We may eliminate the effects of small disasters and mitigate the effects of modest-size ones, but nothing that human ingenuity can muster will save us from the most massive of Nature's tantrums, at least not for the foreseeable future.

It makes sense to believe that disasters are uniformly bad but only in an immediate, reactive, instinctive System 1–thinking sort of way. Destruction all around and deaths in the thousands are certainly tragic. It is fairly indisputable that they are bad in an immediate way—death and ruin can hardly be seen as good (unless by a victorious army)—but the long-run effect is much less clear. It is surprisingly difficult to prove in any rigorous way that natural disasters are bad things in the *long run*.

Using the standard measure of gross domestic product (GDP) to describe social welfare and the statistical tools of econometrics that today's economists and political scientists rely on so heavily, it is possible to gain insight into some of the subtlest socioeconomic processes that influence our lives.

Natural disasters are hardly subtle, yet the few econometric studies that exist give contradictory results. Some say disasters hardly matter at all; some say all have negative economic consequences; others say some disasters under certain conditions can have a positive effect (e.g., floods often appear beneficial[1]); still others say that, on balance, *all* disasters have a positive effect.[2]

Many of today's social scientists use randomized control trials (RCTs) wherever possible as a basis for their research. RCTs were first advanced for testing new drugs by comparing outcomes for treatment groups (whose members got the drug) and control groups (whose members received a placebo). That's rather hard to do with natural disasters. The difficulty of finding rigorous proof of the harm caused by natural disasters may stem, at least in part, from the tools of modern social science, which are not suitable for the problem. Moreover, using even GDP has come under fire from prominent economists, including Joseph Stiglitz, the Columbia University Nobel Prize winner, because it doesn't measure social progress well at all, especially in poor regions where disasters might do the most harm. One of the major issues with using GDP is that a large fraction of the economies of poor countries is "informal," meaning that production is not performed by workers who receive a salary from an employer in the way we are used to in the West. No taxes are gathered on this work, and the government has no real way of knowing how much informal production is taking place. Poor countries often have bustling economic activity that is not captured by GDP. Yet, if the tools of modern social science fail us, how are we to know what disasters do besides the brutally obvious effect of causing death and destruction? How *could* they affect societies positively?

YOU CAN COME UP WITH plenty of examples and counterexamples to support or dispute any variation on the outcomes of econometric analyses. Japan experiences typhoons, earthquakes, tsunamis, and volcanic eruptions, yet until recently it was the second-largest economy in the world. So perhaps disasters are good for Japan, or perhaps the Japanese have learned how to deal with them swiftly because they experience them so often. The recent decline of the Japanese economy has nothing to do with natural disasters and more to do with disastrous economic decisions, a declining and aging population,[3] and a suite of other factors. And the horrifying earthquake and tsunami of 2011 actually didn't set the Japanese economy back, no matter how weak it is often now said to be, by very much or for very long, despite almost universally dire predictions of collapse with global repercussions.

Chile is buffeted by disasters much like Japan, though it does not experience cyclones and is the wealthiest country in Latin America. Does that mean earthquakes are dealt with more easily than cyclones? Argentina has experienced several highly destructive earthquakes but is otherwise almost disaster free, and its economy has been sliding backward for decades now.[4] Until 2010, Haiti hadn't experienced a serious earthquake for 200 years. Yet it has one of the worst economies in the world and is the poorest country in Latin America and the Caribbean—and not by a small margin.

In contrast, the areas of western Europe where the Industrial Revolution took off are fairly safe places. They don't flood much and almost never have hurricanes or serious droughts. Had those regions been prone to earthquakes or massive storms, say, mining the coal that fueled the power plants and factories and ignited the rise in human welfare that came with the Industrial Revolution might well have been more of a challenge.

Detroit is supposed to be the safest place in the United States for people who fear natural disasters. Perhaps the auto industry would not have taken off in Detroit had it been in Tornado Alley or an area prone to earthquakes or flooding. The decline and bankruptcy of Detroit has nothing at all to do with natural disasters but rather with the disastrous decline of the US auto industry and other economic factors. Apart from occasional winter storms that cause a few days of disruption, New York, the financial and cultural capital of the United States (of the world, most New Yorkers would say), has a fairly benign climate.

THE IDEA THAT SOCIETIES could prosper from disaster in the long run, as some econometric studies suggest, is, not surprisingly, quite controversial. Mark Skidmore and Hideki Toya first put the idea forward in an article in *Economic Inquiry* in 2002 with the provocative title "Do Natural Disasters Promote Long-Run Growth?"[5] They used the standard tools of econometrics to show that for meteorological disasters like floods and hurricanes, disasters have positive returns. That is, climate disasters were found to be good for the economy—the more disasters the better, in fact. Not so for what they call geological disasters, meaning earthquakes for the most part. They are negative in their effects. Note that the article described "long-run" effects, and the authors studied economic growth over many years in quite a few countries. Often during the rebuilding phase a boost mainly benefits the construction industry (and not necessarily the local industries, which may be damaged by the disaster), but that boost should be short-lived. Skidmore and Toya say, however, that the effect is lasting.

The explanation for a positive return draws on the work of the Austrian economist and political scientist Joseph Schumpeter (1883–1950), who was on the faculty at Harvard University from 1939 until 1949.[6] The idea goes under the somewhat disarming term *creative destruction*. Schumpeter also called it "industrial mutation" and wrote that it "incessantly revolutionizes the economic structure from within, incessantly destroying the old one, incessantly creating a new one. This process of Creative Destruction is the essential fact about capitalism."[7] Schumpeter wrote about the creation of new businesses rather than the effects of natural disasters, which he never once mentioned. One of the most commonly cited examples of creative destruction is the rise of personal computers, which harmed many mainframe computer companies and put several out of business. What is new is far better than what is old, but the new does harm the old.

It is easy enough to map the thinking behind Schumpeter's theory—the gale of creative destruction, as it is sometimes called—into the analysis of disasters. It is posited that rather than destroying old businesses through new business innovations, disasters destroy old, inefficient capital, clearing the ground for new, more productive capital development. Old capital stocks are replaced by newer, better capital. Disasters force technology upgrades that benefit many businesses and the economy as a whole. But does this really happen? Who really rides the gale to a better life?

There is, in fact, some evidence that creative destruction does happen, sometimes. Two months after the 2008 Sichuan earthquake, journalist Drake Bennett, writing in the Business section of the *New York Times,* quoted a Chinese government source as saying that the rebuilding would boost the economy by 0.3 percent in GDP growth.[8] Bennett also quoted one of the earliest findings of this type by Douglas Dacy and Howard Kunreuther. In Dacy and Kunreuther's *Economics of Natural Disasters,* they reported that government loans and grants for rebuilding after the 1964 Anchorage earthquake meant that many Alaskans actually benefited overall.[9] This is more than getting back on your feet quickly; it is an actual improvement in welfare compared to where Alaskans would have been had they not been knocked off their feet by the earthquake.

Betty Hearn Morrow claimed in a book titled *Hurricane Andrew: Ethnicity, Gender and the Sociology of Disaster* that many homes were improved in the reconstruction and that people often made comments like "come see the new bathroom that Andrew built."[10] Restored public housing was often of better quality, and some people were able to become homeowners for the first time.

This *can* work, and it would be wonderful if it would *always* work. No one with insurance would replace a kitchen that burned in a house fire with the exact same appliances as the ones they had before. Since it is a chance to upgrade, you would get new models—a forced technology upgrade. But the only way this could happen in a poor country would be if the World Bank and other donors acted quickly to build new structures before people simply replaced the old with replicas of what came before. As we'll see later, Haiti is the perfect example of such replacement.

IT IS PLAIN ENOUGH TO ANYONE that disasters *do* bring harm, so the fact that we can construct imagined scenarios in which they don't must, at some level, be a ruse or a flaw in economic logic or methods.

How, exactly, in real situations, can disasters operate as agents of social change, and how will they do so in the future? Do disasters accrue benefits to some while bringing harm to others?

If we are to understand what impact natural disasters have, we need to define what exactly they are. The word *disaster* is used to describe so many different incidents, many of which are completely trivial and, objectively, not disasters at all. Quite a range of definitions can be found in dictionaries, but most include some sense of suddenness and loss. For example, the *Oxford Dictionary* defines the word as:

> **Dis•as•ter** 1. A sudden event, such as an accident or a natural catastrophe, that causes great damage and loss of life. 2. Denoting a genre of films that use natural or accidental catastrophe as the mainspring of plot and setting. 3. An event or fact that has unfortunate consequences. 4. A person, act, or thing that is a failure.

Sometimes the definition includes business failures. Many dictionaries list airplane crashes as examples. The root of the word is the Italian *disastro*, meaning "ill-starred." The sense is astrological, of a calamity blamed on an unfavorable position of a planet.[11] The sense, then, is of something far outside of what human societies can be considered responsible for.

The *Oxford* definition is general to all disasters but encompasses the elements of what we mean by a *natural* disaster. The scale of natural disasters is usually measured in human losses—deaths— and economic losses. Neither is simple to estimate, and they are poorly correlated—a large death toll does not imply large economic loss; nor is the reverse true.

There is no agreed minimum number of deaths required for an incident to qualify as a disaster. The defining factor here is really the number relative to our expectations of what the number should be. If a traffic accident kills a dozen people, it probably would be considered a disaster because we don't expect everyday traffic accidents to claim so many lives. A dozen separate fatalities one at a time would not be a disaster, even though the total number of deaths is the same. A school shooting *is* a disaster, whatever the number of deaths. One death makes it a tragedy because we rightly expect the number to be zero. When more than 300 schoolchildren die in a ferryboat accident off South Korea, it is a disaster. It is the simultaneity and the unanticipated nature of disaster deaths that tell us that something unusual and unusually bad has happened.

For an event to qualify as a disaster, the number of deaths does not need to be large relative to other causes of death. Globally, more people commit suicide and harm themselves in suicide attempts than die or are injured in natural disasters. Suicides almost always happen one at a time and are, for the most part, carried out in private, so they don't draw a lot of attention unless the victim is a celebrity, a well-known political figure or similarly prominent person, or, most distressingly, a young, distraught college student. There are many causes of death that, aggregated globally, far exceed natural disaster deaths. As of 2014 in the United States, influenza takes around 36,000 lives each year, also one by one. Those cases, though relatively small in number, have sometimes triggered forced quarantining and massive searches for anyone who might have come into contact with the victims. Thousands have died in West Africa from the Ebola virus, but it raised little concern in the United States until it appeared *in* the United States, because we simply didn't expect it. We read of the deaths in West Africa, and although most of us were distressed by the numbers, we tended to think that the virus belonged in Africa, so we somehow felt those deaths, though tragic and disastrous, were expected for that continent. But when two people in the United States caught the virus, it became a front-page news disaster. It was even suggested that all flights from West Africa be banned from landing in the United States.

Nor is there a minimum extent of damage that has to occur before an event is declared a disaster. Disasters are worse as urban phenomena because people and assets are concentrated in a city, but does a whole city have to be flattened? It would be very hard to determine a minimum damage level for an event to qualify as a disaster, and the level must be relative also. The market value of a poor person's home may be almost nothing, but its loss would be consequential to the person. When disasters are ranked by "economic" losses, those in poor countries often come out on the lower end of the scale because they appear to be low-loss events, when in fact they are high-consequence events for those affected.

ALL TRUE NATURAL DISASTERS can be analyzed in three phases. The phases are common to earthquakes, cyclones, and floods, regardless of whether they happen in rich countries or in poor ones, how many die, or how much the economy suffers. Even so-called manmade or industrial disasters, such as the explosion of the Deep Water Horizon oil rig in the Gulf of Mexico, can have these phases, as can social disasters, such as a school shooting. A trivial personal "disaster"—an embarrassingly bad haircut—doesn't exhibit these phases.

The important thing is to recognize that disasters are processes, not single events, as they are usually considered. The event—the quake, the storm, the flood—is the second of the three phases. Although our System 1 thinking tempts us to believe that this is the phase that matters most, it is, in fact, the least important.

The first phase takes place before the event occurs. It's the time when societies should be preparing for disasters that will surely come, but typically they do not prepare or do not prepare adequately enough to avoid costly damages and multiple deaths. By analogy, this is the phase when the oil rig operator should have been more careful or the school system or health system or someone should have identified the isolated, troubled youth who later ended so many lives. There are scholars who study this phase and try to measure social vulnerability—the variable likelihood that societies will suffer from disasters, by how much, and the factors that might determine the disasters' impact.

The second phase is the event itself. Although a flood and an earthquake and an oil rig explosion are quite different, each event is characterized by media coverage that is similarly intense and frenzied, sometimes ghoulish. The second phase actually has two parts to it, both media driven. In the first part, the media covers the spectacle of the disaster: the damage, the heroic efforts of first responders, the tragedy of people trapped in collapsed buildings or buried in rubble or stranded on rooftops. But that becomes repetitive fairly quickly, and in the second part of this phase, the media switches its attention from chronicling a terrible mishap to investigating the inevitable claims of antisocial behavior, like looting and rape, or failures on the part of agencies, such as the Federal Emergency Management Agency (FEMA), the local police, and government officials or autocratic rulers. If blame can be assigned, the media will assign it. More often than not, it is the media that first designates an event to be a disaster. It's in this second phase that the effect disasters have on societies—they kill people and destroy property—is most blatantly on display.

The third phase, which is talked about the least, is what happens after the disaster, in the weeks, months, and years after the storm has passed and the floodwaters have receded. The media has packed up and left. Losses have been tallied, the death toll has been estimated. It is the period of time when individuals try to get back on their feet and societies try to function in some semblance of the way they did before the disaster. Here is where we find BP at fault for the oil rig explosion and seek damages. Here is where more stringent gun laws are discussed. No one has a formula for how to recover quickly, effectively, or completely. Some societies succeed very well and might even prosper from the experience; some don't. Just as there are scholars of vulnerability, there are scholars who examine societies for their resilience—their ability to withstand disaster events and recover quickly. Vulnerability and resilience are more or less opposites and have become the lingua franca of many disaster studies.

The media has a passing interest in the first phase, especially if the disaster points up some lack of preparation that might be scandalous—failure to maintain levees, say. The media has almost no interest, or merely a rapidly dwindling one, in the third phase, except perhaps to return to the scene of the disaster on anniversary dates to see how things have improved (or, more likely, to show that things have not improved as fast as they should have). But even that runs out of steam after a while. What happens in phase 3 is largely out of sight. Phases 1 and 3 can be quite long and uninteresting. Phase 2 is typically short, exciting, and terrifying. Droughts can be prolonged, but the transition from drought to famine can be very rapid. Phase 2 makes for the best media stories.

That's not to suggest that the disaster phases are absolutely distinct and separable. Lack of preparation in phase 1 will make phase 2 of a disaster worse than it need be. Failure to reassemble societies in phase 3, after a disaster, will make the societies more likely to experience other disasters, just as failing to build a strong postconflict peace can actually induce a new conflict. Phase 1 can even been seen as the tail end of phase 3—the period after one disaster becomes the period before the next.

Very bad things can happen in the second phase. Whole families can be lost, workplaces destroyed, entire villages swept away, hospitals ruined, schools demolished. Here the human tragedy is most evident and social ills are revealed. This is where we hear of murders, looting, and rape. It is where we see that so many of the victims are poor and neglected. This is where the military may be called in to keep peace, not to help victims, and where victims are criminalized.

The physical damage resulting in phase 2 is, at least in principle, simple to restore. People constructed everything in the first place and should know how to replace it. That reconstruction often happens more quickly than might be expected. In restoring damaged structures, we could and should make them stronger if we can; *build back better* is the rallying cry that motivates this objective. It simply means that we should replace old structures with ones that are more resistant and build protective structures (such as seawalls) that might reduce the scale of future damage. That happens, too, but mostly in wealthy countries; the poor have less capacity to do the better building, and, too often, to meet basic needs, they just put things back the way they were as quickly and as best they can with whatever materials are at hand.

Phase 3, I argue, is where social ills are concealed. The media has almost completely lost interest, and what is left is both physical and social damage. While the physical damage can be handled, the social damage cannot so easily be addressed. In fact, the very idea of social restoration is elusive. You can't bring the dead back to life, but you can certainly build back better when it comes to structures: using bricks and steel beams, et cetera. But can a whole society truly be built back better?

ACCORDING TO NEWSPAPER REPORTS, most societies experience long, miserable struggles back to some semblance of their predisaster states and are permanently set back by these events. You would assume that the more often a society is hit, the more often it experiences a setback, and the setbacks accumulate into permanent penalties. But that assumption, too, is a System 1 reaction (to a System 2 problem), and with a little more deliberative thinking, the opposite conclusion can be reached.

The idea that societies suffer losses but get back up and running fairly quickly after crises is controversial, too, as is the notion that societies sometimes profit from disasters. As early as 1896, philosopher John Stuart Mill mused, "What has so often excited wonder, is the great rapidity with which countries recover from a state of devastation; the disappearance, in a short time, of all traces of the mischiefs done by earthquakes, floods, hurricanes, and the ravages of war."[12] Tellingly, Mill writes "what has so often," as if the "great rapidity" of recovery were common knowledge in the late nineteenth century. His musings applied more to "the ravages of war" than to disasters, but when he says it has "excited wonder," he is saying that the swiftness of recovery is counterintuitive. System 1 thinking would lead us to imagine that recovery will be long and hard, but in many instances it is not. We need System 2 thinking to understand why.

People readjust to new situations quickly, no matter how dreadful those situations are. The formal term for this is "hedonic adaptation."[13] It is the idea that people deal with shocks, both positive and negative, and then settle back to their previous state of happiness.

Most people are not vastly happier when they gain wealth or vastly distressed if they suffer a loss—not for long, anyway. This phenomenon echoes an observation attributed to Dostoyevsky that "man is a pliant animal, a being who gets accustomed to anything."

In *The Other Side of Sadness: What the New Science of Bereavement Tells Us about Life after Loss,* George Bonanno, a professor of clinical psychology at Columbia University's Teachers College, challenges the common notions that for most people, grief is a long, hard slog to be worked through in well-defined stages and that many people never get over the loss.[14] Most of us are actually fairly good at dealing with tragedy. It seems to be a built-in feature of our psyche, something we must have to keep going.

In *The Natural History of Destruction,* W. G. Sebold writes of how people emerged from the ruins of their shattered homes after the Allied firebombing raids on German cities at the end of World War II and immediately began getting about their lives, straightening what could be straightened, and opening shops and businesses if they could. Banks reopened within a week. Sebold tells of a woman who was sweeping and tidying the entrance to a half-destroyed movie theater, getting ready for the matinee show the day after a bombing raid, though it likely would never take place, given the damage to the theater.[15]

THE TRADITIONAL ROLE of natural scientists—climatologists, seismologists, volcanologists, and others—has been to estimate the timing and magnitude of natural extremes or natural hazards, as they are typically called, not the magnitudes of disasters. The difference isn't trivial. If an earthquake at the top end of the geophysical magnitude scale occurred above the Arctic Circle in Siberia, it probably would not kill anyone or damage any structures, so it would not be a disaster of any magnitude. The earthquake that took tens of thousands of lives in Haiti was far from the top of the magnitude scale, but it was a disaster of massive scale. The magnitude of the physical event does not predict the magnitude of the disaster very well at all.

Hazard has a formal definition also, of course. Cambridge's on-line dictionary explains the word as something that is dangerous and *likely* to cause harm. In almost all definitions, the words *danger, risk,* and *unavoidable* appear. Disasters, in contrast, are thought of as avoidable. A *natural* hazard is one in which the danger is presented by Nature. Almost all definitions have a tone of fatalism. The word for *hazard* in French is *hasard* and has a broader suite of synonyms than in English, including *coincidence,* but the deep sense of the inevitability remains. The unavoidability of a hazard and the avoidability of a disaster are implicit in almost all discussions of natural disasters, in the academic literature and in disaster risk reduction (DRR) strategies in UN agencies and within the numerous organizations tasked with disaster mitigation.

With information on hazard distribution, natural scientists also participate in disaster studies by finding ways to estimate natural hazard risk. Using records of past events, they try to map out the regions most likely to experience earthquakes, storms, landslides, and the like. Governments can use this information to make strategic investments in hazard mitigation projects where they will have the most benefit. The World Bank and regional development banks are very interested in this research as well (and have funded hazard assessments) because they often fund mitigation projects or support reconstruction costs following disasters, particularly in poorer countries.

Economists use the term *moral hazard* to mean the temptation to take greater risk because another party will bear the consequences of that risk taking.[16] It is used a little more broadly than that in conversations among economists.

Social scientists most often study disaster phases 1 or 3 or both. That's because this is where human judgment, human actions or inactions, social systems, politics, and institutions most come into play. Social scientists study human reactions during phase 2 as well as the organization of humanitarian relief and the organization and motivation of donor contributions. But social scientists in general do not attempt to predict when disasters will occur or how consequential they will be. Their work most often involves understanding human behaviors and suggesting policy formulations that might lead to a reduction in the social harm disasters bring.

WHILE THERE MAY BE no bright lines drawn between each of the three disaster phases, high barriers mark the disjunction between the social and the natural sciences. Generally the two live in very different worlds; certainly they do in academia. Few social science departments, for instance, have a natural scientist on the faculty, and few if any natural science departments have a social scientist on the faculty. The two are almost immiscible. Although the two areas of intellectual inquiry thrive in their different worlds, their separation creates significant issues for our objective: understanding all phases of natural disasters.

The problem is an old one. In the decades after World War II, scientists such as Richard Feynman, Niels Bohr, Albert Einstein, and others were popular heroes. They were often asked to give opinions on all manner of subjects that had little to do with their fields, and they ventured their opinions on politics, religion, and many more subjects. Feynman, the great nuclear physicist, was publicly vocal on a wide range of topics. One thing he argued was that the doing of science was "doing good." Others—politicians, for instance—may make bad use of the knowledge that comes from science, but creating that knowledge remains a good action. That idea has many adherents still.

British scientist C. P. Snow is most often quoted on the subject of the standoff between science and other intellectual pursuits at the time when science and scientists commanded high regard and public support.[17] In his famous Rede Lecture of 1959, "The Two Cultures," Snow referred to science and humanities; but from the perspective of a natural scientist, he could have been discussing science and almost anything else that isn't science.

Feynman actually wanted a Snowvian separation to exist between the *work* of science and how science is used by those who are not scientists. He, along with many other physicists, had worked on the Manhattan Project at Los Alamos, New Mexico, which built the first atomic bomb. Many of them felt huge guilt and remorse for it. Feynman wanted to separate the act of building the bomb from the decision to drop it, a decision that the Los Alamos scientists did not make. He wanted to draw a bright line—I called it the Feynman line in the introduction—between the work of an atomic *physicist* and the work of an atomic *bomb*. And he really wanted to say (and he was not alone in this) that scientists should be left to do anything they please in splendid isolation and that whatever negative consequences unfold aren't their fault. In other words, if the consequences are good for society, scientists revel in the praise that comes; if the consequences are bad, that is someone else's doing. Feynman thought social problems were much harder to solve than regular science problems because there were no physical principles to call on, no formulas to derive and solve that would resolve the problems.

But the most serious problems of our time lie at the nexus of the physical and the social worlds. They are on neither side of the Feynman line; they sit right *on* it. Climate change is the leading example: Science gives us an understanding of the effect of greenhouse gases but does not tell us how to deal with them. And think about the problem of continued poverty in today's world, the problem of massive economic inequality. What prevents the poor from breaking out of their terrible situation and enjoying the benefits of prosperity? If some can do it, why can't everyone? There is no simple answer, and many factors are cited that are social in nature. Governance, institutions, and corruption are leading causes. But poverty must be a physical phenomenon as well as a social one; why else would poverty today be concentrated in the tropics? That's no accident of history. Why would the actions of Nature be harsher on the poor than on the rich? Why is it that only the poorest among us are brutalized by famine when there is more than enough food in the world to feed us all?

When thousands of children and their teachers die in schoolrooms during an earthquake in China, scientists will say it is because building codes are lax, and they scold the politicians for not making or enforcing stricter codes. The old adage holds true—earthquakes don't kill people, buildings kill people. (Chapter 2 discusses this in more depth.) Those who live in countries prone to earthquakes are the very last people who need to be told that. They know earthquakes are inevitable hazards, but the deaths of schoolchildren should not be inevitable. Natural scientists can answer the question of *how* the children died but not *why* they died. Why are building codes, or their enforcement, often so lax in places so prone to earthquakes? That is a question for social scientists.

Since most natural scientists remain with their colleagues, where they are most comfortable, the result is that a lot of what passes for science on the nonscience side of the Feynman line isn't science at all. You could call it *scienciness,* a riff on Stephen Colbert's *truthiness*—things that are felt to be true and might even *be* true but are often factually incorrect and not logically true. They do not come from the works of science, but they sound like science. These assertions are attempts, often quite genuine, by people not trained in science to communicate some important issue where science has played a part.

But the general reserve and guardedness of many scientists—often out of a fear of being misquoted, which does indeed happen quite frequently—leaves open a space that can be filled with whatever tidbit of science-sounding information that appears to support a position erected for political and other reasons. The debate on climate change in the United States is a leading example. Those who wish to argue against action to reduce greenhouse gas emissions have not made a thorough study of the extensive analyses of climate research available from the UN's Intergovernmental Panel on Climate Change. They have adopted a view that their standard of living will be diminished if any action is taken. People in Congress who represent states where fossil fuel–based industries are a significant part of the economy push that idea very hard and receive considerable funding from those industries to propagate this case. People like the Koch brothers can always dredge up some sliver of information or equivocation on the part of a scientist (or someone who sounds like one) somewhere and twist it to indicate that any action would be a mistake. Senator James Inhofe's book, *The Greatest Hoax: How the Global Warming Conspiracy Threatens Your Future,* and the entire genre of climate change denial books is based on this sort of *scienciness.* If you have your mind made up already, you will believe what books like these say and even convince yourself that they are based on science.

MANY EXPERTS AND NONEXPERTS will tell you that disasters are actually increasing both in frequency and in severity and that we should expect that trend to continue. They mean that the number of disaster events—phase 2 of disasters—is increasing, because the events are reasonably easy to count. Part of the reason for the growing number of events, it is said, is that our climate is changing for the worse, bringing with it more meteorological extremes. In the United States, more than half of the population apparently believes that disasters are indeed increasing, and half of that number believe that it is evidence of the "End Times," the time before the apocalypse and the second coming of Christ.[18] Only a minority in the United States believes disasters are increasing due to climate change.

The most authoritative source for disaster statistics is the Emergency Events Database (EM-DAT) compiled by the Center for Research on the Epidemiology of Disasters (CRED), a group based at the School of Public Health at the Catholic University of Louvain in Brussels.[19] EM-DAT data for 1960 shows about 50 disasters per year. That figure rocketed up to 450 per year in 2010, an almost tenfold increase. (When meteorological disasters are treated as a group, it's not so bad: the increase is about fourfold.) The temperature change from 1960 to 2010 was less than 1°Celsius. Although aspects of the climate system are very sensitive to small changes in temperature, there is no basis in climate science to support a fourfold increase in weather extremes as a response to a globally averaged temperature increase of less than 1°C.

In 1960, there were about 3 billion people on Earth; by 2010, there were almost 7 billion. Thus, the number of people more than doubled in 50 years. By simple logic, you could argue that population increase might cause a bit more than twice as many disasters if the number of natural extreme events themselves stayed constant. But if EM-DAT is right, there are nearly *ten times* as many disasters. To make these two increases jibe, you would have to suppose that most of the population increase occurred in the most dangerous places on the planet rather than in places where there are few disasters.

But that isn't the case. Populations *are* swelling in some dangerous places. Cities are growing at a very rapid rate, and many are in coastal regions and subject to tropical cyclones. Some coastal regions, such as those of Latin America, the US West Coast, and Japan, are also prone to earthquakes. But populations are also growing rapidly in many places that are not especially dangerous. And if population increase alone was the answer, then the increase in all forms of disasters would be the same.

If the number of disasters has increased because of population increase, surely the number of deaths would have gone up by the same tenfold factor as the disasters. But the number of deaths *per disaster* has actually decreased. We are safer from disasters now than we have ever been. The drop in deaths per disaster is about sixfold, from around 120,000 deaths per disaster in 1975 to around 20,000 today. That's a remarkable improvement in people's safety. The world is not becoming a more dangerous place to live; it is becoming a safer place!

THE MOST IMPORTANT FACTOR in the decline in fatalities per event is the well-known effect of poverty on disaster fatalities. Poor people live in fragile, poorly built homes, often in marginal lands like the barrios that cover the slopes behind so many cities in Latin America. Many lack public transportation and rarely own cars or motorcycles or even bicycles, so they settle in near where they can get work, often in floodplains or on riverbanks, unaware of or reluctantly accepting of the dangers. Their wealthy employers know the dangers of such places and never live there. They live in the well-planned, well-serviced, well-policed cities with gentle terrain and rows of trees, lawns, and open parklands.

David Stromberg at the Institute for International Economic Studies in Stockholm has run regressions (the central tool of econometrics) of income against the number of deaths and finds a robust relationship with high reliability.[20] For the same geophysical type of event, high-income countries have only 30 percent as many deaths as low-income countries. Stromberg estimated that had the economic development that occurred globally in the last 40 years of the twentieth century not taken place, the number of disaster deaths would be around 20 percent greater than they are today. Continued development should further reduce disaster risk and fatalities. The wealthier we get, the safer we are, so the best DRR strategy is to become wealthy. An article in the *Economist* that discussed the economics of natural disasters ended with this: "The lesson for poorer countries is that growth is the best disaster-mitigation policy of all."[21] Perhaps that's what you might expect the *Economist* to say, but in this case Stromberg's figures do support the claim.

It's easy enough to understand why. Along with the fragility of poor people's dwellings (in part due to lack of building codes and/or their enforcement), poor countries typically have weak or absent institutions that could help prepare for disasters and reduce harm. They rarely have agencies like FEMA, or a developed science institution like the US Geological Survey with large numbers of seismologists who study earthquake hazards, or climate scientists in the National Oceanographic and Atmospheric Administration (NOAA) who study cyclones. Those institutions are the rewards of wealth and are part of what protects the wealthy from disaster.

ONE THING WE CAN SAY with some certainty about natural disasters is that they take lives, sometimes in tragically large numbers, and many more in poor places than in others. Every effort we can make to avoid these deaths is an effort worth making, through the DRR work of the UN or others. That said, death tolls are actually quite difficult to estimate with any accuracy. You can't be sure of any reported figures, and, of course, deaths are harder to estimate in poor places. You can't just count bodies the way Quartermaster General Montgomery Meigs did after the US Civil War. He searched all the Civil War battlefields, disinterred the bodies of all the slain Union soldiers from the rough, shallow graves dug quickly by their comrades, and made as accurate a count as he could.[22] But even Meigs didn't count Confederate soldiers or civilians.[23]

Disaster deaths are always highly political. The government of Myanmar rarely reports disaster deaths, and the government of North Korea almost never does. No international agency is charged with finding out just exactly how many die, because such a task would be an infringement on sovereignty, so we have to rely on country reports. CRED does the best job of figuring out what deaths have occurred, but it acknowledges significant uncertainties. In Myanmar, international media attention forced the government to acknowledge that they had a disaster on their hands days after Cyclone Nargis made landfall in 2008, but no one seriously believes that country leaders accurately reported the deaths, and it is widely believed that the numbers were much higher than official government figures. Large fatality figures would seem to suggest that the government is not in control, and complete control is one of the central missions of authoritarian governments like the junta in Myanmar; so too for North Korea.

Queasiness about reporting embarrassingly large death figures is not the sole province of authoritarian, xenophobic governments. Eric Klinenberg wrote a classic study of the 1995 heat wave in Chicago, during which Mayor Richard M. Daley challenged figures from the county's chief medical examiner that had been widely reported in the media. Daley said, "It's hot. . . . But let's not blow it out of proportion. . . . Every day people die of natural causes. You cannot claim that everybody who has died in the last eight or nine days died of heat. Then everybody in the summer that dies will die of heat."[24] The mayor was suggesting that the number was lower than the 521 that the medical examiner had determined. The final figure was calculated to be 739.

There's nothing new in this. In his excellent book about the High Plains blizzard of 1888, *The Children's Blizzard*, David Laskin writes of the debate about the death toll from that tragic event: "In the national press an unseemly brawl had broken out over the number of blizzard deaths." A federal judge had asserted that "Dakota papers were deliberately underestimating and 'covering up' the truth about loss of life."[25] The judge claimed the figure might be 1,000, while newspapers reported 300. The judge thought there was a cover-up to prevent the Dakota Territory from getting a bad name, which might dissuade people from moving there. At the time, the blizzard was consistently treated as a freak of Nature, one that was never going to return. Now we know better.

The death toll from the 1906 San Francisco earthquake and fire is still debated. William Bronson, in *The Earth Shook, the Sky Burned,* tells us that the initial death toll was reported to be 375 because no count was made in Chinatown: residents there were not citizens and didn't belong in the official count.[26] Major General Adolphus Greely, who commanded US relief operations in the city, put the number at 664 and included the Chinese victims. I have not been able to access this report, but I suspect it is a straightforward count of actual bodies recovered, in the style of Meigs. A 1972 study by NOAA put the figure at 700 to 800,[27] but the highest figure of all, about 3,000, comes from Gladys Hansen and Emmel Condon's provocatively titled 1989 book, *Denial of Disaster: The Untold Story and Photographs of the San Francisco Earthquake and Fire of 1906.*[28] Hansen, a retired librarian, has made it her life's work to search out documents and account for all those who died in the earthquake and fire, and she might well have the most accurate number.

IN ADDITION TO GOVERNMENTS reducing disaster death counts for political reasons, it is also widely believed, though difficult to document, that they may exaggerate deaths too. Countries hoping for contributions might exaggerate deaths because history shows that donors are more motivated by deaths than by damage, even though contributions are used to tend to the living and to repair damage. High mortality implies a huge number of survivors in great need. The Haitian government is thought to have greatly exaggerated the death toll from the 2010 earthquake, but most NGOs did not question those numbers.

For example, about ten years ago, I was in Taiwan with a group from Columbia University to discuss how climate forecasts could be used to mitigate damage done by extreme weather. Taiwan experiences many typhoon strikes, and they typically bring biblical rainfall. The intense rain causes landslides and flash floods that sweep away whole villages and take the lives of countless people living on denuded steep slopes near the cities where they work, similar to the barrios around Rio and other Latin American cities. As recently as 2009, Typhoon Morakot took more than 500 lives in Taiwan.

The representatives of the Taiwanese meteorological service viewed these high figures with vexation and a distinct sense of embarrassment. On one hand, they were very proud of the rapid economic progress their country had made, but as one government scientist told me, when Taiwan experiences a typhoon, the high death toll "makes us look like we are still a third-world country." They wanted accurate forecast information so they could evacuate people from dangerous areas like the informal housing on the steep slopes of denuded hillsides. I believe they reported death tolls accurately, but they didn't want disasters to make their forward-looking country seem backward.

DEATHS ARE HARD TO ESTIMATE for a number of completely apolitical reasons as well. Just who gets included in the victim list? Many children and adults who died from the effects of the Children's Blizzard of 1888 actually survived the awful night of exposure; they died many days or even weeks later of complications from that exposure or from misguided treatment by doctors and others trying to nurse them back to health. Like the wounded in wars of the past, many of whom survived a battle but died days later from infections in their wounds, people often survive a disaster only to die days or weeks later. When should we stop including a death as disaster related?

Sometimes we see the terms *direct* and *indirect* used to qualify deaths. Direct deaths are fairly obvious: they require that the individual died unequivocally from causes like drowning in a flood or being crushed in collapsed building. But people often die in other circumstances, such as from falling while clearing tree branches from their roofs after a hurricane. People died during Superstorm Sandy and in the days after because they operated gasoline-powered backup generators indoors and were asphyxiated by poisoned air despite usually very clear signage on those generators against such use.

Many people, especially the elderly, have pre-existing heart or respiratory conditions, and they die from the traumatic exacerbation of those maladies. Should they be counted in the disaster death toll? Are they direct or indirect deaths? Perhaps they would have died anyway, maybe only a few days or weeks later. The disarming medical term for this is *harvesting*; the disaster just chopped them down a short while before they would have fallen on their own. Do you count someone who died in a car accident while trying to escape an oncoming tornado? Or someone who fell from a roof while trying to secure windows as a hurricane approached?

The bottom line is this: There are no uniform international standards in mortality reporting for natural disasters. No one really knows how many people die in natural disasters who would not have died otherwise. In the United States, the Centers for Disease Control and Prevention has a set of strict criteria that it uses for all disasters and disease outbreaks, but the criteria are very conservative and typically give minimum estimates.

IT MIGHT MAKE MORE SENSE to estimate injuries rather than deaths. After all, the injured are the ones who need attention. In road accidents and train crashes, many people suffer injuries but relatively few die. In almost all disasters, the number of people injured considerably exceeds the number who die.

It's not hard to understand why. In earthquakes, with furniture falling and glass shattering, it is easy to be struck by a crumbling wall or ceiling. Often people are pinned under fallen structures. In Haiti, many of the injuries caused that way required amputations. (By *injuries* we mean those treated for injuries by aid agencies that keep records, such as the Red Cross and Doctors Without Borders.) Only 63 people died in the Loma Prieta earthquake in San Francisco in 1989, but the number of injured recorded was almost 4,000, a ratio of about 60 to 1. Presumably everyone who suffered even minor injuries was treated.

Tropical cyclones have injury-to-fatality ratios similar to earthquakes, but floods don't injure people in the same numbers: You either drown or you don't. People are beaten around by floodwaters, they survive and require treatment for injuries, but in nothing like the numbers or the severity of injuries seen in earthquakes, for instance. Famines can cause hundreds of thousands to suffer, and vast numbers of people have perished in famines. Like floods, droughts don't really injure people per se, but they can result in huge numbers of people needing medical attention for malnourishment. People weakened by hunger become susceptible to a wide variety of diseases. Many famine deaths are not the result of starvation but of disease.

There is always an issue after disaster events with people who go missing and are unaccounted for. Even in very wealthy countries with very good census surveys, it can be hard to determine the exact number of people who go missing. Making such determinations in poorer countries where governments hardly know how many people live in any given region at any time can be almost impossible. Conducting a census is expensive. The last census in the United States cost taxpayers $13 billion, or about $42 per person counted.

Some of those who go missing after disasters are surely dead and their bodies are never found. People get washed out to sea by storm surges in cyclones and tsunamis. In some cultures, the dead are buried very quickly, usually due to the unwarranted fear of disease transmission. The corpses of people who die of transmittable diseases, such as Ebola, are sources of contagion, but the corpses of people who die disease free are not. The fear that arises in some cultures is based on the sad fact that, in many parts of the world, so many people die of untreated diseases. After the earthquake in Haiti, thousands were buried in mass graves; most were not identified.

Typically, searches for survivors and victims' remains end after several days. Just how long searches continue is based on some guess that anyone not found by a certain time must surely be dead. Cadaver dogs may then be used to systematically scan disaster scenes for bodies. In earthquakes, searches are terminated after a week or so, based on the assumption that anyone still buried in the rubble will have died. It is a gruesome thought, but the fact that some people are pulled from the rubble more than a week after an earthquake implies that others must take many days to die, from starvation or dehydration, in the ruins of the homes, schools, and stores that once seemed safe.

Anyone still unaccounted for in the collapse of the Rana Plaza garment sweatshop in Bangladesh was almost certainly dead. Those unaccounted for after a major tsunami are almost certainly dead also. For weeks after the 9/11 attacks on the World Trade Center, many people remained unaccounted for. Stories of traumatized survivors who wandered around for days before they were found gave false hope to those with missing family members or friends. The death toll in the 9/11 attacks is probably the most accurately estimated of all disasters in which more than a few died. Huge efforts were made to account for everyone. The total figure is 2,726, including those in the airplanes and 13 people who died after September 11.[29]

The *Times-Picayune* in New Orleans published the names of Katrina victims, a practice that has a long history worldwide. Survivors who have family members or someone they know unaccounted for search these lists with a conflicted mixture of hope and trepidation—hoping not to see their loved ones' names but wanting to know their fate. And after some time, most people come to accept that missing loved ones must indeed be dead and just hope that their remains will be found and given a proper burial. Having someone go missing, never to be heard from again, is simply dreadful.

Many people missing after natural disasters are thought to have left the area as the cyclone or floodwaters approached or because their crops failed in a drought and there was no food. Some are forced to leave because an earthquake destroyed their homes and workplaces. If they are displaced to refugee camps, like the tent cities that housed earthquake survivors in Port-au-Prince, Haiti, they can be counted fairly accurately and their names recorded.

But a lot of people, especially in poorer places, move away and don't return. They stay with relatives, find jobs in other places, and send their children to other schools, and they don't always report in. In Haiti, it would have been hard for displaced people to know to whom to report. And to what purpose? In rich countries, people report in and have every reason to expect their government to help; they are vocal in their criticism if they feel they are not being adequately assisted.

Droughts displace many more people for greater distances and for longer periods of time than do most other disasters. Often after a drought there is nothing to go back to but parched land. There may be nowhere nearby to shelter from a drought, which may affect a vast area, typically much larger than a flood. If adequately warned, you can get out of the way of a flood, then wait until the water subsides and return home. Often you don't have to go too far or stay away for long, and in farming areas, people want to get back quickly and replant if possible to ensure a crop to replace the one lost. Droughts operate over much longer periods and over greater areas than floods.

There is a silver lining for some people who actually benefit from being displaced to a location where the residents are generally better off, much the way poor migrants benefit from entering richer host countries. This can be especially true for children who are displaced into areas with better schools and health-care systems. They may acquire better skills than they would have and are around others of their age for whom completing high school and going on to college is a normal expectation, not an impossible dream.

EVEN MORE UNCERTAIN but often reported are the number of people "affected" by disasters. That figure can be extremely high, as it was in 2012 for Superstorm Sandy, a storm of huge dimensions that hit a very densely populated area of the northeastern United States. Tens of millions of people were affected by Sandy in some way, even if they just lost power and shivered for a while. After many disasters, the total number of those affected is often a pure guess. Although the number of people who lose power in a storm in the United States can be determined with accuracy, can the same be said for the Philippines? Most people who make comparative studies of disaster consequences cannot use data on populations affected by disaster events (which CRED faithfully maintains as best as it can) because the data are far too unreliable.

WHEN WE ASK WHAT SOCIAL HARM disasters do, one thing is certain: they take many lives and cause countless injuries and massive displacement, and they do so much more in poor countries than in rich ones. But what this discussion has made clear is that these numbers are not well known. Death tolls, at least, should be simple, but they are not. If an independent agency was tasked with counting body bags, we could have reasonable figures, but the counts are done by local governments with highly variable capacities and motivations for correct reporting. When three people die, you can be fairly sure the number really is three, but when 30,000 die, the number can be higher or lower for good reasons or political ones. After any disaster, we can never state very accurately how many people died, how many were injured, and how many moved away to better lives or worse lives. What we know from directly counting bodies are minimum death tolls.

Most people assume there really is an agency or a Meigs-like person whose task it is to get the numbers right, but there rarely is. Mostly, it seems to me, we don't really want to know. Hardly anyone remembers death tolls. Most people asked to remember how many died in 9/11 cite a figure that is much too high. I have asked the question in classes of graduate and undergraduate students and of colleagues; no one has come close to the correct number. In fact, some people overestimate by a full order of magnitude. Responses to a similar question about Hurricane Katrina yield similar inaccurate results.

AFTER TALKING ABOUT DEATHS, and sometimes even before, the media will cite "economic" losses resulting from the disaster, often without providing a source. This happens most in the United States, where death tolls are typically small, and it's one of the most common ways rankings get made—the top ten costliest. We forget the deaths fairly quickly. But there are many problems with estimating economic losses, more even than accounting for deaths and injuries. In the US media, first you hear about deaths; soon after "economic" losses are tallied. Technical Appendixes I and II explain some special issues involved in the basic economics of natural disasters.

I used quotation marks around the word *economic* because what are so often referred to as economic losses are not that at all; rather, they are losses of capital stocks, mostly manufactured or built capital. Natural capital—forests or beaches, for example—can be damaged, too, but generally those costs are not cited in disaster economic losses unless restoration costs are included. But a stock, like the type of stock lost in a natural (or even industrial) disaster, is not in itself an economic loss. This is not splitting hairs, just as the difference between a hazard and a disaster is not trivial. The economy of a country, a city, or a home includes stocks and flows. The economy is the function of, for instance, the rate at which production of goods and services takes place, not just the capital stock produced. It reflects how much people are regularly paid for the work they do, not just the accumulation of physical assets that they surround themselves with. Your house can be thought of as an important capital stock: it has come to you from a flow of income. If your income goes away, having a house isn't much help unless you sell it.

Not all capital is productive capital. Your home is not really productive capital unless you have a home business, something that happens a lot in poor places and rather less in wealthy places. This sounds harsh, but the things we cherish might not matter very much to the performance of an economy.

The first accounting of so-called economic losses from disasters often comes from insurance and reinsurance companies that cover all manner of capital, including home exercise equipment, which is of no consequence to the economy at all. In fact, losing your flat-screen TV might be good all around: If it is insured, you'll get a newer version with higher definition, and the electronics company will make a sale. Roughly about half of all disaster capital losses are private property losses that are more likely to spur economic growth than detract from it.

Uncomfortable as this fact may make us feel, there is very little relationship between human losses and economic ones. It sounds callous to say it, but the people most likely to be killed in a disaster—the very old and infirm, the very young, and the very poor—don't much influence the performance of the aggregate macroeconomy because economically they are not very productive individuals. Most of the victims of the Chicago heat wave that Klinenberg described were elderly people living on their own and isolated on the upper floors of walk-up apartment buildings. So, too, were the great majority of victims of the western European heat wave of 2003, which killed more than 14,000 people in France alone. Overwhelmingly, those who died in Hurricane Katrina were elderly and alone.

These deaths matter for other, more important, noneconomic humanitarian reasons. But all forms of reporting on disasters equate large death tolls with large economic impacts when in fact the reverse may even be true: if most of those who died were living on welfare, their deaths actually may represent a savings to government coffers.

CAPITAL LOSSES FROM DISASTERS are increasing, but that's just what you would expect as the world economy as a whole grows richer. The cost of capital losses *per* disaster will increase as the amount and value of the capital increases. It is like the poverty effect on deaths but in reverse. Wealth leads to fewer deaths but greater capital losses. Whether global capital losses are increasing at a rate faster than that of the global economy is an open question. Part of the problem is the metric we use to count.

Haiti was said to have lost more than 100 percent of its annual GDP in the 2010 earthquake. Disaster economic losses often are given as a percentage of a country's GDP. That means it is important to understand what GDP is, what it measures, and what losing some fraction of GDP in a disaster means to an economy. Diane Coyle's excellent book, *GDP: A Brief but Affectionate History,* outlines the rise of GDP as the universally adopted way to gauge an economy.[30] Thomas Piketty also discusses GDP in his celebrated book *Capital in the Twenty-first Century* because much of his work draws on national income accounts.[31] Joseph Stiglitz gives a clear picture of what's wrong with GDP in *Mismeasuring Our Lives: Why GDP Doesn't Add Up.*[32] So what is wrong with GDP, and how might that make a difference to how we understand the way disasters affect societies?

GDP became a way to measure an economy in the period before World War II, in the midst of the Great Depression. Prior to this time, there were many different measures of how economies were assessed and considerable debate about what should be measured— what constitutes the "economy," a debate that continues to today. GDP is calculated as the sum of four terms:

GDP = private consumption + gross investments + government
        spending + (value of exports minus imports)

Even though it's a pretty simple formula, if you look up country rankings by GDP or GDP per capita available from the International Monetary Fund, the Central Intelligence Agency, and the World Bank, you will find that they differ and not by small amounts.

GDP does not translate to average income because only a fraction of the income from a country's production goes directly to workers' salaries. GDP masks inequality. A disaster might cause great losses to low-income people but not show up very strongly in GDP.

And while the formula is simple enough, the problem is in totaling up what goes into each of the terms. What exactly are gross investments? What goes into consumption? The UN's *System of National Accounts* manual is hundreds of pages long and provides guidelines on how this should be done. Many countries don't, won't, or can't follow the guidelines very closely. Most poor countries don't have the institutional bodies needed to keep track of the figures that go into GDP.

As noted earlier, in poor countries much of the economy is informal, in the sense that many transactions, including pay for labor, are done in cash or bartered. Hence they are not taxed or regulated and do not show up in government accounts. The size of the informal economy in any country is hard to guess. Even in wealthy countries, the informal economy can be around 20 percent of the total, while in poorer countries it can exceed 60 percent.[33] The greater effect a disaster has on the informal sector, as it does in many poorer countries, the less likely the amount will be revealed in GDP figures.

After Italy started to include in its GDP an estimate of its quite-large informal economy in 1987, the country's GDP rose by 18 percent overnight and jumped ahead of the GDP of the United Kingdom. In an even bolder move, Italy started included drug trafficking, prostitution, and alcohol and tobacco smuggling in its national accounts in late 2014.[34] The United Kingdom followed a week later. Illegal businesses are big businesses in many countries, and it makes good sense to include their output in GDP figures, but the very fact that they *are* illegal makes them difficult to estimate. There is no reason to think these illegal activities decrease following a disaster. In fact, with law enforcement distracted by dealing with the disaster, criminal activities may even increase.

Low GDP can indicate low production of goods and a weak position in global markets. But comparing GDP outputs across countries
is no simple business. Anyone from a developed country who has
visited a relatively poor country knows that goods you buy there seem
cheap. It is not uncommon for travelers to conclude that, although
poor people have low incomes, goods are cheap, and perhaps people can live reasonably well on a small income. But goods that seem
cheap to wealthy travelers still are out of reach of many poor people.

This difficulty is what gave rise to the Big Mac Index created
by the *Economist*. You can get a Big Mac practically anywhere. To
calculate the index, first take the price of the hamburger in the
United States—say, $2.50—and in another country, such as Mexico,
where you pay in pesos. Then convert pesos to dollars using current exchange rates and get the price of a Mexican burger in dollars.
If currency exchange rates were perfectly aligned, the Mexican Big
Mac would also cost about $2.50. But that never happens. After con-
verting to dollars, the Mexican burger costs less than the American
burger, which indicates that the peso is undervalued compared to
the dollar. The same burger in Sweden is more expensive; the Swed-
ish currency is overvalued relative to the dollar. The Big Mac Index
calculates these relative valuations; it is a way to show what is more
formally termed the purchasing power parity (PPP) adjustment.[35]

One very serious problem with GDP is that capital stocks are
not explicitly involved in the equation, and capital stocks are what
are lost in a disaster. Capital and capital depreciation are included
implicitly because capital stocks are needed to achieve production.
But the effect of capital on production is quite variable and is very
different in economies at different stages of maturity. The marginal
return to capital may be quite low in comparison to total GDP in very
advanced economies. If that is true, a marginal loss of capital should

mean less in a rich country than in a poor country. In fact, if those losses give rise to new investment and consumption, as they so often do, capital stock losses actually can benefit GDP.

GDP also does a poor job of measuring the output of the service sector of an economy because there is no physical product as such. What is the product of nursing, dentistry, or teaching yoga classes (or prostitution for that matter)? According to economist Diane Coyle, what the financial services industry produces is especially difficult to measure. Economic development typically is associated with a move away from agriculture and manufacturing (areas GDP measures fairly well) and toward services (an area GDP does not measure well at all). This move is hugely consequential. At both the high and the lower ends of development, GDP is notably imprecise. For that reason, disaster consequences measured in GDP have to be viewed with great caution.

Discussing the flaws of GDP also gives an important insight into the reason wealthy countries and wealthy people might have the ability to rebound after a disaster. Disasters destroy manufactured capital more than anything else, and wealthy countries are not so reliant on this form of economic activity. Thus, the capacity of wealthy countries to keep going after a disaster is greater than that of an economy in which physical capital and capital production are more important.

The general implication (of our flawed measuring of disaster effects) for the socioeconomic consequences of natural disasters is fairly clear. Disasters mainly cause a rapid loss of lives (human capital) and a loss of physical capital stocks—built assets or crops in case of drought and floods—but that may have little or no effect on GDP because they are not explicitly included in the GDP formula. They would be seen in GDP only in places where the marginal return to capital is high, and hence a marginal loss of capital would cause a strong negative return. Rebuilding following a disaster, in contrast, can involve at least the first three components of GDP in a very positive way—private consumption, gross investments, and government spending. It isn't hard to see how the effects of a disaster could also be well hidden in GDP figures—or, perhaps worse, may be seen in GDP in some countries and not others, depending on the constituents of the economy. And it wouldn't be totally surprising if GDP were to *rise* as the result of a disaster in some settings, but that increase would be meaningless from the viewpoint of social progress.

SO HOW CAN WE THINK about how disaster losses affect the rich and the poor? Technical Appendix I presents a series of diagrams and some logic that might help explain, in a simplified way, how disaster loss and recovery possibilities can be conceptualized. Technical Appendix II presents some of the basics of so-called neoclassical growth theory that economics has relied on for decades, with suggestions about how disasters might be viewed in that framework.

According to neoclassical growth theory, as an economy starts to grow, at first there is a rapid gain in human welfare from year to year, and then that gain eventually flattens out. Very mature economies, such as those in the United States and Europe, are in the flattened, slow-growth phase. They have a large stock of wealth, but it is not growing very rapidly. China and India are the poster-child twins of high growth; Japan and Argentina may not be growing at all.

This implies that very poor economies should be growing rapidly, yet there are many instances in which they simply are not. Something must be wrong with the theory's treatment of the early stages of growth, even if it properly predicts the later stages. What might more realistically be happening at the start is what is called negative growth, a phenomenon described as a poverty trap.

Here is the classic description of a poverty trap:

- If you live in a poor country, you are very likely to get sick—due to poor sanitation, lack of health care, and the like.
- But if you are sick, you can't work or go to school—you can't earn, and you can't learn.
- So you get poorer. The poorer you get, the more likely you are to get sick. And so on.

The poverty trap is a self-amplifying feedback of bad consequences.

A country locked in this situation can do nothing to cause growth. In particular, additions of capital are ineffective in promoting growth because the economy isn't capable of making effective use of the capital. Haiti is a good example of this problem.

It also raises an interesting and unexpected factor in thinking about the economic consequences of disasters. If *additions* of capital are ineffective in promoting growth for poverty-trapped economies, then rapid *subtractions* of capital, as might be caused by a natural disaster, may have limited measurable impact as well, especially if GDP is the measure. If the economy is dead, it can't be made more dead. This leads to what has been called a vulnerability paradox: even though you might think, using very good System 1 reasoning, that poor countries are more vulnerable to the impacts of disasters than rich ones, they may in fact not be.

It also says that for very wealthy economies where growth is slow but absolute levels of capital wealth are high, the loss of capital may not be very damaging because the loss represents only a small proportion of the total value of the economy. This might be why the impact of Superstorm Sandy was fairly minor. New York's economy is hugely driven by service-sector activities, which barely lost pace for a moment.

Likewise, some individuals have large capital reserves, and others do not. For that reason, individuals will be able to manage quite differently. The owners of capital are better off than those who don't own it, even though most disasters are primarily events that cause loss of capital.

Imagine that an economy is halfway between rich and poor—say, India or Brazil. At a certain time in the history of a country's development, the economy has just managed to get out of poverty and is racing toward prosperity. At this stage, returns to capital are very high. Typically such economies are moving along at full capacity but with no reserves to fall back on in times of crisis. If a disaster happens at this stage, losses of capital could be very consequential. It is not hard to imagine such an economy being thrown back into a poverty trap after a disaster. So it could be, contrary to what System 1 thinking might lead you to believe, that robustly growing economies full of promise might be the most vulnerable.

SO WHAT DOES ALL THIS tell us?

We can see that the impact of disasters—economic and social, short term and long term—can be extremely difficult to discern. Many factors contribute to, and obscure, any assessment of what disasters actually do, including a natural-enough tendency to focus more on immediate disaster events with their attention-grabbing scenes of destruction (phase 2) than on their denouement, willful political obfuscation, and the disconnect between the approaches of the natural and social sciences that creates a void often filled by sci-enciness. Overall, however, it's clear that prosperity provides a shield against the worst that nature can do.

On the pathway to prosperity, societies face many barriers. Natural disasters compete with many other challenges, political and economic. Natural disasters probably do more harm to the prospects of poorer countries than to those of richer ones, but so do economic disasters, political crises, incompetent leadership, corruption, conflicts, and public health emergencies. All these crises are more likely to happen in poor countries and are more difficult to get under control. The Ebola crisis in West Africa is the leading example at the time of this writing. The very poorest countries may not be made poor by disasters, but disasters of all sorts may stand more firmly in the way of progress in poor countries than they do in rich countries.

Most free-market economies work, or are thought to work, because the holders of capital are far better off than those who do not hold capital. Holders of capital don't actually need to work; their capital works for them. The work they do amounts to ensuring that they remain among those with capital and that they can keep acquiring capital. For this reason, being close to the center of power, which may or may not be the government itself, is important because it allows holders of capital to manipulate policy, and hence laws, that will be most favorable to them.

Postdisaster situations—like postconflict situations and times when countries are rapidly emerging from autocratic rule and closed markets (Myanmar and Cuba)—are fertile ground for some and wastelands for others. An elite few make out-of-sight decisions about rebuilding or not rebuilding, about who will benefit from the lucrative contracts that will be part of any reconstruction and who will not. But more important still are the actions of another elite group (perhaps with some of the same members as the first), operating outside media scrutiny, to exploit an opportunity to reshape society in order to secure its hold on power and capital. Wealth is clearly a factor in long-term disaster outcomes. So let's now turn to a geographic view of disasters and wealth.

CHAPTER 2

THE GEOGRAPHY OF WEALTH AND POVERTY

KNOWLEDGE AND NATURAL DISASTERS

WHERE DO WEALTHY PEOPLE LIVE? WHERE DO POOR PEOPLE LIVE? WHERE IN the world are people most productive? Where are people at high risk from natural disasters? Is there any relationship between these different geographies?

The maps of the world shown in figure 2.1 tells us where wealth measured in gross domestic product (GDP) is generated. Most ways in which the wealth of countries is compared is in the form of tables and graphs. This depiction of the geography of wealth gives a sense of where people are wealthy and where they are poor rather than simply who is wealthy and who is poor. An earlier version of the map at lower resolution was first published by Jeff Sachs and colleagues in 1999.[1]

Some regions are obviously very high producers of GDP; some are very low. Coastal regions are often more wealthy than interior regions. There seem to be oases of prosperity amid economic deserts.

Figure 2.1

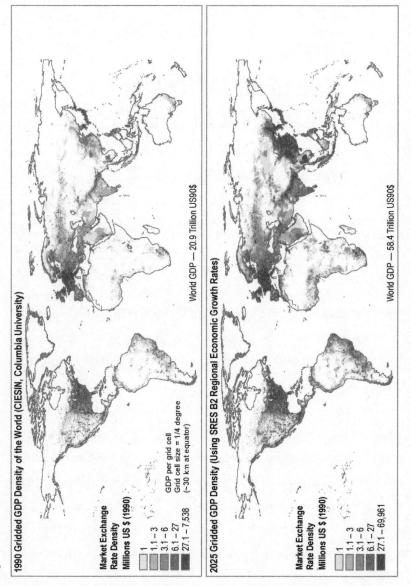

1990 Gridded GDP Density of the World (CIESIN, Columbia University)

Market Exchange
Rate Density
Millions US $ (1990)

1
1.1 – 3
3.1 – 6
6.1 – 27
27.1 – 7,538

GDP per grid cell
Grid cell size = 1/4 degree
(~30 km at equator)

World GDP — 20.9 Trillion US90$

2025 Gridded GDP Density (Using SRES B2 Regional Economic Growth Rates)

Market Exchange
Rate Density
Millions US $ (1990)

1
1.1 – 3
3.1 – 6
6.1 – 27
27.1 – 69,961

World GDP — 58.4 Trillion US90$

Source: Columbia University Center for International Earth Science Information Network (CEISIN), a NASA Socioeconomic Data and Applications Center | SEDAC.

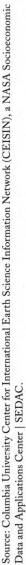

Some of the economic deserts are true deserts (or mountainous dense forests or frozen places) where few people live, but many are not. What these maps make clear is that the geographic distribution of wealth is tremendously uneven, both worldwide and within many countries. Economists know this but seldom portray the distribution of wealth in this manner.

Economists Jeffrey D. Sachs and William D. Nordhaus and their colleagues compiled these data and asked whether something as straightforward as latitude is a factor in determining wealth. They found something surprising—although there is no "Global South," a term that is in common use to mean the poor countries to the south of Europe, there is a global middle. With few exceptions, the poorest places on Earth lie closest to the equator, and the most productive parts on Earth are in the temperate zones north *and* south of the equator. Other economists, most notably Daron Acemoglu, have suggested that latitude has nothing at all to do with it; what matters are institutions, and the apparent geographic effect is just that, apparent or happenstance.[2] It is striking nonetheless that the most advanced countries are, for the most part, located in regions with fairly benign climates.

Another way to look at the geographic distribution of wealth is with night lights data—composite satellite images that show how Earth is lit up by light sources, as shown in figure 2.2.[3]

The most brightly lit places are the places of greatest wealth and correspond fairly well to the first map. Poor regions are dark. Economists are starting to use these data to give information on economic growth patterns, especially in poorer places where standard economic data are hard to come by and not especially reliable. It is far more spatially detailed than a countrywide figure like annual GDP growth.

"Night Lights 2012," a NASA night lights image that illustrates the geographic distribution of wealth across the globe.
Source: NASA Goddard Institute for Space Sciences (GISS).

Figure 2.3 is a night lights image of the Korean peninsula, the kind commonly used to display the stark difference in wealth between two geographically adjacent countries. The one tiny spot of light in North Korea is Pyongyang, the capital. On this map, with its finer level of resolution than that of figure 2.2, we can pick out cities and thin bands of light that show development along major roadways. A comparison between Haiti and the Dominican Republic or between Israel and Palestine is similarly (but not quite as) stark.

You can't hide economic activity from night light observations, unless it is performed underground. Night lights are blind to the difference between, say, formal and informal sectors of an economy, and they show everything that is going on that produces lights. In analyzing such data, you have to be sure you are not including forest fires and other sources of light that do not reflect economic productivity, and you must recognize that agricultural lands are not going to produce much light. When assessments are controlled for such factors, night lights provide a proxy economic output statement that does not

Figure 2.3

"The Koreas at Night," a NASA satellite image of North and South Korea, taken January 30, 2014. Pyongyang is the small, bright dot in the center of the image.
Source: NASA Earth Observatory.

rely on country reports with all the biases and differing standards that are inherent in them.

These maps give part of the answer to this chapter's opening question: Where do rich and poor people live? Although the maps are ways to represent where GDP wealth is produced, that does not imply that the average person living in a region that produces a lot of wealth is wealthy. The reverse is also true. Some very wealthy people live in very poor places. In most countries, no matter how poor the people are in an aggregate sense, there are rich people around.

GDP AND NIGHT LIGHTS MAPS are proxies for many types of activities.[4] The most brightly lit places typically are also cultural centers, places where theater and the arts thrive. And, importantly, for the purpose of our inquiry, the most brightly lit regions are, by and large, the places where science is produced. Science and wealth go more or less hand in hand. The National Science Foundation requested $7.255 billion from the US Congress for 2015. Most of the science funded by the NSF has little, if any, direct connection to social needs. A connection may come in the very long term or not at all, but immediate application to the welfare needs of US citizens is not required for a project to be funded. This is especially true of most fundamental forms of science, such as the search for the Higgs boson, which involves the use of a massively expensive apparatus. Our lives are not going to change very much because the Higgs boson has been confirmed or because a vehicle has landed on a comet.

No poor country has the luxury of resources to do this kind of research, and committing funds to such efforts would be an insanely wrong priority relative to other pressing needs. Many poor countries have no institutional science structure at all. Some have remnants from what was begun under colonial powers. A few of those have maintained a reasonable presence in higher education, but most have nothing resembling the research programs of wealthy countries. Where poorer nations have developed a capability in scientific research, it typically is focused on immediate needs. Agricultural research to improve crop yields in water-stressed areas is a good example.

NOW LOOK AT THE MAP in figure 2.4 of earthquakes of magnitude greater than 4.5 since 1973.

This map is formed of numerous small dots, one for every earthquake that occurred within the last 30 years with a magnitude greater than 4.5 on the Richter scale.[5] Like wealth, the distribution of earthquakes is far from even but in a different way. Earthquakes occur in fairly tight bands or long smudges rather than in islands of intense seismic activity, and large regions of the planet are more or less free

Figure 2.4

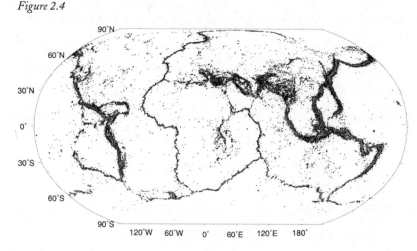

A map highlighting all the occurrences of earthquakes that exceeded a magnitude of 4.5 since 1973.

Source: US Geological Survey.

of earthquakes. The map shows how seismologists see the world, as a filigree of seismic disturbances that originate deep within Earth and pay no attention to human societies and how they might choose to divide up the world. In fact, the map shows none of the usual outlines of continents or countries. It represents how Earth is figured, or disfigured, by earthquakes, not by humans.

The bands of earthquakes occur at tectonic plate boundaries, and their configuration on Earth today reflects the location of those boundaries right now. The boundaries shift very slowly.[6] A map like this drawn 50 million years ago would look quite different, but one drawn 5 million years ago would look very much the same. Earthquakes will continue to occur where they do now for millions of years to come. Night lights maps or GDP density maps for 1900 would have looked much different from those of today, and they will be vastly different in the future.

Figure 2.5 is another geophysical map, this one showing the tracks of tropical cyclones (also called hurricanes and typhoons depending on the region).[7]

Tropical cyclones also have a very distinct distribution, with regions of intense activity and others completely free of cyclones, but the distribution is utterly different from that of earthquakes because the forces that give rise to earthquakes have no connection to those that produce cyclones. Earthquakes originate from forces caused by ultraslow movement of the deep mantle within the solid Earth, while cyclones are the product of atmospheric disturbances. Although the pattern of earthquakes will change only very slowly because the forces that drive them are very slow, significant changes are anticipated in the magnitude spectrum of strong storms (how many cyclones will be of a particular strength each year) and their geographic range as climate change alters temperatures and thus the atmospheric temperature gradients that drive these phenomena. One way to think about

Figure 2.5

Tracks and Intensity of All Tropical Storms

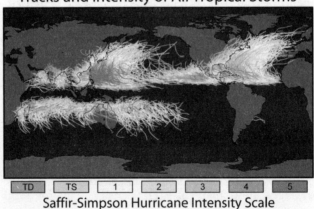

Saffir-Simpson Hurricane Intensity Scale

Gray-scaled version of a plot where colors indicate hurricane intensity.
Source: NASA.

the effects of climate change is to recognize that it implies an expansion of the tropics that could mean extensions both north and south to the range of tropical cyclones and tropical diseases. Because of this extension, cyclones may become common in places where previously they were rare or unknown. New York may experience a Sandy-like storm every few decades rather than once a century. Brazil, currently spared the wrath of hurricanes, may begin to experience them.

OF ALL NATURAL DISASTERS, earthquakes (including those that induce tsunamis) and cyclones do the most damage, much more than landslides, lightning strikes, volcanic eruptions, and most floods.[8] Volcanic eruptions have a distribution much like earthquakes because they too result from plate boundary processes, but, with notable exceptions, they rarely cause damage on the scale of earthquakes.[9] None of the other disasters has the same distinct, and distinctly different, geographic patterns. Here we focus our discussions mostly on cyclones and earthquakes.

In some settings, droughts and floods may be very damaging and economically very consequential. Droughts are the leading natural disasters in poor countries, which typically have economies dependent on agricultural exports, and they can have long-term effects. In contrast, most settings can recover fairly quickly from the effects of floods. Floods, as I noted before, may have positive economic effects in the years that follow. For example, among other factors, floods can recharge groundwater reserves, which can benefit crop production in the following year or years by providing ample water for irrigation.

SCIENCE, MAINLY GENERATED in the rich world, can tell us exactly why earthquakes happen in some places and not in others. It can also tell us how likely it is that earthquakes of different magnitudes will occur in different places. Happily, very large–magnitude earthquakes don't occur often, but very tiny earthquakes occur all the time. For example, about a million magnitude 2 earthquakes occur every year. No one but seismologists knows that because they are rarely felt and cause little or no damage. Only about 20 magnitude 7 earthquakes occur yearly, and most of those are sufficiently far from populated areas that they also are not usually felt.[10] Truly huge earthquakes, around magnitude 9, are mercifully very rare. In the last 100 years or so, there have been only five earthquakes at the top end of the magnitude scale—two in Chile (1960 and 2010), one in Indonesia (2004), one in Alaska (1964), and most recently the 2011 event off Japan. The storied 1906 earthquake in San Francisco, at magnitude 7.8, wouldn't make it into an earthquake hall of fame.

Remarkably, a simple mathematical expression describes exactly how often small and medium-size earthquakes happen compared to the biggest ones. In fact, all earthquakes of all sizes scale to one another. The expression is called the Guttenberg-Richter relationship (the same Frank Richter who gives his name to the commonly used magnitude scale) and is in a class of formulas called power law relationships. The Guttenberg-Richter relationship tells us in mathematical form what we know already—that very large earthquakes don't happen very often—and it gives a quantitative measure of how often we can expect very large quakes to occur based on how often smaller ones occur. An extraordinary number of phenomena can be described by power law relationships. For example, if we know how many small cities a country has, we can reasonably estimate the number of large cities it has, because we know, statistically, that for every big number X of small cities, there is a smaller number x of large cities. The same is true for earthquakes. The surprising thing is that there is such a rigorous and dependable relationship between small and large earthquakes. The distribution is not random, with the most common value lying in the middle of the distribution, like people's height.

Science has a very good understanding about why earthquakes occur where they do but much less understanding of why magnitudes *should* obey a power law function. And the goal of predicting exactly when a large earthquake will happen and exactly where within the elongated bands of earthquakes has eluded science. Most seismologists have serious doubts that this goal will ever be met.

METEOROLOGY PROVIDES AN UNDERSTANDING of why cyclones occur where they do and why they exhibit distinctly curved tracks that look a little like fish hooks. The prediction challenge here is to calculate the track a cyclone will take once formed and what strength it will attain. The critical issues to predict are where the cyclone will make landfall, what its sustained wind speed will be at that time, and the size of the storm surge along the coast so people can be warned and evacuated from areas most likely to be impacted. Storm surge height and maximum wind strength are related, but not in a strictly linear way; seafloor topography and coastal features like bays and inlets influence storm surge height as well. In most parts of the world, storm surge heights can be predicted reasonably well from wind speed data. In wealthier parts of the world, where the seafloor structures have been mapped, very accurate and detailed predictions are possible. Storm surge, rather than strong wind, is responsible for most cyclone-related damage and deaths. Winds are responsible for power outages, most often caused by trees falling on power lines.

Meteorology can explain the geographic distribution of cyclones and why they are sometimes very large and don't amount to much at other times. Cyclones almost always start off traveling from east to west, whether in the Northern or the Southern Hemisphere. The Earth rotates toward the east, and cyclones are obliged to travel in response to the rotation.

In the Atlantic Ocean basin, storm tracks usually look as if they originate from about the same place, a region just off the west coast of Africa. They don't all form there, however, especially in the early months of the hurricane season, when they form more often on the western side of the Atlantic. Hurricanes form where very warm air and very warm water combine; these conditions are present off the Atlantic coast of Africa when extremely hot winds blow off the Sahara and ocean waters are unusually warm. Those conditions create intense evaporation; clouds form, and a disorganized collection of small storms emerges. As they grow, these storms begin to be influenced by a natural phenomenon known as the Coriolis effect, which adds a spin to their motion.[11] The several smaller storms then build into one large storm that can eventually become a hurricane.

To keep growing, the storm needs warm water in its path as it works its way westward on the trade winds. Tropical oceans provide that water. If an Atlantic hurricane ventures into the Gulf of Mexico, it can quickly grow in strength because the waters of the Gulf are fairly confined and often very warm. The overall path of a hurricane—a westward initial track that gradually hooks north—is also a consequence of the Coriolis effect. A hurricane is influenced by the patterns of atmospheric pressure as well. The Bermuda High, for instance, is a quasi-stable feature in the Atlantic during hurricane season that essentially pushes or holds hurricane tracks to the south of where they would otherwise go; hurricanes head north only when they have escaped the influence of the Bermuda High. Superstorm Sandy's somewhat unusual track—taking a sharp landward turn after heading northward well offshore—was the result of a high-pressure ridge that blocked its northward track.

Hurricanes diminish in strength as they head northward because they encounter colder and colder water. When they make landfall, they tend to peter out fairly quickly as they are deprived of warm water. They can still dump a tremendous amount of rain while traveling inland; freshwater flooding is common. In many wealthy countries today, inland flash flooding causes almost as much loss of life as storm surge because storm surge warnings are usually accurate and people can evacuate the affected areas. However, flash floods, as the name implies, develop very rapidly and much less forewarning is possible.

Just as there are places that seldom experience earthquakes, there are also places that seldom experience cyclones and others that experience more and stronger cyclones than elsewhere. South America hardly ever suffers from cyclones, and most of Africa is spared except for Mozambique and Madagascar. The whole South Atlantic is spared cyclone activity, as is the very middle equatorial belt.[12]

The equivalent of the Richter scale for cyclone strength is the Saffir-Simpson scale, a five-level scale based on wind speed.[13] At category 5, sustained winds may exceed 157 miles per hour (mph). Wind speeds in Typhoon Haiyan in the Philippines in late 2013 had sustained winds of nearly 190 mph; Haiyan was one of the strongest storms on record. The strongest cyclones on record formed in the Pacific Ocean, where they are called typhoons. They can become so strong because they have such a large expanse of warm ocean to cross, which gives them plenty of time to build in strength. They often cross the Philippines, losing some power, then build again as they head for China. Because the Atlantic and Indian oceans are much smaller than the Pacific, cyclones that form there typically do not reach the same size.

The understanding of tropical cyclones is such that in most parts of the world and at most times, it is possible to warn of their approach in sufficient time to allow for societies to prepare in a way that minimizes fatalities, primarily through evacuation. In Bangladesh, where evacuation would be difficult and communications are imperfect, permanent cyclone shelters have been constructed. These are very simple places of refuge built on strong pilings that are taller than the level of the highest historic storm surge. They proved their worth in 2007 during Cyclone Sidr; although 3,000 people were killed, many lives were saved. In comparison, Cyclone Bohla in 1970 is thought to have taken 500,000 lives in Bangladesh, making it one of the deadliest natural disasters of all time.

NO WARNING IS POSSIBLE for earthquakes, although science does have a very good understanding of the type of quake that gives rise to tsunamis and how tsunami waves propagate across the ocean. Very large earthquakes beneath the ocean floor off Japan, Indonesia, and elsewhere can cause tsunamis because the quake rapidly displaces the ocean floor, causing the ocean waters to move too. Tsunami heights usually are predicted quite accurately, although, as with storm surges, local seafloor topography and coastal features are important factors and are not always known in detail. Warnings can be made up to several hours in advance of a wave's arrival, depending on the distance of ocean it crosses, and this can save lives. The survival strategy is simple in principle: move to high ground as quickly as possible. But, of course, these warnings cannot save capital assets, most of which are immovable and difficult to protect.

What makes earthquake prediction so hard and cyclone track prediction relatively easier? One way to think about it is in terms of what scientists would call realizations: the number of repeat events. Almost every year, somewhere in the world a cyclone will form and reach the maximum strength on the Saffir-Simpson scale. Due to cyclone frequency, over a period of just a few decades, a data set can be collected that covers all possible cyclone strengths and all parts of the oceans where cyclones occur. In fact, cyclone records have been kept for more than 100 years, and there are thousands of tracks—realizations—stored for analysis. Hundreds of these tracks are of category 5 cyclones.

Because the largest earthquakes happen so infrequently, we have only a handful of realizations.[14] Although that is lucky for human societies, it is unlucky for scientific analysis. Oddly enough, those few that have occurred affected wealthy to middle-income countries— the United States, Japan, Chile (twice), and Indonesia. Luckily, very few historic large earthquakes have occurred in very poor countries. It's hard to imagine what would have happened in Haiti had the 2010 earthquake been magnitude 9 rather than the much smaller 7.0. From a statistical standpoint, the data set of earthquakes is sparse at the top end. To have a suitable data population that includes very large quakes, we would need seismograph recordings for thousands of years. The modern seismograph network is only a little more than 60 years old.

The fundamental reason why earthquake prediction is extremely difficult is that it requires predicting several factors at once: the time when a rupture will take place, on which of the many thousands of faults the rupture will occur, how much of the fault will rupture, and how much the shift will displace the crust. It would also be good to know how deep in the Earth fault rupture will occur, because for an earthquake of any given magnitude, the shallower the rupture, the more ground motion occurs and the more damage potential there is. And the ability to predict relies heavily on knowing the current state of stress in Earth, and that is something we really don't know in enough detail to be very helpful.

Attempts have been made to track large earthquake occurrences into the distant past using historic information. Both the Japanese and the Chinese keep detailed records of the damage done by major earthquakes, and these records, plus descriptions of ground shaking, can provide estimates of what is called the "recurrence time" of large earthquakes. The devastating Tohoku earthquake and tsunami of 2011 was at first thought to be unprecedented in magnitude for the region at 9.1, but after examining the historic records, seismologists found evidence of a very similar event 1,000 years earlier. Just how helpful that is seems somewhat debatable: How should a society prepare for a once-in-1,000-year event?

Another reason earthquake prediction is so difficult arises from the very nature of quakes. They occur when Earth's outer crust, or shell, fractures. Forces that arise beneath the crust (mostly due to the great heat of the inner Earth) constantly exert themselves on the planet's rigid outer shell. When these forces overcome the strength of the crust to resist movement, a fracture occurs to relieve the stress. These fractures occur mostly at weak points in the crust. Faults are some of those weak points—places that have already failed before. Like a dinner plate with a crack in it, chances are that if the crust breaks, it will find a fault to break along.

Large, active faults are often very easy to see in the landscape, as shown in the photo in figure 2.6, which is a satellite image of the Enriquillo-Plantain Garden Fault, which moved in 2010 in Haiti. (Actually, a splay, or secondary offshoot, of this fault moved, not the main fault itself.)

The Haitian capital of Port-au-Prince is located on the natural harbor to the right in the image. A heavy black arrow guides your eye to the location of the fault. Once you know where to look, the fault is quite obvious. It runs just south of the city. There appears to be a road running almost east-west on top of a ridge that is part of the expression of the fault. The San Andreas Fault in California is similarly easy to see at this scale. People without training in geology would not recognize these features at ground level, and the danger they pose is not especially evident. A fault that has not moved in hundreds of years is even more difficult to recognize from ground level.

Geologists, however, do know the locations of almost all faults. Even in very poor places like Haiti, where few, if any, local scientists

Figure 2.6

"Quake Aftershock Damage Seen by NASA Satellite," a NASA Image of the Day. The image, taken on January 21, 2010, reveals damage from the aftershocks of the quake. The Enriquillo-Plaintain Garden Fault line, indicated by the black arrow, is highly visibile in this image.

Source: NASA/GSFC/METI/ERSDAC/JAROS, and U.S./Japan ASTER Science Team.

are mapping faults, their pattern is usually reasonably well known because at some point a colonizing power sent geologists to assess the land's potential for minerals and other raw materials. Faults appear on maps made in the earliest years of the British colonization of Africa and India.

It is very difficult to forecast when a fault will slip to generate an earthquake because we don't know much about either the state of stress in the Earth or how much stress faults can endure before rupturing.[15] Weather forecasts use computer models to see forward in time, and these require data that describe the state of the atmosphere now: atmospheric pressure, wind speed and direction, temperature, humidity, and many other factors. These data have been acquired over a long period of time from satellites, weather balloons, and ground-based measurements. It is fairly easy to interrogate this long record to build up an understanding of how weather systems develop and to use that understanding to make predictions.

The same idea applies to forecasting what will happen in Earth's crust in the future, but we don't have detailed measurements of what is going on in the crust beneath us. So seismologists are like weather forecasters before there were satellite measurements or even weather balloons. If we could somehow measure *stress weather*—the buildup and movement of stress in a broad region around a fault—we could reconstruct the conditions that evolved in Earth as a fault gradually inched toward rupture. But getting these data would require thousands of boreholes embedded with thousands of stress-measuring devices and continuous measurement of their output before and after every earthquake for years to come. Then maybe we would have a better sense of what happens in the prelude to earthquakes and be able to make predictions. Even then several accurate predictions of damaging earthquakes would be required before a prediction scheme would be thought reliable and could be used operationally.

Right now, there are no reliable precursors—signals from Earth that warn it is about to rupture—though many people claim they had some sort of premonition of when an quake would occur. You may have heard of foreshocks and aftershocks, particularly the latter, which very commonly follow the main shock. Aftershocks represent the continued release of built-up stress, because the main shock doesn't release all the stress. The magnitude of aftershocks decreases with time, and they become less frequent in a very predictable way.[16] Those that happen soon after the main shock can have a magnitude near to that of the main shock and can be damaging.

Foreshocks are much more poorly understood. It might be reasonable to suppose that as a fault is stressed nearer and nearer to its moment of failure, it sends out some recognizable signals that we could read as warnings. But no such signals have been found yet. In fact, typically we don't recognize foreshocks that have been recorded until *after* the main shock occurs. Earthquakes often come in swarms of tremors, many smaller quakes over a period of days or weeks, sometimes building in magnitude, sometimes not. It is essentially impossible to tell if a swarm of tremors is or is not the portent of a main shock. About 1 in 100 tremor swarms is a rehearsal for a main shock; in other words, even if a tremor swarm is recorded, the likelihood that a large earthquake is imminent rises by only 1 percent.

MISUNDERSTANDING THE MEANING of tremors was probably at the heart of a tragedy in L'Aquila, Italy, in 2009. In the early morning, a 5.8-magnitude earthquake—not very large—struck, causing 309 deaths. Earlier there had been a series of tremors that frightened the residents, many of whom chose to sleep outdoors. Earthquakes are at their most dangerous at night when people are asleep. Italy's Major Risks Committee was called in to assess the situation. Part of what its members said was correct but unhelpful: They saw "no reason to suppose a sequence of small earthquakes could be the prelude to a strong event" and believed that "a major earthquake in the area is unlikely but can't be ruled out."[17] That's completely correct, but the committee did not tell the people of L'Aquila how they should behave. They left it up to the people themselves to decide whether to continue to sleep outdoors.

A week before the quake, one statement was reported that people did act on because it was much clearer. Dr. Bernardo De Bernardinis—deputy head of the Department of Civil Protection and acting as spokesman for a group of government scientists that included the six seismologists who formed the Major Risks Committee—is said to have told a member of the press that "the scientific community tells me there is no danger [of a large earthquake] because there is an ongoing discharge of energy."[18]

The tragedy of the L'Aquila quake hasn't ended. A year later, De Bernardinis and the six members of the scientific panel were charged with manslaughter on behalf of 29 residents who allegedly had taken those words of assurance to heart. All seven were convicted and faced significant jail sentences and large fines, not for failing to make an accurate prediction (which almost all seismologists think they were convicted of) but rather for doing a shoddy job in assessing the situation and making the public aware of the risks. In effect, they were convicted of professional malpractice.

On appeal, six committee members had their convictions overturned; De Bernardinis was only partially exonerated. His sentence was reduced but not overturned.

The take-away message has at least two parts. First, it is important to get the science right. De Bernardinis was close. He may have had in mind the fact that sections of some faults creep, moving as we hope all faults would do: little by little, releasing stress in small packages instead of one large event.[19] Second, accurate and clear communication is critical. Most people have a very difficult time assessing risk and expect experts to spell out clearly what risks they face. In this case, De Bernardinis's statement was clear but wrong.

It does, however, have a ring of plausibility to it. It is easy enough to imagine that the bit-by-bit release of energy could indeed be making things safer. I introduced the idea of *scienciness* earlier. De Bernardinis's statement is an example of scienciness committed by a scientist that may have had deadly consequences.

A SIMPLE COMPARISON of the two maps in figure 2.1 and the map of earthquake distribution in figure 2.4 shows that there isn't an obvious relationship between past earthquake occurrences and present-day poverty and wealth. Afghanistan and Pakistan have high earthquake risks, as does Bangladesh. Northern India and the Himalayan countries are at high risk also, but it would be quite a stretch to suggest that earthquakes gave rise to these countries' low levels of development or are currently inhibiting their development.

But that's not really the point. Roger Bilham, a seismologist at the University of Colorado in Boulder, worries most about what might happen in the future and paints a very grim picture. In an influential paper titled "The Seismic Future of Cities," he argues that rapid population growth, particularly in poorer parts of the world, will require vast additions of building stock that are unlikely to be seismically safe, given the history of building practices in those regions. He thinks the world will soon see a million-fatality earthquake.[20]

Bilham emphasizes that disasters are worse killers if they affect cities, and many cities in poorer areas are growing rapidly and often chaotically, with little, if any, attention paid to construction standards or enforcement. Bribery and corruption are rife. The 2010 earthquake in Haiti might serve to make the point. So too might the earthquake in the province of Sichuan, China, in 2008. Both of these rapidly growing regions are noted for the poor quality of their buildings, especially public buildings. In China, the tragedy was amplified because so many schools were destroyed; the fatalities among schoolchildren (and their teachers) were appalling. China even has a term to describe structures of such poor construction quality: they are "tofu dreg" projects, referring to the remains that are left over after making tofu.[21] The term refers to both the building materials—such as cement building blocks in which the sand fraction is far too high, for instance—and the construction process itself, in which too few steel-reinforcing elements (rebar) might be used in columns.

The message here is simple. As the adage familiar to all seismologists and well known to the citizens of L'Aquila says, earthquakes don't kill people; buildings kill people. Sometimes earthquakes trigger landslides that bury people, but the point is that, *Superman* movies notwithstanding, the ground does not open up and swallow people. Death comes when your home, workplace, or a shopping center collapses and crushes you. Buildings are more deadly at some times of day than others. For example, schools are more deadly during the daytime hours when students are inside.

In homes, earthquakes are deadliest at night, when people are asleep. A shaking home may wake residents, but when half-awake and in the dark, people have trouble thinking quickly enough to find somewhere safe to shelter or to get out into the open. The L'Aquila earthquake struck at 3:32 in the morning; most victims were found in their beds, crushed to death by their collapsed homes.

The amount of shaking needed to cause a building to collapse depends on the integrity of the building itself and of the surface on which it was built. In vast sections of blighted areas of Detroit and other US cities that have fallen on hard times, the buildings often are partly collapsed. Water has invaded the structures, causing critical beams to rot and be unable to bear the weight of roofs and walls. The Rana Plaza building in Bangladesh collapsed on its own in 2013 without any earthquake, killing 1,129 people, mostly female garment workers on the four upper floors—unauthorized additions to the original building, which consisted of a bank, stores, and apartments on the lower floors. Cracks in the building the previous day had caused all but the garment factories to be evacuated. The garment workers were forced to work under threat of being fired or having their pay withheld.[22] After a power outage in the morning, a diesel generator was started up on an upper floor. Soon after the building collapsed. The upper floors of the building were so badly built and contained so much heavy machinery that the vibration of the generator may have been enough to shake it into rubble.

A contributing factor in the collapse was the ground on which the building was constructed. The area included a pond that had been roughly filled in. The building was partly located on the in-filled pond, so part of the structure rested on very soft ground and part on firmer ground. This is a recipe for serious problems. Part of the overweight building would have slowly sunk into the soft ground while part would have resisted. The cracks that opened in the building the day before its collapse were most likely the result of differences in the underlying support that caused parts of the building to subside while other parts stayed firm. Rana Plaza was ready to topple at any moment.

To get a sense of how important ground conditions are in determining the highly variable nature of damage that can be done by an earthquake, look at the image in figure 2.7.[23]

Figure 2.7

Evidence of liquefaction during an earthquake in Christchurch, New Zealand, in 2011.

Source: NZ Raw. Photograph by Mark Lincoln of marklincoln.co.nz. Used with permission.

In the figure, it looks like the back end of a car has been sawn off at a bizarre angle and dumped on the ground, but the car has actually sunk into the ground. On the window, you can actually see a high-water mark, suggesting it was even more deeply submerged at one point. You might think someone had the misfortune of driving into a deep pool of mud, but the mud was actually created by shaking during the Christchurch earthquake in New Zealand in 2011. The process, called liquefaction, commonly happens when very soft, wet soil is shaken during an earthquake. Liquefaction typically is seen in portside areas that have been built out with landfill. Much of the Marina District in San Francisco and the southern tip of Manhattan were formed that way using material excavated for the foundations of tall city skyscrapers. Houses in the Marina District were all but submerged in the 1906 earthquake and again during the 1989 Loma Prieta earthquake.

The image in figure 2.8 appears in almost every textbook description of liquefaction. It shows a group of buildings in Niigata, Japan, that look identical in construction type. They all experienced the same earthquake on June 16, 1964, but one building is flat on its side, one is tilted half over, another is tilted just a little, and others remain upright. Soil liquefaction is the reason for the earthquake's variable effects, which are obviously very localized. It wasn't bad luck that the one building toppled; it was located on especially weak soil.[24]

There are many causes for the very uneven distribution of damage in most earthquakes, but when a fully intact building topples, as shown in figure 2.8, it is a sure sign that ground conditions were the issue.

Look back at figure 2.7, the photograph of the sunken car. In the background, next to an apparently undamaged house, is a car in a driveway that is in perfectly good shape, sitting high on what must be solid ground. The fact that it is perhaps 30 yards away from the vehicle in the foreground indicates that the effects of liquefaction and soil conditions in general can be highly localized.

Figure 2.8

Liquefaction during an earthquake is illustrated in this photo of the aftermath of a quake in Niijata, Japan in 1964.

Source: U.S. Geological Survey

Just as scientists can map faults, they understand how to assess ground conditions. The equipment required is neither expensive nor difficult to operate. Operators do not require high-level training. So like faults, ground conditions can be mapped in almost any setting around the world.

When earthquake waves propagate through the Earth, they shake different types of ground by varying amounts with distinct results. Even if the ground doesn't fully liquefy, it responds very differently according to the type of rock layers, their age, the extent of weathering, and many other factors. Very loose soil shakes more than very solid ground.[25] This variable effect often accounts for much of the difference in damage from place to place. Liquefaction is an extreme expression of this effect.

Topography makes a difference too. Just as the shape of a glass lens in a telescope or magnifying glass focuses light energy, the shape of Earth's surface and the rock layers beneath can focus seismic energy. Sharply peaked ridges, for instance, can show particularly severe fracturing (sometimes described as shattering by geotechnicians). Small depressions of softer rocks can cause seismic energy to reverberate and amplify, causing more severe local shaking than in surrounding areas.

The net result is that the damage caused by an earthquake can appear capricious, with completely collapsed buildings next to others that show little if any damage. Older buildings may remain in good condition while newer ones are severely damaged. Of course, more damage might be expected in poor countries where governance is weak and/or corruption levels are high. But good governance and low corruption are no guarantees of suffering less damage. New Zealanders were fairly astonished when the relatively modern Canterbury Television Building collapsed, causing more than half the total deaths in the 2011 quake. It had been inspected several times after earlier earthquakes and was found to be in good condition. The construction was sound and up to code. The ground was solid and suitable for the size of the structure. No one was bribed. No one cut corners. No one cheated. Yet the building collapsed. After a royal commission investigation, no one was charged.

Many people in the New Zealand governance system are well versed in earthquake hazard assessment. The island country experiences many earthquakes, and people there have learned a lot about how to make buildings earthquake resistant. In fact, almost everyone trained in seismology anywhere in the world has studied the earthquakes of New Zealand. The nation has very stringent building codes and strict enforcement. After every quake, no matter how small, buildings are inspected and their safety is assessed. Unsafe buildings are closed until they are properly repaired and have passed inspection or are torn down. In 2013, New Zealand tied with Denmark as the least corrupt place in the world, as rated by Transparency International.[26] Haiti ranked number 163 of 177 countries rated. For comparison, the United States came in nineteenth, tied with Uruguay.

It is important to recognize that buildings collapse and people die in well-governed countries with almost no corruption and in highly corrupt countries with almost no governance. There is little doubt that many fewer buildings typically collapse during earthquake disasters in advanced countries than in poor places. We can hope that what happened at Rana Plaza is an extreme outlier, but there can be little doubt that other buildings of the same sort are ready to fall at the slightest tremor and that tens of thousands of people—perhaps millions, as geological sciences professor Roger Bilham suggests— risk their lives by working in them or visiting them for school, shopping, or any of the most common acts of daily life. Corruption in the building industry is a major problem, but it is wrong to point the finger of blame at corrupt officials every time a building collapses and people are killed in an earthquake.

THE BOTTOM LINE IS THIS: Earthquakes cannot be predicted, so the best thing any country can do is understand how prone it is to quakes, how likely large quakes might be, how the risks are distributed, and how strong the ground is and then not build in risky places. If there is no chance to restrict areas for development, then the strength of built structures in risky areas should be assessed. Any built structures that can be made stronger should be, especially schools and bridges. But because doing so can be very expensive, abandoning the most unsafe structures may be required.

NOW COMPARE THE MAPS in figures 2.1 and 2.2 with that of cyclone tracks in figure 2.5. There might seem to be a strong case that cyclones have a role in determining poverty levels, but it is not wholly convincing at this coarse level of analysis. Atlantic hurricanes primarily affect the Caribbean and southern United States. Those states (and Washington, DC) are the poorest by far in the United States. Latin America is on the whole progressing fairly well economically, but the Caribbean region is doing less well, with Haiti the leading example of economic struggle. The Central American countries are poor as well and are impacted by numerous natural hazards—hurricanes, earthquakes, and volcanic activity. The Philippines sits at the dead center of where Pacific typhoons reach their maximum strength; it is also a poor country compared to its neighbors, which are less impacted by typhoons.

Tropical cyclones are, after all, tropical in their geography. As Sachs and Nordhaus have pointed out, tropical regions are the least productive in the world.[27] Tropical cyclones rarely reach into the temperate, most productive parts of the world. Look at the maps in figure 2.1, and you will see that much economic activity is coastal in its distribution. The reason is that it is much easier to manage trade from the coast than from inland. Many of the world's greatest cities are on the coastal outlets of rivers, which allow goods produced inland to be shipped easily to port. New York on the Hudson and London on the Thames are leading examples.

Of course, scholars might argue that there many reasons why these countries and states have evolved to different levels of development, including important factors like the legacy of colonial rule. Proneness to cyclone strikes might well be part of the reason for the uneven distribution of wealth, but it would be hard to make the case that it is *the* reason.

But, as in the case for earthquakes, that's not so much the point. Cyclones will keep happening, just as earthquakes will. But with climate change we can expect cyclones to change their strength distribution to include more cyclones in the highest category and to range farther to the north and the south. People will continue to live in places prone to cyclone strikes because of the advantages those areas offer and will do their best to improve their own welfare. The best thing cyclone-prone societies can do is understand the risks as much as possible, try not to build in the most hazardous places, and provide protections in places that are already populated. Protections here don't mean structural features of buildings but rather seawalls and other barriers to withstand storm surges. The strategy is essentially the same as for earthquake: assess the physical risks, then protect or move.

THERE IS A PROBLEM HERE, and it is not trivial. It goes back to the maps in figure 2.1 and what they tell us. As noted, these maps indicate both where wealth is produced and where science is produced. There is almost nowhere in Africa, except in South Africa, where someone can obtain a PhD in seismology or climatology. Some countries on the continent have never registered a patent for anything (a measure often used to judge scientific acumen), and many of these countries lack the institutional structure to issue patents anyway. The same is true for Haiti, which has one seismologist. What results is that there is little local notion of the risks that poor countries face based on the work of their own scientists.

The paradox is that scientists working in relatively safe places like Europe, where earthquake and cyclone risks are low, know more about risks to poor countries than people in those countries know themselves. The largess of wealthy countries is needed to provide poor countries with information about their risks, to help train local scientists, and to set up monitoring networks, but typically funds are hard to come by.

There is only one working seismometer in Myanmar, and it is over 50 years old. There was only one in Gujarat, India, when the

Bhuj earthquake struck in 2001, killing perhaps 20,000 people. In the wake of that earthquake, and with the help of funds from the Asian Development Bank, an Institute of Seismological Research was established in Gandhinagar; a network of 60 seismometers and 54 strong motion accelerograms has been set up as well.[28] In a decade or so of recording, Gujarat will have a much improved idea of its seismic risks.

The fact that poor countries have few, if any, seismometers typically is not due to poor governance. Myanmar had established a larger (though still inadequate) network in the 1960s. The seismometers were donated by the United States, Japan, or China, and all but one fell into disuse during Myanmar's period of military rule.

Many poorer countries have much higher priorities than determining their earthquake risks. For example, in poor tropical countries, malaria typically kills many more people annually than do earthquakes. Death comes from poor-quality water more often than from the shaking of the ground, so the national priority should be to clean up the water supply. More souls would be saved per dollar spent on water improvement than on earthquake engineering.

A SIMILAR SCENARIO APPLIES to cyclones—in fact, to most natural disasters. Superstorm Sandy may have been a perfect storm in many meteorologically interesting ways, but it was close to a perfectly predicted storm as well. All forms of media provided constant warnings for days in advance, evacuation protocols were determined, and people were moved out of low-lying areas. There was considerable storm surge damage, especially to beachfront towns, and power was lost in many inland regions for four days or more. Transportation systems were interrupted for much longer. Many people were inconvenienced, but relatively few were killed. Using Red Cross data, the Centers for Disease Control and Prevention put the total number of fatalities in the United States at 117. New York suffered more deaths than other states. Many who died drowned in their homes in areas where evacuation orders had been issued. This was also the case for sea-front residents of Mississippi when Hurricane Katrina came ashore in 2005. The death toll would likely have been around half the total had everyone been willing or able to heed the evacuation orders. Com-pared to the many millions of people who experienced the storm, 117 deaths is a tiny number. Statistically it could be treated as effectively a zero fatality event—completely characteristic of a disaster in a rich country. A storm like Sandy would certainly have killed many more people had it made landfall in a place like Bangladesh, the country that may hold the all-time record for cyclone fatalities.

Generally, poor nations have much less access to disaster-related information, and even if they have access, the information itself or its dissemination is compromised in some way.[29]

The result? In poorer countries, an elite few with higher educa-tion and an ability to be part of a global community of scientists, or educated enough to know how to understand scientific information, know the risks they and others face. They also know how to protect themselves and have the means to do so. They know when a warn-ing to evacuate makes sense and probably make their own decisions anyway. They can build strong houses on strong ground. They would never allow their houses to be built below standard.

Members of that elite may be part of the government or they may not be, but either way they control wealth and political power. The massive inequality in wealth across the globe and within coun-tries—which, as discussed in chapter 1, determines the highly vari-able outcomes of disasters—is matched and exceeded by the massive inequality in the natural science–based knowledge of the dangers people face in risk-prone places. And just as the chasm between the natural and social sciences discussed earlier creates a void that can be filled and exploited by scienciness, those who have knowledge can exploit knowledge inequalities for their own profit. Poor people in poor countries generally know the least and thus are most at risk both during and after disaster events. Which brings us to Haiti, the focus of the next chapter.

CHAPTER 3

CARNAGE IN THE CARIBBEAN, CHAOS IN CONCEPCIÓN

IN HAITI, PROFITEERING IS PART OF EVERYDAY LIFE. IT TAKES MANY FORMS, depending on where the profiteer fits within the society's structure. In 2010, there were two very different ways of life in Haiti. And those two ways life changed (or ended) when an earthquake shook the capital, Port-au-Prince, senseless on the twelfth day of that year.

In his book *The Big Truck That Went By*,[1] Jonathan Katz devotes a chapter to describing the two classes in Haiti—*blan* and *neg*. *Blan* derives from "white," but it is used to mean "foreigner" regardless of skin color; *neg*, though derived from "Negro" or "black person," is less related to skin color than to class. The neg are the lowermost class. It's a them-and-us distinction that Katz describes as the "cardinal division of Haitian society." You are part of one or the other, and there is no movement between the two and no mixing.

The blan is made up of a very small group of wealthy people who run most of the businesses in Haiti. At the time of the quake, if you were part of that elite, you lived extremely well by any global standard. If you were in this group, you were probably not Haitian by birth and you may not have had Haitian nationality; more likely you were French, Lebanese, Syrian, or German.

As one of the elite, you probably lived in the lush enclave of Pétionville, in a large mansion behind a strong high gate and protected by high walls topped with razor wire, broken glass, or steel spikes. You also had high levels of personal security—armed guards. The razor wire or broken glass on those high walls would be the main clue that, although you lived very well yourself, you lived well in a very poor country where the great majority did not live well at all. Those were the people the walls were meant to keep out.

Gated communities with high protective walls as barricades are hardly unique to Haiti; they are common in almost all major cities in Africa and Latin America and in many other places, the United States being no exception. You can sometimes mistake them for prison walls meant to keep people in, but they are meant to keep people out.

If you were living behind the wall in Haiti, you were certainly connected to the government in some way, even if quite indirectly. Many of the top government officials were your neighbors. The business you had, legal or illegal, relied on an almost complete lack of regulation and government oversight. You may have paid taxes in Haiti but probably not, and if you did it was a trivial amount. You didn't comply with labor laws, and you didn't provide your workers with decent wages or benefits. You may have been a government crony. And whether you were or not, you saw the government as a sort of theater of the absurd because it was so completely nonfunctional. The outcome of elections mattered little because the government didn't really govern. You had no interest in seeing effective government. A functioning government would charge taxes on business profits and impose regulations that governed how workers were paid and should be treated. That wasn't in *your* interest. The government led by Jean-Bertrand Aristide, champion of democracy and the poor, was threatening to you because it might have imposed such regulations. For that reason, it was never allowed to function.

So you profited from the fact that nothing functions well in Haiti, especially the government.

In 1994, while Jean-Bertrand Aristide was still in exile after one of the coups that ousted him, the US ambassador to Haiti called your group the "morally repugnant elite."[2] You thought that was funny and joked about it with others in the elite, using the acronym MRE to refer to yourselves.

THE OTHER CLASS IN HAITIAN SOCIETY in the first days of 2010 was comprised of the people in the overwhelmingly poor and overwhelmingly numerous lower group—the 99-plus percent who lived down the hill from the elite. If you lived that life, you lived in the slums of Port-au-Prince or in the destitute farming communities of the interior of the country, where poverty is at its worst. Your home was not much like the places where the rich lived, and there were no high walls protecting you. Your home typically was a rough cinder-block structure or reinforced concrete building. But many dwellings in Cité Soleil and other slums were nothing more than corrugated iron sheets put together as a sort of container for people, with a crude opening as an entry but probably with no actual door. No electric power, no running water, no toilet, no cooling, no real place to cook—just walls and a roof, not much more. And in the same way the homes of the rich in Pétionville looked much like the homes of the rich anywhere, your home in Port-au-Prince looked like the slum dwellings of the poor practically anywhere in Latin America or Africa.[3]

Cité Soleil is home to maybe 400,000 (no census is available[4]) of the very poorest people in Haiti, some of the poorest people anywhere in the world. Eighty percent of Haitians are thought to live below the poverty line, and 54 percent live in abject poverty.[5]

The unemployment rate in Haiti is around 40 percent, as best as can be estimated,[6] but two-thirds of those in Haiti who do "work" have informal jobs, meaning they don't receive regular wages or benefits from an employer. They try to sell things—anything—in tiny stalls or on foot by the side of the road. It's hard work but it just doesn't get counted as employment when figures are tallied. And gross domestic product (GDP) doesn't include the productivity of people who work in this way.

Katz makes an important point about this sort of labor. In Haiti and in most poor countries, almost everybody actually *does* work. They are working hard to survive, often harder than many people whose work *is* tallied. The product of this work, however, never finds its way into GDP.

Living in Cité Soleil, the chances that you had a high school education were practically nonexistent. You probably couldn't read: Haiti's literacy rate is only 53 percent. That means that the chances that you had any sort of real job were virtually zero. You probably suffered malnutrition as a child. One in ten children dies before the age of five in Haiti, and malnutrition is the leading cause of death. Of those who survive, one-third show signs of severe growth retardation, and 40 percent of five-year-olds are stunted and have reduced brain development resulting from inadequate nutrition.

You were probably born in a rural area and migrated to the city for a chance at getting out of poverty, a chance that didn't materialize. Still, you were better off than if you had stayed on the farm. You didn't have a car. You might have had a bicycle or even a motorcycle, but chances are you mostly walked to get from place to place or took a "tap tap," a converted pickup truck that carries passengers in a brightly painted enclosure over its bed.

Cité Soleil was established as a workers' community close to the former Haitian American Sugar Company factory; it was intended to give workers easy access to their place of work. Later it housed laborers for the export-processing zone established by the dictator Papa Doc Duvalier. But all that has collapsed, in no small part due to policies imposed by the United States. Now the walk to work is long, arduous, and dangerous.

Cité Soleil is also one of the most violent places on Earth.[7] Gangs run the slums, and their foot soldiers are known as the *chimeres* (ghosts). Chimere is a highly derogatory term and is applied as an invective to slander people of a different political persuasion or class. It is used widely to describe the poorest people in Haiti and to associate them with criminal behavior.[8] The gang structure is, in fact, very complex. People's motivations for joining gangs vary considerably and may include genuine political reasons.[9] But all gangs profit from the absence of effective law enforcement, and their members rob, extort, and rape with impunity.

One of the chief activities in Haiti is the random work of the countless nongovernmental organizations (NGOs). The word *countless* is not accidentally chosen—no one knows for sure how many there are. Working for one of these NGOs is one of the few ways a neg can make a reasonable salary and be treated reasonably well. UN peacekeepers make up a massively omnipresent force in Haiti. They are the troops of MINUSTAH—the United Nations Stabilization Mission in Haiti. As of January 31, 2015, there were 6,892 uniformed personnel comprising 4,658 troops and 2,234 police.[10] They come from an astonishing array of countries. The cholera outbreak in northern Haiti that began ten months after the earthquake (and had nothing at all to do with the quake itself, though it may have advanced more aggressively because the state was weakened by the quake) was brought by MINUSTAH troops from Nepal.[11] The

UN pays countries to provide troops for MINUSTAH, which is why troops so often come from poor countries like Bangladesh.

HAITI IS THE MOST UNEQUAL of all countries in Latin America, which is one of the most unequal regions in the world.[12] Even Chile, the least unequal of the Latin American countries, is still well down the list on global standards. Pétionville is a tiny oasis of wealth and Cité Soleil a broad desert of poverty in Haiti. There are many ways to express social inequality, but one way to get a sense of its magnitude is this fact: The 85 wealthiest people in the world today have a combined wealth equal to that of the bottom half of the world's entire population.[13] That comparison might be even more stark in Haiti, where the poor are so very poor and so numerous, and the elite so wealthy and so few by comparison. Individuals in the Haitian elite may have wealth equal to the sum of the income of as many as 2 million of the poorest Haitians. The World Bank has estimated that the richest 20 percent holds more than 65 percent of the country's total income, while the poorest 20 percent holds barely 1 percent.[14]

THE EARTHQUAKE STARTED blanket bombing the city of Port-au-Prince at 4:53 p.m. on January 12, 2010. The most intense barrage was short, shaking the ground for only 10 or 11 seconds. The onslaught came from the west, from a region near the town of Léogâne, which was flattened on the way. Destruction was indiscriminate; the homes of the rich and the homes of the poor were all targets. Even the presidential palace scored a direct hit.

The first shock was followed by more than 60 aftershocks in the next days and weeks. The capital city had no defenses. These aftershocks knocked down just about anything still standing, much of which was weakened by the first attack. When the aftershocks ceased, more than 200,000 homes had been destroyed or severely damaged;

most of them belonged to the poor.[15] Damage maps and photos of the Port-au-Prince area taken from high altitude look like damage maps from the firebombings of German cities toward the end of World War II. Vast tracts of buildings were brought to rubble heaps in both places. The damage seems almost capricious—some buildings stand essentially undamaged among the ruins of others. Some areas look to be 100 percent flattened; others appear unscathed.

Just how deadly the sacking of Port-au-Prince was will never be known. In massive events such as the Haitian quake, most morgues fail to function. In New Orleans, after Hurricane Katrina struck, the US Federal Emergency Management Agency established a DMORT (Disaster Mortuary Operational Response Team) facility, a temporary morgue with volunteer morticians, in the town of St. Gabriel, a considerable distance from New Orleans, to compensate for the submerged and mostly inoperative morgues in the city itself. Nothing of that sort happened in Haiti. Bodies, mostly unidentified, were brought to vast open burial sites by the truckload.

In the early aftermath of the Haitian earthquake, the Red Cross[16] estimated that around 50,000 people had died, in accord with the initial estimate from the Haitian government (which may have merely been a repetition of the Red Cross figure). Several revisions followed, until the official death toll was put at 220,570—though figures as high as 300,000 had been mentioned.[17] If the official toll is correct, it equals or exceeds the death toll from the 2004 Great Sumatran earthquake and tsunami, which affected a vast area around the Indian Ocean. Such a high mortality figure is not entirely unreasonable. Port-au-Prince was a densely crowded city. Almost no buildings were constructed to be earthquake resistant.

The Haitian government eventually raised its total count to 300,000. Most major relief agencies—Oxfam, Catholic Relief Services, Doctors Without Borders, and others—adopted a figure closer to an earlier government estimate of 230,000 or else finessed the issue by stating that "several hundred thousand" had died. On the first anniversary of the quake, the government put the death toll at 316,000. A very high death toll was inevitable, but that number is probably an overstatement.

Two sources of information have suggested that the Haitian death toll may be exaggerated. Netherlands Radio Worldwide claimed that "only" 52,000 people had been buried at official burial sites, the only places where any attempt was made to keep a count of the dead.[18] The article also asserted that the government reported 20,000 to 30,000 deaths in the coastal town of Léogâne, close to the quake epicenter, whereas Léogâne authorities themselves said they had buried 3,364. The article further reported that the government claimed 4,000 dead in the town of Jacmel, whereas a French aid group whose workers were involved in burying the Jacmel dead reported only 145 bodies. Jacmel authorities, the report went on to say, settled on a death toll of between 300 and 400.

The uncertainties and inconsistencies were further underscored in a "post-disaster needs assessment" created by the Haitian government in the weeks after the earthquake.[19] In that report, injuries were put at 300,000 and deaths at 220,000. A 3:2 ratio of injuries to deaths is actually quite low; typically, it is closer to 3:1 and often much higher.[20] If the injury figure is correct (and injury counts are somewhat easier to determine accurately, since they can be based on actual cases recorded by relief agencies), the more customary injury-to-death ratio implies a death toll closer to 100,000.

The second source is LTL Strategies, a consulting firm specializing in international and business development. In a report to the United States Agency for International Development (USAID) on building assessment and rubble removal (BARR), LTL took a quite different approach to estimating mortality: The group surveyed some of the most heavily affected neighborhoods, asking the remaining residents for information about those killed or injured.[21] The BARR survey specifically asked people how many of the residents in a building died, where the survivors went after the earthquake, and the current location of the survivors if known. The survey focused on the hard-hit area of lower Port-au-Prince, which had a high concentration of heavily damaged houses. With these data, investigators were able to make some inferences about the number of people killed, the total number of people who went to camps, and the total living as absentees from earthquake-impacted houses, as well as the whereabouts of the absentees. Deaths per residence were calculated by using average occupancy per house and average death rate by damage characteristics of the houses. The area impacted by the quake had an estimated population of 3 million people. An estimate based on these findings suggests that between 46,190 and 84,961 people were killed in the earthquake.[22]

The LTL estimate is derived from a cluster survey: based on the interviews, the analysts extrapolated from their samples to estimate the overall mortality. Estimates based on cluster surveys (including this one) are necessarily imprecise, but the authors of the LTL report do suggest that the discrepancy between their estimate and that of the Haitian government cannot be accounted for by factoring in all potential errors in their method. Despite the large range of the LTL figure, it is sure to be more accurate than the official government assessment.

WHAT WOULD BE THE MOTIVATION for overstating the deaths? No one profits from disaster deaths very much, if at all, in any direct sense. Morticians don't really make out because there is a sudden rush of business. Coffin makers may see a bump in their business; so might businesses that produce gravestones. But none of this is especially significant, and I am unaware of any instances of bribes or corruption in these businesses to take advantage of disaster mortality. Perhaps it happens.

Large profits *were* made by morticians who followed troops around the US Civil War battlefields, collected bodies, notified families, and sent the bodies back home in caskets made to the families' specifications. Mostly fallen soldiers were buried by their comrades in shallow graves, and some article of identification, carried by soldiers for that express purpose, was sent home. Some morticians were unscrupulous in their fees, but most were doing a service that is now performed by military personnel. Stores like Macy's had special sections for funeral attire and mourning clothing.

No one in Haiti made much directly from the disaster deaths. Very few of the thousands who died were attended to by morticians, and not many were buried in coffins in marked graves. But if the 300,000 figure was an intentional exaggeration to elicit sympathy and donor contributions, it worked. By late 2013, ReliefWeb[23] estimated the total donations at over $3.5 billion with a further $1 billion pledged. You would hardly call it profit for the country, but it was a large influx of money, especially in comparison with other disasters.

Elizabeth Ferris at the Brookings Institution in Washington, DC, analyzed the different levels of donation following the flooding in Pakistan in July of the same year and the Haitian quake[24] and found that the level was far greater for Haiti than for Pakistan. While human losses were relatively small in Pakistan (1,539), physical losses were much greater—six times as many schools, four times as many hospitals, and ten times as many homes were damaged or destroyed. The Pakistan floods submerged one-third of the entire country. No matter how devastating, earthquakes are usually fairly confined in spatial extent compared to major floods.

Maybe the smaller donations to Pakistan resulted because it is a Muslim country and that makes many people nervous, given the way in which Muslims are often viewed by the media in the United States and other non-Muslim countries and the association with extremist movements. But most likely, I expect, it was the comparatively small number of deaths in Pakistan compared to those claimed in Haiti; deaths tend to prompt a more compassionate response than physical losses.

NATURAL DISASTER SCENES are very often compared to war zones and vice versa. It really is difficult to tell the difference when looking at scenes of damage. That's one reason why I used the analogy of a bombing raid to describe the fall of Port-au-Prince. The camps of earthquake survivors are essentially identical to those for people escaping conflict, though people in war zones may need more security.[25]

There was no way the residents of Port-au-Prince could have been warned. Earthquakes can't be forecast, so there can be no shrill air-raid type siren telling of the seismic waves to come. No one in Haiti had undertaken earthquake safety training. First responders were not trained in rescue and recovery operations.

If you were there and had your wits about you, and you felt the first motions of the ground begin and you were near enough to the door of a building or happened to be outside, you might have run for the open spaces and suffered only minor injuries or none at all. But I expect few, if any, people in Port-au-Prince knew that it is buildings that kill people, not earthquakes.

The last time an earthquake of this magnitude had struck Haiti was in 1770, and it probably occurred on the same fault system as the 2010 earthquake. It destroyed much of what was Port-au-Prince at the time and took around 200 lives. The population of Port-au-Prince in 1770 is hard to guess, so that mortality figure may represent a significant fraction of the residents. It had been almost five lifetimes of the average Haitian since an earthquake had seriously rattled

Port-au-Prince. There was no equivalent of a Major Risks Committee like that in Italy. Even if there had been one, what could it have said? Even if a mystic with the power of clairvoyance had made an exact prediction, what could the government of Haiti have done? Buildings can't be rapidly retrofitted to be earthquake resistant.

Certainly, the overwhelming majority of buildings in Haiti *were* poorly built. Little shaking was needed to crumple them into a mass of fractured cement with jagged edges that could sever limbs. Remember that the Rana Plaza building in Bangladesh collapsed on its own. The humble buildings of most Haitians had survived many hurricanes, disasters that recur and that people prepare for as best as they are able. Even so, hurricanes in Haiti often kill many hundreds of people.

In a rich country with a relatively effective government, like Italy, we could point the finger of blame at public officials, but not in Haiti. No one in government, ineffective though it is in Haiti, failed in their responsibility to issue a warning; no one misled the public about the risks. That's not why people were unprepared, why so many died. None of the survivors will bring charges against Haitian government scientists who specialize in seismic risk—there are none. No one in government was to blame for the deaths in Haiti; *poverty* was to blame.

And it is simply not correct to say, though I have heard it many times, that Haiti has no building codes. After the Haiti earthquake, many claimed that the heart of the problem lay in lack of adequate building codes. Jonathan Katz,[26] in the early part of his book, describes how he met then President Préval at the site of a school collapse that had occurred without any seismic activity months before the 2010 quake. The school collapse was similar to the Rana Plaza collapse in form and in tragedy (though many fewer were killed). New floors had been added to the building, which sat on a substrate that was too weak to hold the weight. The school collapsed without encouragement, just like Rana Plaza.

Katz asked Préval why there were no building codes. The president angrily answered that there *were* building codes. The problem, he insisted, was lack of a stable government. In other words, the government lacked the institutional capacity to enforce existing codes. So poor people build as cheaply as they can and once in 200 years suffer the consequences.

Shoddy building is by no means a peculiarly Haitian problem, nor is it always a reflection of a weak central government. Sometimes tragedies are caused by blatant violation of well-known building codes, combined with inadequate and corrupt oversight. Vastly fewer children, teachers, teaching assistants, and school nurses would have died in the Sichuan earthquake in 2008 had the buildings not been made of tofu dregs. China has been both criticized and praised for its rescue and reconstruction efforts after the quake. The World Bank, which helped finance the rebuilding, has a piece on its website titled "What China Got Right When Rebuilding after Sichuan."[27] China and the World Bank spent lavishly on the reconstruction and did not wait for a long time to get started. They devised a system of partnering with neighboring provinces that were not damaged, a reflection of a method adopted by the Kremlin during the Soviet era in which each unaffected state was assigned a specific role. More than 40,000 reconstruction projects were completed less than two years after the quake. Public buildings like schools and hospitals have now been built to high earthquake-resistance standards.

But an investigation by National Public Radio titled "Five Years after a Quake, Chinese Cite Shoddy Reconstruction" is much more critical.[28] The crux of the article is that almost all the mistakes and malfeasance of the past have been repeated in an effort to rebuild quickly—build back fast rather than build back better. Construction is poor, corruption is high, building standards are not being met. Several new schools that were supposed to have been built to earthquake codes were heavily damaged in a quake in 2013. A national audit showed that $228 million of reconstruction money had been embezzled. Some officials have been convicted on corruption charges. Some claimed their districts were far more damaged than they actually were and took for themselves funds that weren't needed. Eleven thousand farmers had their land appropriated for new housing, but there are still no buildings, and the government's asking price for the land is 100 times what the farmers were paid. At the same time, reconstruction workers have not been paid.

The NPR version of the reconstruction story rings truer than the World Bank story. At least it fits the typical narrative reported by both the foreign press and Chinese journalists who have been able to get their messages out of the country. The earthquake came at a time when China was embarking on a spending stimulus package to boost the economy. A quarter of that money was spent on earthquake reconstruction; much of the rest went to national infrastructure. A real chance existed for a Schumpeter boost that would bring lasting benefit to those who suffered. But if the critics are right, new tofu dreg buildings have replaced the old, and the gale of destruction will again be tragic, not creative.

A rapid influx of reconstruction money is viewed as manna from heaven by the unscrupulous, a chance for new profits. In the aftermath of a terrible cataclysm of destruction, it is typical (though, as we will see later, not universal) for governments to want to rebuild as quickly as possible, as China did. It is another way in which postconflict thinking modulates responses to disaster. The urge to reconstruct often overwhelms the need to be thoughtful and provide proper oversight. Postdisaster, local governments are stretched and normal government activities are challenged by reduced staff and weakened operational capacity. Postdisaster chaos opens up irresistible opportunities for the corrupt.

Corrupt profiteering is well known in zones of conflict. Sarah Chayes, in her book *Thieves of State: Why Corruption Threatens Global Security*,[29] claims that conflict and corruption are so interactive that, while conflict provides opportunities for the corrupt, corruption itself may give rise to conflict. Her thesis is that ordinary, honest people get so frustrated with being shaken down by police and other government employees that they are vulnerable to taking up arms against the government.

Roger Bilham, whose work I mentioned in Chapter 2, is sure that corruption in the building industry is the leading cause of earthquake mortality in many countries, particularly in South Asia. In a paper in the journal *Nature*, written with Nicholas Ambraseys and provocatively titled "Corruption Kills,"[30] Bilham lays out a case that the far most telling factor in predicting earthquake mortality is the intentional violation of building codes permitted by inspectors who are paid to look the other way.

So we always need to ask *why* buildings collapse and kill people. Buildings need not kill people. In Haiti, first and foremost, poverty, neglect of the poor, and lack of strong government cause people to be killed by buildings in earthquakes. But Haiti is also even more corrupt than China and falls near the bottom of corruption listings made by Transparency International.[31] Yes, buildings collapse because they are poorly built, but to say buildings kill people is like saying that guns kill people, when it is people with guns in their hands who kill people.

AFTER THE FIRST SEISMIC WAVES reached Port-au-Prince, more destructive surface waves followed a few seconds later. Just what seismic energy feels like when it arrives unwelcome on your doorstep depends a lot on the nature of the fault on which the earthquake takes place. Faults are not much like a spherical pebble being dropped into still water. They are generally elongated features, more like a crack or a tear, so they don't radiate energy equally in all directions. If you can imagine a fault with a more or less east-west orientation, it is very possible that the region north of the fault will shake more than that to the south or vice versa, and areas at one end may shake more than at the other. That was true when the Paganica Fault moved in the L'Aquila earthquake in Italy. The region to the southwest of that fault moved more than the region to the northeast. Unfortunately, the town of L'Aquila (pop. 73,000) is located to the southwest.

What's more, passing through Earth is nothing like passing through a perfectly still pool of water. Earth is made up of an irregular mélange of rocks of different ages and types—some rigid, some soft—that break up, focus, and disperse seismic energy as it travels away from the site of the earthquake. Port-au-Prince wasn't very far from the epicenter of the earthquake, but the energy arriving was broken up somewhat, arriving just a little sooner and stronger in some parts of the city than in others.

That's part of the explanation for the variation in damage that the earthquake caused. But as every geotechnical engineer[32] knows, there are many factors that go into determining how well a building will do when shaken by an earthquake. In fact, knowing an earthquake's magnitude isn't especially helpful. What matters is the amount the ground shakes where people are located. A large-magnitude earthquake many miles from a town will have much the same effect as a smaller earthquake much nearer to the town. Earthquakes as small as magnitude 2 can be felt if people are essentially on top of them.[33] A more useful measure used by seismologists is peak ground acceleration (PGA), which describes the movement of the ground and is a much better predictor of damage.

A bizarre and perverse piece of "good" fortune can work in your favor if you live in a shanty in a slum. Your home may be so flimsy that if it shakes down on you, it won't kill you. Most people can survive the impact of a few sheets of corrugated iron falling on them, but only luck will save you if a reinforced concrete building collapses on you. And oddly enough, flimsy structures may remain standing more than seemingly more rigid structures. That's because they can sway a little with the motion of the ground. Everyone who has been high in a skyscraper in strong winds knows that they are built to give a little. Tall skyscrapers are designed to move several feet. A little yielding is a good thing. It prevents a buildup of stress and sudden failure. Newly constructed skyscrapers, like the 1,483-foot-tall Petronas Towers in earthquake-prone Kuala Lumpur, have elaborate bracing and absorbing systems, not unlike the shock absorbers in a car's suspension, and they buffer the motion of an earthquake by allowing the structure to yield somewhat.

This idea is not new. In the rebuilding of Lisbon after the massive earthquake and tsunami of 1755, an elaborate bracing system of stout wooden beams—called the Pombaline cage after its inventor, the Marquês de Pombal, who led the rebuilding of the city—was designed to allow buildings to give a little when the ground shook. All new housing was required to be constructed around such cages. Some restaurants in Lisbon today display exposed parts of the original cage structure as a part of their decor.

WHAT HAPPENED IN PORT-AU-PRINCE? Everything that causes damage and death—poorly built buildings, weak ground conditions, weak governance, corruption, and poverty—came into play. You can find a description of the physical causes in the geotechnical extreme event reconnaissance (GEER) report made with funding from the National Science Foundation.[34] This group surveyed 90,000 structures in the capital city, assessed the damage in relation to geology, soil conditions, and topography, and compared it to damage assessments made from satellite observation by the UN.[35]

The group found that severe damage was pervasive. That's certainly the impression you get from looking at the UN satellite-based damage assessments of the city as a whole. It looks like hardly anyone, rich or poor, escaped. But, in fact, the satellite data suggest that only 9 to 12 percent of structures were completely destroyed; 7 to 11 percent were described as badly damaged; and 5 to 8 percent were moderately damaged. Even taking the upper end of these numbers, that is a total of 31 percent that suffered damage; 69 percent of structures suffered no damage at all. Taking the lower end of those ranges, you would conclude that maybe 79 percent of structures were undamaged.[36] These satellite-based estimates are from UNISAT,[37] the UN technology arm that provides support for relief and development. They are quite marvelous in the detail they show, but inevitably they can only reveal the damage visible from straight above. From ground-based observations, the GEER authors suggest that 30 percent of city structures suffered damage sufficient to be seen from above, but in places the actual damage could be much higher. That's not a trivial loss of structures, but it is far less than the percentage of buildings lost in German cities firebombed by the Allies in World War II.

The other surprising observation in the GEER report is that the percentage of damage in shanty zones, high-density areas, and moderate-density areas was almost the same—28, 30, and 27 percent, respectively.

So just like estimates of mortality, it can be extremely difficult to get a true sense of how much physical damage actually takes place in a disaster. And you can't trust the press. They will always show tight-focus images of the damage and not what survived undamaged.

In places, the GEER group saw distinct boundaries between areas of severe damage and areas hardly damaged at all. The report describes one case in this way: "The structures to the north [of an imaginary east-west line] are larger buildings that appear to be nice homes (some with swimming pools). They are also constructed on more gradual topography. Very few of these homes were damaged. The structures to the south are shanty-type structures, and the ones that are damaged most severely are located near the top of the hillsides/ridges. This could be evidence of ridge-top focusing of seismic energy."[38]

Some "larger buildings that appear to be nice homes (some with swimming pools)" were quite badly damaged; they did not all escape. But reports from Mac McClelland,[39] writing in *Mother Jones,* tell us that generally they suffered relatively little damage. That makes sense. The January 2010 earthquake was not so very large. While there is no strict seismological definition of "large" in regard to an earthquake, earthquakes of magnitude greater than 9.0 have been recorded, and the Haitian quake measured 7.0. About ten earthquakes of this magnitude occur each year on average. The Haitian quake compares in magnitude to two recent earthquakes in California: Loma Prieta in 1989, which killed 63 people (3,757 injured) and had about the same PGA, and Northridge in 1994, which killed 57 (over 8,700 injured) but had PGA values three times larger than those in Haiti.[40]

Those California earthquakes caused extensive damage to critical public infrastructure, private housing, and businesses, but they resulted in very low death tolls (if expressed as a percentage of population) compared to even the smallest plausible figure for Haiti. In the California earthquakes, the ratio of those injured to those who died is enormous compared to Haiti; this in part reflects the fact that services for the injured were much more available in California.

The number of injured, of course, counts only those who made it to a treatment center and had injuries serious enough to be prioritized for immediate treatment. In Haiti, many poor people had injuries that were never treated. Treatment of injuries relied almost entirely on foreign assistance because there was so little local capacity. Just how many injured Haitians went untreated is impossible to know. So the injury total in Haiti is the total of *serious* injuries, while in California, with its well-functioning emergency response capability, a higher percentage of the injured are likely to have been counted and treated.

HOW DID THE DIFFERENT GROUPS of people in Haiti cope? Did the blans suffer along with the negs, unifying them in their common plight? The answer is absolutely not.

If you were in the Haitian elite, your fate was not unlike that of a well-to-do Californian. In fact, your life wasn't very different in most ways. You might have been injured, but probably not seriously. By and large, if you have a lot of money to put into a home to live in (even if you don't live there full time), you have it built well, meaning strongly and with high-quality materials. Hurricanes are common, so you build to resist hurricanes; as an unintended benefit, you make the house somewhat more earthquake resistant as well.

And if you were injured in your mansion in Pétionville, you were attended to quickly. The elite have never relied on Haitian government services for anything, especially anything to do with their health, and were treated by private doctors living in the same neighborhood.

After the earthquake, if your house needed repairs, you had money to pay for them without straining your budget, and you were able to effect repairs quite quickly. You didn't rely on any assistance from the government or international agencies. You probably left

Haiti with your family and left your home guarded and didn't return until things were back in shape. You may even have had a choice of several other homes to go to.

So just as a country's wealth provides a potential shield against the worst that a natural disaster can do, an individual's wealth also provides a shield. What is disaster to some is nothing more than an inconvenience to others.

THE "OTHER HOMES" to which nonwealthy Haitians retreated were blue tents provided by the UN or one of a multitude of NGOs. Other Haitians stayed in the yards of their homes and slept outdoors, much as the residents of L'Aquila did. Aid organizations have an aversion to using the word *refugee* to describe people forced out of their homes by natural disasters. According to the UN definition, refugees are people who have been forced to *leave their country* by actual or perceived threats.[41] Definitions matter. People who move inside their borders are considered "internally displaced persons." Nevertheless tent cities, like those occupied by tens of thousands of the poor of Haiti, are often described as refugee camps because, for all intents and purposes, that's what they are. They are indistinguishable from the camps set up for refugees from conflicts or oppression.

Too often the help disaster survivors get is meager. Their shelters are often hardly even tents. More likely they are sheets of plastic stretched over sticks. One and a half million or so people took refuge in 1,500 camps after Haiti's 2010 quake, and at the end of 2013, roughly 150,000 still lived that way, their homes still in ruin.[42] Others lived in the remnants of their homes. It's not so obvious which is better. Life was hard enough in the slums of Port-au-Prince before the earthquake; it became immeasurably worse after.

Desperate people do desperate things. The rate of violence is always highest in the poorest places, especially when poverty is linked in the public mind-set with injustice. In the United States, violence on Native American reservations is 2.5 times higher than the national average, and alcoholism is rampant.[43] Before Katrina struck, the murder rate in the poor parts of New Orleans was ten times higher than the national average.[44]

In places where rape and other violent crimes are common and seldom prosecuted, and where people are deprived of basic social services and employment, safety, and the rudiments of governance, the aftermath of disaster can be especially grim. Those who suffer most will be those who are the least well regarded in normal times.

Haiti had always been a place where women and young girls were at high risk of rape and other forms of sexual violence; it was common and difficult to prosecute and control. But after the earthquake, in the tent cities and around Port-au-Prince, sexual violence surged to ghastly levels. It is one of the saddest stories of life in Haiti after the earthquake. There was nowhere in the world where a young woman was at greater risk of rape.[45] Why?

The dictators "Papa Doc" and his son "Baby Doc" Duvalier used rape as a weapon of oppression, but they were far from the only ones to do so. US soldiers are known to have indiscriminately raped women and children during the occupation of Haiti from 1915 to 1934 and to have kept women as sex slaves.[46] After the Duvaliers' regime came to an end, Raoul Cédras used rape as a way to suppress opposition to his regime by supporters of the populist president Jean-Bertrande Aristide, whose ouster Cédras had helped to engineer. Rape and threats of rape are one of life's many challenges for Haitian women.

But why do incidences of rape rise after a disaster? Don't think it happens only in poor places with weak or despotic governance. Instances of violence (not only sexual) rose strongly after the Loma Prieta earthquake in California, and Hurricane Katrina brought many forms of misery to the poorest people of New Orleans, including an increased risk of rape and domestic violence. Disaster rape is, it seems, something to be expected. It is so common, in fact, that the US National Criminal Justice Reference Service publishes a guide for the prevention of and response to sexual violence in disasters.[47]

The incidence of rape in Haiti also rose after other shock events. In 2006 Athena Kolbe and Royce Hutson published a controversial paper in the highly prestigious medical journal *Lancet*. They used survey data (1,260 households, 5,720 individuals) from Port-au-Prince families to establish that in the 22-month period following the 2004 coup that ousted President Aristide, an estimated 8,000 murders took place and 35,000 people were raped; more than half the victims were girls under the age of 18.[48] The perpetrators were most often common criminals, but victims also identified as perpetrators a significant number of political actors as well as UN and other peacekeepers.

These same researchers plus eight colleagues published similar findings about the upsurge in crime and rights violations after the 2010 earthquake.[49] They estimated that nearly 10,500 women and girls were raped in the aftermath.

Most accounts of sexual crime after disasters posit that the cause is loss of social order, and the two papers just mentioned support that. This proposed cause of the upsurge in rape supposes that men are held back in their persistent desire to rape by forces of law; during the disaster these forces are removed, diminished, or diverted to other responsibilities, such as search and recovery. Much the same argument is used to account for looting[50]—we are all suppressed thieves just waiting for the cops to be distracted so we can grab luxury goods at will from upscale stores and take them home or sell them. And we will invade other people's homes as well, not just stores.

Would most men really be tempted to rape just because the opportunity presents itself and there is virtually no chance of being caught? Does this include men who have never done such a thing before? Could that explain the postdisaster rise in sexual assaults?

I find that idea hard to fathom and hard to live with if it is true. Certainly for some in the desperate slums of Cité Soleil, rape was a part of everyday life. If you had been encouraged and perhaps even paid to use rape as a way of domination for political reasons or personal gain or to suppress a group ethnically different from yourself, this behavior could have become normal. And, as noted, violence is often highest in the poorest places because many lack institutions to enforce rule of law.

But I believe that there is something else beyond this "time bomb" view of the poor. Remember that the word *neg* is a form of derision, a term used by the elite as a way to slander poor people (though not exclusively) and associate them with criminal actions. Negs are portrayed as thieves at the best of times; in a disaster, it is believed that they will rise up as a looting mob. Therefore, vicious actions to suppress them are justified. If you are a poor neg in Haiti and you are seen looting, or even suspected of looting, you can expect to be shot dead—possibly by a UN peacekeeper.

That was the fate of 15-year-old Fabienne Cherisma. The loot she made off with comprised three framed pictures.[51] In color images of the scene, you can see that the picture facing upward is of brightly colored flowers in a vase.[52] For stealing these pictures, she was shot in the head, presumably by a policeman, and died instantly.

Numerous versions of this image can be found online. In one, the girl's anguished mother is seen being restrained by friends. In another widely circulated image, no less than seven news photographers are seen in a group just a few feet from the body, crouched in the classic photographers' pose, getting close-up pictures of the girl's face.[53] The

Figure 3.1

Fabienne Cherisma, a 15-year-old girl, was shot and killed by police for stealing three framed pictures after the 2010 earthquake in Haiti.

Source: Photograph by Edward Linsmier. Used with permission.

photographers must have come to the scene in a crazed rush, because even though they are down the slope from Fabienne (that must have been the best angle), blood has yet to flow down the incline from her head, beneath the framed pictures. The person who shot Fabienne is unknown and will likely remain unknown.[54]

How could anyone think the crime Fabienne committed would merit punishment by death, without being charged and without a trial? The person who carried out the death sentence could not have believed that she was a threat of any sort. The sentence and its execution are so vile we want to believe the scene is not from our world. But this sort of punishment is more than permitted; it is the norm and is encouraged in the aftermath of a disaster in poor countries. That punishment is yours if you are poor in Haiti and you want some colorful pictures to brighten up your home in the slums.

Why did Fabienne steal the pictures? Why did others loot non-essential items, such as luxury goods? In most of the polite litera-ture and reporting, stealing food and other necessities is frowned on but forgiven. After all, perishable food will go bad soon if there is no electricity for refrigeration, so why not take it? And shop owners might well be insured so they are not actually taking a loss.

Here is what I think or, rather, speculate. Perhaps Fabienne had seen those pictures in her neighborhood before. She had walked past the store where they were sold and stopped each time to admire them and wished that she had enough money to buy just one. But she didn't and was never likely to have the money. When the front of the store broke open or was broken into, she could not resist. She could have not just one but two or three of the pictures—unimaginable. Maybe she wanted to give them to her mother. She took the pretty things she admired so much and ran with them—into a fatal bullet.

This never happens to the daughters of the elite in their mansions in Pétionville. Their risk of death by a policeman's rifle shot or of rape or any other form of violence remained about the same in the wake of the disaster—near zero. In fact, by the time Fabienne was killed, they were probably long gone, jetted off the island to another home in another country. And they don't care much about the stores being looted in Port-au-Prince; that is not where they shop, and they know their mansions will be safe because they have security guards to keep looters out.

Most of the looters probably were motivated by the same things that might have motivated Fabienne. People took essentials first, but then they took things they knew they would never be able to afford, things the blans could always have. Some people may have vandal-ized for the sport of it. No doubt criminals stole luxury items for resale on the black market. But while looting for personally desired objects, as Fabienne appears to have done, is wrong, the reaction far outweighs the crime.

IN THE ACADEMIC LITERATURE and elsewhere, a comparison is often drawn between the earthquake in Haiti that I have just been discussing and one of much greater magnitude—8.8[55]—that occurred on February 27, 2010, in Chile. That earthquake released 500 times the energy of the Haitian quake. The shaking lasted three minutes rather than ten seconds. The earthquake was so large that it slightly shifted the Earth's spin axis and shortened the length of the day (the Earth now spins a little faster on its axis)—1.26 millionths of a second. The death toll, however, was much smaller: 525 dead, 25 missing and likely dead. So a hugely more powerful earthquake caused a fraction of the deaths of the smaller earthquake. Why?

Part of the reason lies in geophysical aspects I have already described. Remember, what matters is how much the ground shakes where people live, not how much energy is released at the earthquake at the hypocenter deep underground. (The more commonly used term, epicenter, is the point at the surface of the Earth immediately above the hypocenter.) The Chilean earthquake was more massive than the Haitian quake, but it was much deeper in the planet and much farther from the nearest populated towns. In Concepción, Chile, the ground did shake more than the ground in Haiti, and for longer, but not 500 times more—only about twice as much, actually.

Almost every scientist will give the same reason for the difference in destruction: building codes. Chile has them and enforces them; Haiti has them too but can't enforce them. Even Haiti's National Palace suffered massive damage because it too was poorly built.

What Haiti has in vast supply and Chile has in much shorter supply is poverty and corruption. Only 14 countries in the world are thought to be more corrupt than Haiti, according to Transparency International. Only 21 countries are considered less corrupt than Chile as measured by the same organization. Haiti and Chile are poles apart.[56]

They are polar opposites seismically as well. Almost everyone in Chile besides the very young would have experienced an earthquake before February 27, perhaps several. Everyone there is well aware of the risks.

Haiti's earthquake losses were greater than 120 percent of GDP in a stagnant economy; Chile's were 0.06 percent in an economy growing at over 5 percent per annum. Chile had made a transition to democracy in 1990 after the harsh period of rule by General Augusto Pinochet, who took power in a coup d'état in 1973. Even while living under the dictatorship created by the coup, the country had begun to build many stable and well-functioning institutions of government. Chile is now a representative democratic republic and another coup is unlikely. Haiti, although nominally democratic, has almost no functioning institutions of government, and fears of another coup are constant. Chile has more seismologists per capita than any other country in the world. Educational attainment is high. Far more than building codes separate these two countries.

And in a somewhat perverse way, experiencing a lot of earthquakes can help. This may be part of the Schumpeter creative destruction scenario. Old buildings destroyed in quakes are rebuilt to withstand future earthquakes, while at the same time, the building stock is renewed and updated. It is certainly a significant reason for the relatively low mortality rate in Chile's 2010 quake.

CHILE AND HAITI ARE ALSO more alike than you might imagine. The Pinochet dictatorship, like those of the Duvaliers, was cruel and repressive, characterized by human rights abuses and brutal suppression of opposition. But the Pinochet government led open-market economic reforms that saved the economy from collapse and started robust growth. With robust aggregate economic growth came a widening income gap between the rich and the poor—not as wide as in Haiti, but wide nevertheless. The Gini measure of inequality places Chile 124th out of 147 ranked countries.[57] Chile does better in the Human Development Index rankings, coming in at number 41 out of 187, but it loses 20 percent of its score when HDI is adjusted for inequality, causing it to drop to number 52 in overall rank.[58]

The elites of Chile are not as small in number as they are in Haiti, but income distribution is highly skewed and highly problematic. There were student protests from 2011 to 2013 over these inequalities. Similar to Haiti, there are really two Chiles, one that profits from the fruits of growth and one that doesn't. Seventy-five percent of Chile's growth in 2011 went to the wealthiest 10 percent of Chileans.[59] The small, wealthy elite is made up of the family owners of major businesses, such as banks, the media, and mining. Gonzalo Duran, an economist at Chile's Universidad Católica and director of the nonprofit Fundación SOL, puts it even more strongly: "They are the owners of Chile, the elite that configure and decide day to day the nation's economy." Journalist Fernando Paulsen said that Chile is "hijacked by 3,000 or 4,000 people."[60] Chile's population is over 17 million.[61] The country's export revenues, mainly from copper, helped to create a large reserve that the government was able to use in the reconstruction after the earthquake. In fact, President Michelle Bachelet said that Chile would be able to manage reconstruction without the need for external aid.[62] But in the end, Chile did have to appeal to the World Bank and others for loans to cover rebuilding.

Another thing that happened in Chile is in many ways similar to what happened in Haiti—looting and other criminal and antisocial behaviors broke out soon after the earthquake, particularly in the southern region around Concepción, which had been hardest hit. The earthquake generated a tsunami that caused most of the damage in that area as well as the majority of deaths. Concepción is no stranger to earthquakes and tsunamis, having been devastated five times since its founding in the mid-sixteenth century. Because of this, the town was moved inland from its original coastal location and reestablished on the shores of the Bío Bío River. The 2010 tsunami ran up the river, gaining in height from the river's funneling, and inundated the new Concepción.

Bachelet has been criticized for her response to the quake on two counts. One is that coastal and island communities did not receive timely warnings of the tsunami. The first waves from the tsunami reached the coast 34 minutes after the quake; the tsunamigenic nature of the earthquake was known only a few minutes after the quake occurred. The Chilean navy has acknowledged that the warnings it put out could have been clearer and more timely, and might have saved lives. The officer in charge of the emergency warning unit was fired. The new president, Sebastián Piñera, who took office only two weeks after the earthquake, vowed to examine the warning system and improve it.

The second and probably more important criticism is that Bachelet failed to quickly deploy the military to quell the crime that erupted in the southern towns.[63] Although she had clear reports of criminal behavior, including television coverage that, like coverage of other similar situations worldwide, very likely exaggerated the severity of the situation, she did not deploy troops for 48 hours. There has been speculation that she was mistrustful of the military. She had been a political prisoner during the Pinochet military regime and had been tortured while in prison. She may have been reluctant to unleash the power of the army, which is quite strong in Chile and remains a largely independent institution even today. Perhaps she hoped the situation would calm down and the local police response would be sufficient. She ended up sending 14,000 troops who helped keep order but also were engaged in rescue and other activities not related to law enforcement. That might sound like a lot of soldiers, but it's insignificant compared to the 70,000 soldiers sent to New Orleans just to restore order after Hurricane Katrina.[64]

People were said to have come from nearby villages that experienced little or no damage just to take part in the looting, to get something for themselves before the troops arrived.[65] People in the towns where looting was reported were afraid, as their text messages and tweets reveal—they were pleading for help. Looted buildings were set on fire as a blatant act of aggression against store owners. Chileans outside the affected areas watched television, listened to news broadcasts, and read newspaper accounts in horror and dismay as their fellow citizens appeared to be plunging further and further into anarchy. There were, however, no reports of rape or murder.

The citizens of Concepción were slowly but inexorably descending into hunger and thirst as food ran out and the water supply failed, and into the cold and dark because there was no electricity. The city was essentially cut off from the outside, and it was difficult to get relief assistance in. The main road is the Pan-American Highway, which begins in Mexico, crosses through Central America, then stretches along the coasts of Ecuador, Peru, and Chile. In many regions it is the only road that can accept motor vehicle traffic. It had been made impassable by the earthquake. Anyone who did not have supplies of canned food and bottled water was in trouble.

Surely that is part of the reason that looting broke out in this region. Tired and worried residents of Concepción expressed relief when the troops finally arrived. But not everyone was pleased at the troop deployment, and many saw very different signals in it. Jose Aylwyn, codirector of a Chilean human rights group, said, "These lootings, at least in some cases, are explained by the perception of injustice that exists in segments of the population that, in moments of emergency such as this one, consider it legitimate to empty the shelves of superstores and supermarkets that, with the backing of the State, have accumulated wealth at their expense, while they remain poor."[66] Andrés Schuschny, a blogger, posted an article that read, in part:

> It is terrible how a natural catastrophe unmasks the face of inequality in a country whose officials refuse to acknowledge it. Because, for example, if 10% of copper revenues had been, long ago, destined to public education and social services (debts always outstanding in the region) and not to increase military budgets, the purchase of sophisticated weaponry, and a passport to a life of luxury for high-rank militiamen, maybe history would be different and the communicators of the system would not be referring to the LUMPEN (lowest social group) as a horde of loose aliens that surfaced with no reason.[67]

Another wrote: "Can we expect something different in a system that generates segregation and social exclusion? Is it a product of a society that forces competition and to fix things oneself?" And another: "Our bubble burst and the truth hurts. Now we ought to understand it, accept it and work for the reconstruction of our buildings and society."[68]

These quotes suggest that the looters—not all of them, perhaps, but many—were marginalized people who had been left behind in the Chilean boom. When they got their chance to even the score, even just a bit, with the 3,000 to 4,000 families that Fernando Paulsen claims have "hijacked the country," they took it. They took luxury items—that is, items that *to them* are luxuries beyond their economic reach.[69]

But when looting goes beyond just taking things—necessities or luxuries—and includes acts of personal aggression against targeted groups or the property owned by those groups, the public mind views the actions as rioting, not looting, and that's very different. That pits one group squarely against another and threatens the established power structure.

The actions of those in authority and especially the statements they make publicly can have a profound influence on a volatile situation. Concepción's mayor, Jacqueline van Rysselberghe, appealed frequently for more military personnel, sending the strong message that the situation was out of control. She entreated the minister of the interior to take responsibility. Many Chileans felt her reaction was detrimental to both the relief efforts and security. One commented, "I feel that Jacqueline Van Rysselberghe scares people more than helps them." Some leftist organizations, including the Chilean Communist Party, were blunt in criticizing the deployment of the army: "We reject the distortion encouraged by the media with regard to the prioritization of emergencies. [The media] has placed an emphasis on the protection of the right to private property of the supermarkets and the mobilization of the armed forces under the pretext to maintain public security, instead of pressuring for an effective and efficient response in the restitution of connectivity, public services, and nutrition of our affected fellow countrymen."[70]

So, different as Chile and Haiti are in so many ways, in the immediate aftermath of the earthquakes, some dramatic and tragic events took place in both. Marginalized groups form majorities in Haiti and Chile. Because they believe they are held in poverty by a political and economic elite, they pounced on the opportunity to take what they believed they deserve. They knew they might not have another chance. The elite panicked and overreacted, inflaming the situation and criminalizing the victims, transforming them from survivors to thieves.

The one extraordinary aspect of the Chilean earthquake is the outstanding positive way in which economic recovery was achieved. Using numerous on-site interviews and access to government documents, Michael Urseem, Howard Kunreuther and Erwan-Michael Kerjan explain clearly and in detail in *Leadership Dispatches*[71] how the incoming government of President Sebastián Piñera, which took office only ten days after the quake, acted without delay and set out an uncompromising, all-encompassing plan for recovery, involving all levels of government, the private sector, and the affected citizens. The fast recovery—just a year—can be attributed to strong leadership that understood delegation as well as strong institution that benefited from extremely sound fiscal management. For countries at the development level of Chile, the process of recovery is exemplary.

HOW HAS HAITI RECOVERED, and who has benefited? First of all, it is extremely difficult to answer such a question based on standard figures like GDP for reasons already discussed. It also is difficult to come up with something like an average wage.

Before the earthquake, there was a plan for Haiti's economic revival. Its author was Paul Collier, professor of economics and public policy at Oxford, but after a time it might have been thought of as the Clinton plan because Bill Clinton embraced it so completely when he became the UN special envoy to Haiti. Collier is an expert on development issues in Africa (not the Caribbean) and has served as director of research development for the World Bank. He has written several books, the most popular being *The Bottom Billion*.[72] The title is now an oft-repeated and very appropriate phrase to describe the poorest of all the world's people.

The core of Collier's 19-page report[73] was fairly simple and not a new idea in developmental economics. It involved securing foreign investment to develop a vigorous garment industry that would produce export earnings and create tens of thousands of low-skill jobs. Inducements would include low taxes and a special economic zone. Haiti has a large, able, young workforce with low wage expectations. The formula had worked well elsewhere, particularly in Asia; in fact, it wasn't so very different from a plan crafted earlier by Papa Doc Duvalier with assistance from the US government. Haiti had about 30 garment factories already. It also had in place a special trade relationship with the United States under the HOPE II agreement (Haitian Hemisphere Opportunity through Partnership Encouragement Act), which allowed Haitian-made garments to enter the US duty free until 2018.

After the earthquake, the Collier/Clinton plan became the guiding light for rebuilding Haiti's economy. Clinton, appointed head of the recovery commission, spoke enthusiastically about prospects for recovery and overall economic revitalization rolled into one. The best thing about it was that so much money had been donated to Haitian relief that there was less need to encourage foreign investors; some of the aid money could be used for economic development instead. And used it was.

Not everyone was pleased about how these relief funds were used. A widely cited 2011 report from the Center for Economic Policy and Research (CEPR) showed that since December 2010, no contracts had been awarded to Haitian companies. Of the 1,490 contracts awarded prior to that time, only 23 had gone to Haitian companies. Their total share of the $195 million awarded was only 2.5 percent. A large fraction of these contracts were no-bid contracts, which were justified, as is typical, by the need for urgency.[74]

CEPR's analysis showed that all the other contracts went to US firms, half of which were so-called Beltway contractors (firms from Maryland, Virginia, or Washington, DC). USAID contracted with Beltway firms for 92 percent of its work; it contracted with no Haitian companies at all.

Of the Haitian companies that did get contracts, one, Sanco Enterprises, was initially awarded nine contracts, mostly for waste removal. Sanco is the largest waste removal company in the Port-au-Prince area. But soon after a cholera outbreak occurred in the north of Haiti, well away from the earthquake-affected areas, Sanco was found to be the contractor that provided waste removal services to the Nepalese UN peacekeepers believed to be the source of the outbreak. Sanco was suspected of being responsible for the outbreak, as improper human waste removal is a leading theory for the spread of cholera, but its culpability was never proven. Sanco improved its performance at the UN base, but by that time it was too late; the cholera epidemic had caught hold and was heading south.

Another contract went to a Haitian company, GDG Beton & Construction, the largest supplier of cement in the country. The leader of the reconstruction commission that awarded the contract is Haiti's minister for tourism, Patrick Delatour, who acknowledges he has a 5 percent share in the company, which he started with a cousin in 2000.[75]

A few members of the Haitian elite who owned contracted companies have benefited from the reconstruction, and many American companies close to the political elite in Washington have benefited also. It's hard to see how ordinary Haitians have benefited, if at all. The negs still suffer in poverty.

And things haven't gone very well. Initially, an industrial park was planned near Port-au-Prince, but it proved difficult for the government to obtain the necessary land. The new location is far away on the northern coast; you can't get any farther away from Port-au-Prince and remain in Haiti.[76] The cost of construction so far has been about $300,000. The Clinton Foundation says:

> In collaboration with the Government of Haiti, the Inter-American Development Bank, and the U.S. State Department, the Clinton Foundation assisted with the development of the Caracol Industrial Park, which could ultimately create up to 60,000 jobs and help to decentralize the Haitian economy. In October 2012, President Bill Clinton joined Secretary of State Hillary Rodham Clinton, President Martelly, Prime Minister Lamothe, and President Moreno of the Inter-American Development Bank (IDB) for the opening of Caracol Northern Industrial Park. Today, the Korean apparel manufacturer Sae-A is the anchor tenant and will create 20,000 jobs alone.

Well, not quite. To date Sae-A is the only major tenant, and 2,000 jobs have been created. Other companies have pledged to join but have been slow to move. Most of the land was acquired from several hundred farmers at minimum compensation, and no alternative form of income has taken its place. Those who have jobs at Sae-A are not so thrilled with their working conditions, security, and pay. They get $4.56 a day. At that rate, a worker would have to work 29 days a month just to buy food.[77] And there have always been critics of this sort of development who argue that it is too insecure, because companies can easily relocate if they find a country with even lower labor rates and greater tax and other incentives. These companies have no allegiance to the country. More important, the establishment of a garment factory does little for Haiti's drastic food insecurity. A few more people may be able to pay for imported food, but it will do little to reduce rural poverty.

But to be less critical, the project *is* going forward. A power plant was built on time and under budget and supplies power to the park and to surrounding villages. And based on the celebrities who attended the opening in 2012 and are identified as supporters of the project—Hillary Clinton was master of ceremonies and Bill Clinton was prominent, and guests included Donna Karan; Brad Pitt; Ben Stiller and his wife, Christine; Haiti's current and former presidents; and Czech supermodel Petra Nemcova, who is ambassador at large to Haiti—then the project is a certain success. I certainly hope so.

I DON'T WANT TO THROW a wet blanket over Caracol, but there is a serious problem that none of the planners appears to have considered. In the north of the island of Hispaniola, the western half of which is Haiti, lies the deadly equivalent to the Enriquillo-Plantain Garden Fault that ruptured in 2010, devastating Port-au-Prince: the Septentrional Fault (literally, the fault of the north). It forms the opposite side of the Gonâve Plate and runs under the Dominican Republic and almost exactly along the north coast of Haiti.[78]

The Septentrional Fault is the same class of fault as its southern counterpart (technically a right-lateral strike-slip fault like the San Andreas). In 1842 this fault ruptured in the Cap-Haïtien earthquake, which had an estimated magnitude of 8.1. About 5,000 people died in that quake, and another 300 in the tsunami that followed. That is far fewer people than were killed in the 2010 event, but there were far fewer people in the exposed area at that time. The site of the planned Caracol development park is just as close, maybe even a little closer, to the Septentrional Fault than Port-au-Prince is to the Enriquillo-Plantain Garden Fault.

A *New York Times* article that discussed the fault was highly critical of the project and pointed to the possibility of environmental damage as well as poor planning and execution. However, if all goes well and the critics are wrong, Caracol could become a thriving center of production that could help lift Haiti out of postdisaster torpor and contribute to economic renewal. Though seismologists cannot say when or exactly where it will happen, they can say with certainty that the Septentrional Fault will move again. None of the new buildings has been built to resist an earthquake the size of the 2010 quake, and the Septentrional Fault has generated larger events. Because the fault has supported a magnitude 8 earthquake in the past, another earthquake of that magnitude is possible. A north-coast counterpart to the Port-au-Prince tragedy is likely to result.

Haiti has suffered so many tragedies in its history. To avert the next one, factories and houses in the new center must be built to very high earthquake-resistance standards. Including earthquake-safe features in new construction adds just a few percentage points in costs but can ensure that many lives are saved and that businesses can keep running or get back online fairly quickly after a quake. Haiti need not lose so many people, and the economy need not lose more than 100 percent of GDP, as it did in 2010.

Every seismologist who read the *New York Times* article and saw the location of Caracol must have put their head in their hands and cried *Oh no, not there.* A safer place would be on the western coastline near Gonaïves or Saint-Marc. Although these areas suffer from repeated flooding from hurricanes, they are far from active faults; hurricanes here are far more manageable than earthquakes.

The die was cast for development in Caracol a long time ago, and changing the location of the new industrial center is not feasible. But the catastrophe in Port-au-Prince should have heightened sensitivity to earthquake risk in Haiti. Since the project began so soon after the 2010 quake, you would think that *someone* might have looked at a seismicity map.

The map shows that for most of its length in northern Haiti, the fault is just a few miles offshore. If a significant earthquake does occur on the Septentrional Fault, the motion on that submarine segment of the fault could cause the seafloor to shift and give rise to a tsunami. The Caracol complex, with its worker housing, power plant, and nearby villages, is close to the coast, and the topography is fairly flat. Caracol Park itself is about two miles from the shoreline. A river runs through the complex into Caracol Bay. The river could funnel tsunami waves from the coast into the complex just as the earthquake in Chile in 2010 found the relocated Concepción by traveling up the Bío Bío River. From a geophysical viewpoint, Caracol is in just as dangerous a place as Concepción.

I HAVE IDENTIFIED SOME WAYS in which we can look at the earthquake disasters in Chile and Haiti that occurred within a few weeks of each other in 2010, with an excursion into an earlier earthquake in China. In absolute magnitude of energy released, the order goes: Chile, China, Haiti. In order of the misery caused, we could argue for the reverse ordering. In order of speed of reconstruction, China wins hands down, even though Haiti received by far the largest donations of relief monies. Haiti is easily last in recovery.

Each place has a markedly different form of government, and each is at a different stage of development. In GDP per capita, of 185 countries assessed in 2013, the World Bank ranked Chile the highest at 51, China at 85, and Haiti at 165. Transparency International ranks Chile very highly at 21, China quite low at 100, and Haiti even lower, at 161 out of 175 countries assessed for perception of corruption. The countries are closest to each other in income inequality: the Central Intelligence Agency (CIA)[79] ranks all three in the top 20 percent of the world's most unequal countries, with Haiti number 7 (the most unequal country outside Africa); Chile, number 14; and China, number 27 of 141 countries assessed. (Haiti and Chile are in the top 10 percent.)

It is hardly unexpected that countries so different in character would experience different disaster outcomes—death tolls, economic setbacks—from geophysically similar natural events. Chile and Haiti can be thought of as the best and the worst in Latin America. But their inequality gives rise to disaster outcomes more similar than might be expected. The small, wealthy governing elite barely notice. It is an inconvenience to them but not much more. Their income is essentially unchanged because they have the capacity to buffer the losses. The poor die or are badly injured and made homeless. They suffer more than they suffered before. What little they had is diminished. *They* suffer setbacks even if the economy doesn't because their production isn't counted and the economy is in the hands of so few. Their deaths don't count, and their suffering doesn't matter.

Do the elite actually profit? Not directly, you might think. But by losing less and recovering more quickly than the poor, they set themselves even further from the poorest. A society of unequals becomes even more unequal, and power and wealth become even more concentrated.

We turn next to examine the colossal disaster of tsunamis. Tsunamis are the quintessential black swan event,[80] an occurrence so unexpected that most people would think it impossible. In most languages there is no native word for them, and the Japanese word is adopted. When they do come to your shoreline, they come with a horror multiplied during centuries of quiescence.

CHAPTER 4

WALLS OF WATER, OCEANS OF DEATH

EARTHQUAKES CAUSE THE MOST DESTRUCTION WHEN THEY GENERATE tsunamis—that is, when the quakes are, as seismologists say, tsunamogenic—because they are capable of causing damage much farther from the earthquake hypocenter than is caused by the ground shaking. These earthquakes occur at special places in the tectonic fabric of the planet, mainly around the Pacific Ocean but also along the western coast of Indonesia. To be tsunamogenic, an earthquake has to be large (magnitude 8 or so) and displace the floor of the ocean. The more the ocean floor is moved, the larger the height of the tsunami wave.

When an earthquake triggers a tsunami, the damage far from the site of the quake itself can be enormous. Places that were not affected by the ground shaking can be devastated by a tsunami running silently across the ocean at speeds as fast as that of a modern commercial airliner. It is very hard to prepare for a tsunami and get out of the way before it is too late. There is no rumbling; the skies don't darken in advance of the wave. Often the sea does retreat hundreds of yards in advance of the tsunami wave, which gives a very good indication that a tsunami will arrive soon—if you know to watch for that signal. That can give people enough time to escape to high ground or a tall, robust building, the only means to ensure survival when the wave comes.

But not many people recognize this warning signal. It's like knowing that buildings kill people in earthquakes; not everyone knows that. There are countless stories of people venturing onto newly exposed beaches to pick up shells and look at stranded sea life, only to be swept to their deaths by the tsunami wave just a few minutes later.

The tsunami that came to Sri Lanka in 2004 was not anticipated; in fact, there isn't even a word in the Sri Lankan language for tsunami. The Japanese word meaning "harbor wave" has been adopted in other languages without translation. The term *tidal wave* is often used, but tsunamis have nothing to do with the tides. Hardly anyone on the eastern coast of Sri Lanka that day would have been familiar with a tsunami. Although the region had experienced tsunamis in centuries past, no one had any memory of them. There were no folktales, no songs of ancient tsunamis. People on the eastern coast of Sri Lanka were as unprepared for the tsunami as those in Port-au-Prince were for the earthquake in 2010.

A tsunami detection and warning system basically consists of a suite of instruments, some deployed on the ocean bottom and others set in buoys on the ocean surface. They measure tiny pressure changes at the seafloor and changes in sea surface height. Seismometers detect earthquakes. Once a quake is detected, computer codes can quickly analyze the seismic data to determine if it might cause a tsunami and, if so, the wave's maximum height and how long it will take to reach various locations. This information is sent to areas that might be affected. For the information to be useful, however, there has to be a way to broadcast it to a public educated about what to do in case of a warning—for example, there can be signs giving guidance as to where people should go for safety. In principle, reaching safety is fairly simple—you take the shortest route to high ground or go to the upper floors of a sturdy building.

If you are not warned, you may see the wave arriving as it enters the shallow regions and grows ever larger. If you are on the ground, your instincts will tell you to run away as fast as possible, as if it were a very large but otherwise normal ocean wave. Over 20,000 people died making futile efforts to escape the 2004 tsunami in Sri Lanka.

Why was there not a warning system in place in the Indian Ocean in 2004? The UN's Intergovernmental Oceanographic Commission (IOC)[1] could have established a suitable system, and it had been an agenda item at meetings for some time. Although the instruments themselves are not very costly or sophisticated, the countries around the Indian Ocean are quite poor and don't have much clout at the IOC. The countries around the Pacific Ocean are exactly the opposite. They are wealthy and have plenty of clout, as well as large numbers of scientists, scientific institutions, and infrastructure that they can contribute cost free to the Pacific warning system. The Indian Ocean countries have far less. So they lost out.

Scientists at the Pacific Tsunami Warning Center in Hawaii detected the earthquake off Sumatra on December 26 and calculated that it would not generate a tsunami that would threaten any of the member countries to which it provides warning—none of which are in the Indian Ocean region. Although those scientists knew that the earthquake was tsunamogenic and posed a threat to Indian Ocean countries, there was no established way for the Hawaiian warning center to contact appropriate authorities around the Indian Ocean. The scientists made calls and sent e-mails to whomever they could think of, but no tsunami warnings were issued in any Indian Ocean country. Sarath Weerawarnakula, the director of the Sri Lankan

Geological Survey and Mines Bureau, later acknowledged receiving word of the earthquake and its tsunami potential, but, it seems, he did nothing.[2] And it's not so clear what he could have done. There was no system in place whereby he could have broadcast a message of warning to people by the coast.

One fascinating story that emerged from the 2004 tsunami in the Indian Ocean is that despite the massive human death toll, very few animals died. It made me wonder if that was true in general in disasters of all types. I don't know the answer, though it has been argued that animals have a sort of sixth sense about impending danger and take off in a direction away from the danger. Elephants in particular are believed to be highly sensitive to unusual sounds, and their feet can sense low-frequency vibrations, which tsunamis *do* create. There are many stories of elephants trumpeting and moving to high ground five minutes or so before the tsunami arrived.[3] Other animals apparently saw that the elephants were upset and, even if they did not sense anything themselves, followed the elephants' lead. Still, it would be fairly impractical to post elephants along the coastline to act as a tsunami warning.

There was no warning system in place in the Indian Ocean before the tsunami of December 26, 2004, but there is a system now. The new system is much like the one that has been in place for many years in the Pacific Ocean and provides accurate and timely warnings of tsunamis generated by earthquakes in the Aleutian subduction zone off Japan and other Pacific regions.

SRI LANKA DID NOT COLLAPSE economically from the tsunami. The World Bank's overview says that "the Sri Lankan economy has seen robust annual growth at 6.4 percent over the course of 2003 to 2012, well above its regional peers"; it doesn't mention the tsunami at all.[4] Why did the economy not suffer from such a severe blow?

First, although the extent of disaster damage is terrifying in its scope, the total damaged area does not take up a very large fraction of Sri Lanka as a whole, just a strip a few miles wide, mostly on the eastern and southern coasts. The capital city, Colombo, is on the western side of the island and was not greatly affected. Government was not disrupted. Conflict between the government and Tamil separatists took a short break, then continued as fiercely as before.

Second, the businesses most affected were fishing and tourism because they were and are concentrated in the coastal strip. In the tsunami, 150,000 lost their main source of income.[5] There was a massive loss of fishing boats and fishing nets (1 million or more nets). But revenues from fishing make up a small part of the Sri Lankan economy.[6] So, while fisheries were important to the local economy of affected areas, their loss did not upend the aggregate economy. Textiles, tea, and rubber products are the largest exports; all are produced inland, and none were damaged by the tsunami. The port facilities through which these products move were largely unaffected also.

And the losses were fairly easily overcome as well. Fishing in Sri Lanka is conducted by hundreds of small-scale fishermen in very small boats. Dozens of nongovernmental organizations (NGOs) saw the opportunity to assist here. To do so, they donated and/or repaired boats to get the fishermen working again. It worked—almost too well. So many boats were made available that it led to overfishing in some areas. In some places, near-shore fisheries, where the small boats could go, became so depleted that fishermen opted to work on large foreign fishing vessels that operate on the high seas.

Tourism is important to Sri Lanka's economy. Fifty-three large hotels and 248 small hotels were damaged or destroyed in the tsunami, as well as around 200 small businesses that relied on tourism. But by the end of 2005, just a year later, 41 of the 53 large hotels were in operation again. Tourism revenues dropped sharply in 2005 but have risen slowly since.[7] Recovery of tourism relies mostly on companies that own the tourist hotels, which will rebuild or repair them, and on the government, which reestablishes transportation and other infrastructure. The challenge is to convince tourists to return.

But tsunamis are such rare events that few people imagine that an area already struck by one will experience another one soon after. And in a first-order way, they are basically right. Tsunamis *are* rare events. And repeat rare events in the same place are even rarer. People living on the eastern coast of Sri Lanka should not think that they live in a region prone to tsunamis. It is prudent to have a warning system, because such systems do save lives, but it makes little sense to declare the coast of Sri Lanka off limits for development indefinitely.

Immediately after the disaster, the government declared a no-build zone 100 meters inland from the high-tide mark. This meant land had to be found for many thousands of people who had to move. Land is scarce in the region, and it is generally privately owned. Many of the largest and best hotels, which produced considerable tax revenues, were located well within 100 meters of the waves, and relocation would have been very difficult. Many were not so badly damaged that repairing them was too costly to consider.

One hundred meters is a fairly arbitrary no-build zone. The tsunami reached much farther inland in many places; in others, due to the nature of coastal topography, it did not come ashore at all. Would an undamaged house 50 meters from the shore have to be destroyed due to the government declaration? More than a year after the tsunami, the no-build zone was dropped, sensible as it might have seemed in the immediate aftermath of the tsunami.

By November 2006, 46,531 partially or fully damaged houses had been rehabilitated by the government or NGOs, amounting to an "85 per cent completion rate."[8] In some places more houses were built than had been destroyed, a remarkable achievement. In chapter

6 we will discuss the effects of Hurricane Katrina on New Orleans. In parts of that city, in the world's largest economy, the rehabilitation rate has been precisely zero.

Did Schumpeter's gale of creative destruction blow in anyone's favor after the Sri Lankan tsunami? Maybe. Many people say their new homes are better than the ones they had before. Yet almost everyone who was relocated is farther from schools and clinics than they were before.[9]

Furthermore, the disaster came during a less-than-stellar time in Sri Lanka's economic life. Growth as measured by GDP was slow, there were fears of inflation, deficits in current account balances were growing, and the currency was on a downward slide. Since the amount of money donated for recovery seemed at the time to be quite a bit more than was needed to restore what had been destroyed, some of the money—the surplus, if you will—was used to put right some macroeconomic problems the country had been facing. In addition, the very typical boom in construction that accompanies rebuilding gave a short but strong surge to the economy. In fact, GDP growth went from very small figures to 6.2 percent in 2005 and 2006.[10]

Is that Schumpeter's gale at work? The World Bank said Sri Lanka's economy is "well above its regional peers." It has also done extremely well at poverty reduction since 2003, meeting the Millennium Development Goal of reducing extreme poverty by half. The World Bank is almost giddy in its praise of Sri Lanka. Prosperity has been "broadly shared," and the Gini coefficient has dropped from 0.41 to 0.36.[11] The World Bank does warn that the effects of climate change may erase all this because Sri Lanka has a variable climate, with areas of high and low rainfall, both of which could become more extreme. But overall, the World Bank is bullish on Sri Lanka.

The problem with ascribing any of this growth to the tsunami is that we do not, and never do, have access to the counterfactual—what would have happened had there not been a tsunami. We don't know what would have happened had the tsunami not occurred and the vast influx of aid money not been received. In my view, the influx of aid money *was* important in the overall economic progress of the country. There is little doubt that it had a stabilizing effect on the macroeconomy, one that may have allowed other forces to lift the economy.

THE ONE PLACE WHERE THERE is fairly clear evidence for creative destruction from the December 2004 tsunami is in the hardest-hit areas of Indonesia in Aceh. First, the long insurgency by the Free Aceh Movement ended in late 2005 with a peace agreement that is widely said to be the direct result of the tsunami. The same did not happen in Sri Lanka where, after a brief truce, fighting by the Tamils continued—if anything, more aggressively.

And there is no doubt that what has been rebuilt in Aceh is universally better than what was destroyed. Everything from the new roads to schools to hospitals is now far better than it was before. Recovery was not hurried; instead, it was very deliberate, and donor funds were used effectively to make improvements to almost every facet of life for the people of the region.

JAPAN'S TOHOKU EARTHQUAKE and tsunami in 2011 has an especially terrible twist because it led to the failure at the Fukushima nuclear power plant. It is impossible for me to erase from memory the video images of the tsunami coming ashore, picking up everything in its path—thousands of cars, entire factory warehouses, buildings on fire in the water like ships burning at sea—and in slow motion relentlessly pushing everything in front farther and farther inland. It seemed like it would never stop, like it would just keep going until it covered all of Japan, penetrating even farther inland than the 2004 Indian Ocean tsunami penetrated anywhere.

Looking at the videos made from helicopters, by people in tall buildings, and even one by someone in a car floating in the water, you could imagine the corpses in the ugly mélange of churning water and shattered buildings. We never saw any bodies in those videos, but you knew they had to be there—16,000 or more of them. The earthquake and tsunami caused 127,000 buildings to collapse totally; another 749,000 were partially damaged.[12] And then compounding the awfulness of the tragedy, the Fukushima Daiichi nuclear plant was seriously impacted. Although it shut down automatically, failure to maintain its cooling systems caused large-scale damage to the reactor and fears of air, marine, and soil contamination and of large explosions.

Japan is a manufacturing economy and has been in a stagnation period for around 20 years. There are apparently two issues. One, things look a lot better if you adjust for Japan's unusual demographics: The total population is shrinking, mass immigration is discouraged, and its population pyramid is inverted with few young people and many elderly—the opposite of Haiti, but similar to many developed countries. Second, Japan calculates growth in an extremely conservative way so GDP figures provided by the government understate the true economic growth. If you adjust for both of those factors, the picture turns out to be much rosier.

So what did the earthquake do to the economy? Data from the Japanese Institute for International Studies and Training offer one way to look at the economic impact.[13] Using the industrial production index for the Tohoku region and for the country as a whole, the effect of the quake is striking, but so is the recovery.

Nationally, production dropped around 15 percent, but in the Tohoku region, it dropped an extraordinary 35 percent. The drag on the total economy caused by the Tohoku earthquake is strong and clear, but recovery started almost immediately. In fact, within the same year, national production had returned to its prequake level. It took much longer for the Tohoku region to recover, and you could argue that it has yet to fully do so. But clearly the region is not so very critical to the aggregate economy of Japan.

The earthquake struck in the northern Tohoku region of Japan, well away from the major centers of manufacturing. The reason that it had any effect on the aggregate economy at all is not due to the farmlands and fishing vessels that were destroyed—they play very little part in the Japanese economy as a whole. Rather, the loss of the Fukushima Daiichi nuclear power plant, which provided power to areas well beyond the region in which it is located, affected the economy. Molly Schnell and David Weinstein, both economists at Columbia University at the time, studied the difference in recovery time for the Japanese economy after the Kobe earthquake in 1995 and the Tohoku earthquake.[14] The most important difference they found is that there was no loss of power production after Kobe whereas the loss after Tohoku was substantial. The current anxiety about nuclear power generation, though understandable, has led to a transition back to fossil fuels that the authors suggest will have far greater negative health effects than nuclear power, even considering the accident. The effect on greenhouse gas emissions could be substantial too.

In 2013, about 300,000 Japanese people were still living in temporary housing.[15] Their repatriation to their home area has been slow and difficult because of the vast extent of damage. Many people need to be relocated to higher ground, and new protective barrier systems must be established. The process promises to be slow and arduous, in contrast to the economic recovery. Social recovery takes much longer. As the aggregate economy has not suffered significantly, the 300,000 displaced people must have provided little productive input to the economy. From the point of view of standard economic indicators, it doesn't matter that those 300,000 people have had their lives turned upside down.

Had the power plant not been affected, there likely would not be much discussion of the Tohoku earthquake beyond geophysical circles. At magnitude 9.0, the quake was much larger than many scientists thought possible on the fault system that ruptured. Few previous earthquakes in the region have been larger than magnitude 7.5. In fact, the Tohoku was almost a "double earthquake," rupturing first in a westward direction down deep into the Earth and then to the east and toward the ocean floor. That is extremely unusual behavior, and it seems that the reason was fault gouge—the thin layer of material within the fault produced by the grinding up of rocks as the fault moves. The fault surface turns out to be extremely slippery, permitting the fault to slip by a large amount.[16] That motion disturbed the ocean floor, pushing the entire water column upward and creating the massive tsunami.

Slipperiness is not known from direct measurement of gouge properties but by the amount of heat released when a fault moves. Although slippery, there is still friction between the fault surfaces, and the motion generates heat, just as when you rub your hands together or use sandpaper vigorously. The amount of heat radiated from a fault when it moves is a very good, though indirect, measure of the fault strength. After the earthquake, a Japanese scientific drill ship, the *Chichyu,* not unlike a commercial oil drilling vessel but set up for scientific research, drilled through the fault that moved in the Tohoku earthquake and set in the region instruments that can measure heat flow. And there wasn't much.

But what do these scientific data mean for the people of Japan? Because all the previous estimates of the likely earthquake magnitude in the region came in around 7.5, the seawalls constructed along the local coast were designed for a tsunami generated from an earthquake of about that size. Like levees and seawalls everywhere, their design height was based on what was imaginable, not the unimaginable. In fact, by looking back to the year 869 and using geological markers that indicate how far inland a tsunami wave traveled, we can find evidence of a similar earthquake and tsunami.[17] The observation period scientists had used to assess the maximum likely earthquake magnitude was long but not long enough to capture this ancient monster. Now we know such large events are possible. To be completely safe, the new seawalls would need to be built much, much higher, and existing walls would need to be made taller. The Japanese people would have to live in the shadow of giant structures stretching for hundreds of miles along the coast.

Will the Japanese government undertake such a project? It doesn't appear so. They will probably build the walls a little higher, maybe a lot higher around nuclear power plants and other critical systems, and keep improving earthquake building codes and construction materials and sponsoring research into earthquake science.

But there is a conundrum at the very center of almost all natural disasters, and the two tsunamis discussed exemplify it well. It's a vicious cycle that goes like this:

1. It's only the very big ones that really matter.
2. The big ones happen very infrequently.
3. The big ones present the most difficult prediction problems.
4. It's relatively easy to protect societies from small- to medium-size events.
5. It's extremely difficult to protect against the monsters.
6. Return to point 1.

And there is another, more important dilemma that compounds and amplifies the first point on the list. The huge numbers of deaths that sometimes accompany the largest of disasters prompt the largest donations of aid from the UN, individuals, and agencies. We saw this in the response to the Haitian earthquake. But the aid is not needed for the deceased; it is needed for the living. Most often, death tolls are high when countries are poor and are poorly governed, with the weakest institutions and the highest levels of corruption. Some outspoken economists, such as Dambisa Moyo and Bill Easterly, have claimed that these countries should not be provided any aid, even in good times, because it creates a dependency sometimes referred to as the Samaritan's dilemma.[18]

The rebuilding in Sri Lanka relied heavily on external funding, but the Japanese rebuilding less so. Sri Lanka was in no position economically to take on the huge task. It would be quite wrong to suggest that Sri Lanka should be denied aid for fear of the Samaritan's dilemma. Or for fear that donor funds might be misappropriated. That fear, perhaps quite understandable, exists whenever disasters occur in poor countries and makes all attempts to recover even more difficult. Donors first pledge, then withhold, looking for evidence that money is being spent well.

This sets up a dynamic in which the most well-to-do are certain to be the winners in the race to recover from a disaster regardless of the losses they take in the disaster itself, and the least fortunate are most often the losers.

CHAPTER 5

MALEVOLENCE BY NEGLECT IN MYANMAR

AS IN HAITI, THERE ARE REALLY JUST TWO GROUPS OF PEOPLE IN MYANMAR. The elite world of the paranoid, xenophobic military junta that rules by cruelty and oppression, along with their political and business cronies who reap the benefits of that rule, makes up one group. Just about everyone else makes up the other group. There are a few people high up in economic status and many more low down and to the bottom, in a poverty trap with no way out. There are plenty of small businesses in Myanmar and Haiti, run by people who make enough to stay just out of the most extreme poverty. In Myanmar, the government provides jobs, especially if you would like to be a soldier, but there is not much of a middle class at all.

The military government in Myanmar is predominantly from one ethnic group, the Buddhist Burmans, who make up 68 percent of the population[1] and speak the dominant language. There are believed to be more than 130 other ethnic groups in Myanmar and a similar number of languages or dialects.[2] Many of these smaller groups, especially the Shan (less than 10 percent),[3] have been engaged in ongoing armed conflicts or insurgencies against the government ever since the military gained power in 1962 after a chaotic period of weak postcolonial governance, only 14 years after the country gained independence from Britain.

Myanmar's history is one of repeated battles for power: both internally—between different ethnic groups and others who would periodically hold power over the country, then be overthrown—and externally—notably the British during their colonial period and the Japanese during World War II.[4] The generals who took power in 1962 have compared themselves to warrior kings and liberators of the past and erected statues depicting themselves in just that way. Overthrow of the government by force is the norm in Myanmar. When they took power, the generals saw themselves as following an established historic tradition of violently contested leadership.

Myanmar's history in the mid-twentieth century followed the path of so many other postcolonial countries, but with its own unique meanders: from independence to initial optimism for self-governed prosperity, to troubled corrupt governance, to ethnic conflict, to violent overthrow and dictatorship. In the last case, dictatorship by a military junta.

As in Haiti, it is very difficult to know the state of economic and social welfare in Myanmar. It is, for example, one of a handful of countries that the World Bank typically doesn't include in listings of wealth measured in gross domestic product (GDP). Figures are available in the CIA's *World Fact Book*, but many of them are acknowledged to be rough estimates.[5] It is virtually impossible to get the information needed to accurately calculate GDP or any other indicator, like the Human Development Index. No figures provided by the government are believable. Even total population size is not known accurately. Had it attempted a census, the junta would never have included the Rohingya or other Muslims who have experienced a long history of persecution.

Myanmar (then called Burma) had one of East Asia's strongest economies during the colonial period and was the largest producer/exporter of rice, cultivated mainly in the Irrawaddy Delta. Well before 2008's Cyclone Nargis devastated the rice-producing areas of the delta, home to a mixture of the Burman majority and the Karen minority, rice production had dropped to the very lowest in the region. Almost nothing was being exported.

Although the Karen people are just one of the ethnic minority groups that have been in conflict with the central military government, they are perhaps the most persistent and dedicated to ethnic independence. They have sought a Karen state through armed conflict since 1949. In fact, Myanmar holds the dubious distinction of being host to the world's longest-running civil war. The Karen people sided with the British in World War II in hope of obtaining an independent state, while the Burmese government originally collaborated with the Japanese in hope of gaining independence from Britain. Both groups saw the war as an opportunity to move their cause for independence forward, and both lost. The history of internal and external conflicts in Myanmar is decades old. The southwest region of the Irrawaddy Delta is today and has long been a region where Karen insurgents operate and foment resistance to the government.

In 2008, the military government in Myanmar was by no means an exact mirror of the government of Haiti. It was more like Haiti under the Duvaliers, who were strong, dictatorial leaders who repressed all opposition with cruelty and violence. "Papa Doc" Duvalier was originally elected to the presidency, unlike the junta in Myanmar, which seized power by force. Papa Doc then progressively centered power around himself; jailed, murdered, or exiled all opponents; faked elections (including one in which he claimed to have received 100 percent of the vote); and eventually declared himself president for life, which, he supposedly believed, was the people's will. All power was centralized around Papa Doc and Port-au-Prince, the capital city.

The junta in Myanmar was almost as intent on centralizing power and suppressing dissent. Power was not as physically centralized in Myanmar until the capital was moved from Yangon to Naypyidaw in the center of the country in 2005. The generals did allow one election in May 1990, and it was not faked. The National League for Democracy clearly won, and Aung San Suu Kyi should have taken power as president. Although the generals initially said they would honor the election results, they changed their minds, nullified the election, and then ruled by decree, much like Papa Doc Duvalier in Haiti. Apparently they were so isolated from and indifferent to the mood of average citizens that they were actually surprised not to have won the election. Papa Doc may also have believed he was genuinely popular. It is astonishing to think that the generals may have thought themselves genuinely popular, given the way they had viciously put down popular protest by students and monks in 1988.[6]

The government in Myanmar is also known for its bizarre and incomprehensible actions as well as its brutality. A prime example was the move of the capital from Yangon in the south to Naypyidaw, a wholly new, vast city built specifically to be the capital in the central region of the country, about halfway between Yangon and Mandalay. It is a city of opulent buildings and astonishingly wide boulevards, twice the width of the Champs-Élysées. The official reason for the move was that Yangon had become too congested, but many have speculated that it was fear of an amphibious invasion by Western powers, a repeat of British tactics in the Anglo-Burmese wars. Others believe the new location may be strategically better for dealing with the many insurgent groups trying to overpower the government, some of which occupy territory well to the north.

When I first heard of the move of the Myanmar capital, I couldn't help but recall that the capital of Australia, Canberra, where I worked for five years as a government geophysicist, was also a wholly constructed government capital (in its own territory, like Washington, DC, and called the Australian Capital Territory, or ACT). Canberra was located well inland and partway between Australia's two major cities, Sydney and Melbourne, strategically placed in a high mountain valley so that it could be more easily defended than the former capital, Melbourne, located on the southern coast. The capital of Brazil was moved inland from São Paulo to Brazília for much the same reasons.

BOTH THE HAITIAN GOVERNMENT and the generals in Myanmar led their countries to economic ruin. Haiti and Myanmar both lie within the world's economic deserts. Perhaps it is more correct to say that both countries' leaders led average citizens of their countries into economic ruin while concentrating wealth and power to themselves.

In Myanmar, the defining philosophy was known as the Burmese Way to Socialism,[7] a peculiar mix of isolationism, socialism, Buddhism, and superstitions, especially about numbers. The Burmese Way actually was little more than a collection of Marxist-like slogans mixed with nationalistic ideology that doomed the country to economic failure. But there *is* money in Myanmar, and, unlike Haiti, there is very strong centralized control over that money.

When I visited Myanmar in March 2012, I stayed at a delightful small hotel called the Alamarda Inn on Golden Valley Road, a sometimes roughly paved, winding road north of the main part of Yangon; a very pleasant and leafy place. From the inn and walking around the area I could see, behind high walls and steel gates, quite large homes with sophisticated architecture and luxurious appointments. *Someone* in Myanmar has money. New high-end cars sat in the driveways.

There were advertisements for luxury cars and swimming pools in the center of Yangon. I couldn't help but think of the area's similarity to Pétionville in Haiti. And just think of the cost of the new capital at Naypyidaw, which was built entirely with government money.

Myanmar's wealth comes from abundant natural resources: oil and gas, teak, gems (rubies mainly), and minerals. Agricultural products are no longer a significant source of export revenues. Gas exports are the main source of foreign revenue, not rice and timber, as in colonial times. Most of the resources are extracted in the ethnic states—Kachin, Shan, Kayah, Karen, and Mon—but very little benefit accrues to those states themselves. The nongovernmental organization (NGO) Arakan Oil Watch published a report on Myanmar's extractive industries under the title "Burma's Resource Curse: The Case for Revenue Transparency in the Oil and Gas Sector."[8] The second section of the report is titled "Burma's Black Hole, Where Did the Gas Money Go?" Since gas is sold on international markets, it is possible to make rough estimates of how much wealth is derived from gas. But by manipulating the exchange rate—effectively by claiming a very low official government exchange rate more than a hundred times less than the market rate—the government can hide billions in revenue.

Myanmar is a classic rentier state and suffers the resource curse—the "paradoxical situation in which countries with an abundance of nonrenewable resources experience stagnant growth or even economic contraction."[9] In many ways it is similar to Nigeria, which is the poster-state for the curse. Grievances with the government are many, but one of the most prominent grievances mirrors that of Nigerians in the oil-producing Niger Delta: the people see vast revenues generated locally, but with little to no return to their region.

That government of Myanmar has made utterly bizarre and catastrophic currency blunders. One morning in 1987, government radio informed the citizens of Myanmar that as of that moment, all bank notes denominated in 25, 35, and 75 kyats would cease to have any value. They instantly became nothing more than pieces of paper with numbers and images of generals printed on them. New 45- and 90-kyat notes were issued, but people could not exchange old notes for them. The new notes had the very important attribute that their value was divisible by 9, which the ruling general at the time, General Ne Win, considered lucky. Only members of the elite who were close to the junta were prenotified of the change. They cashed in their old money for gold and jewels and were thereby protected. Everyone else took a hair-raising plunge deep into poverty.

The generals running the government earn their revenues from foreign sales, so the currency change meant almost nothing to them. While superstitious, they are not reckless, unless it comes to the lives of ordinary people. The riots that followed soon after the currency catastrophe, led by students and joined by monks, protested the junta's oppressive regime. The students' grievances were deeply rooted in the currency fiasco, which made it impossible for them to pay school fees.

Cyclone Nargis battered the people of southern Myanmar in May 2008 with winds and water, but the entire country was already badly battered by corrupt, xenophobic, and fanatically irrational leaders.

CYCLONE NARGIS CAME ASHORE in Myanmar's Irrawaddy Delta almost exactly where the British first established a trading post in the early 1800s. The path of the cyclone was most unusual. Even a day or so before landfall, forecasters were predicting the storm would cross the coast much farther north, as most have before. Four days earlier, the Japanese Typhoon Warning Center was expecting landfall almost 100 miles to the north and described it as an intense storm, not a cyclone. Had the storm followed its predicted path, the outcome would have been far less devastating.

No known storm had plowed a similar track across the Bay of Bengal since the British began their conquest in 1842. The cyclone's unusual track meant that people of the delta were as unaware of the risks they faced as the people of Port-au-Prince would be in 2010 or the people on the coast of Sri Lanka had been in 2008. These events are genuinely rare for those locations. No living person would have had any memory of such a storm in the Irrawaddy Delta. Local legends didn't speak of them. The surprise factor accounted for a significant part of the high death toll.

Cyclone Nargis was probably more deadly than the three Anglo-Burmese wars summed together. The cape region, where Nargis made landfall, is extremely low-lying—typical of most major river deltas—and is one of the lowest-lying areas of the country. The inevitable storm surge that accompanies almost every cyclone is driven ahead of the storm by high winds and (to a much lesser extent) by low atmospheric pressures, and it can travel very far inland if it comes ashore in a delta region. Deltas, in fact, are one of the worst places a cyclone can make landfall. Nargis's storm surge reached as far as 30 miles inland into the Irrawaddy Delta, which contributed significantly to the very high death toll.

Often cyclone storm surges do more damage and take more lives than cyclone winds. Coastal relief and seafloor topography govern the inland penetration of storm surges, just as they do with tsunami waves. After making landfall, Cyclone Nargis acted as if it intended to follow the most destructive path possible, running along the length of the delta about ten miles inland from the coast. In following this track, it also traveled across one of the most densely populated regions of Myanmar. Most cyclones significantly lose strength when they cross onto land, where they are deprived of the warm ocean water that provides their energy. But because deltas are swampy—containing more water than dry land in many places—Nargis sustained more strength than usual. By the time it had moved almost directly over Yangon, it was still a category 1 cyclone.

The British were responsible for starting rice farming in the delta and had drained many swampy areas, built levees for flood control, and removed extensive mangrove stands. But more than that, they made people migrate from the northern areas into the delta to help grow rice for export. Rice is a very labor-intensive crop. So the population of the delta grew and grew until it became one of the most densely populated regions in Myanmar. The British colonials have to take some responsibility for Nargis's high level of casualties.

Nargis was never a superstorm; it had nothing close to the strength of Typhoon Haiyan, which hit the Philippines in 2013. At its top strength, it reached category 3 on the Saffir-Simpson scale, the same strength Hurricane Katrina was when it made landfall east of New Orleans. The National Oceanographic and Atmospheric Administration's National Weather Service classifies category 3 as a "major" storm, and its website states: "Devastating damage will occur: Well-built framed homes may incur major damage or removal of roof decking and gable ends. Many trees will be snapped or uprooted, blocking numerous roads. Electricity and water will be unavailable for several days to weeks after the storm passes."[10]

Hundreds of trees fell in Yangon, but there were few recorded deaths in the city. Businesses there were up and running pretty quickly. Not far away, across the Yangon River in the delta, the story was very different. Nargis came nowhere near the new seat of government, which is well inland.

The true death toll, according to the Red Cross, was 84,500 with 53,800 people unaccounted for.[11] If it is accurate, those figures are unusually large. Assuming most of the missing are actually dead, that would place the death toll as high as 138,300.[12]

WHAT IS SO DISTURBING about Cyclone Nargis is not this very large mortality figure—we have grown inured to reports of high death tolls from poor countries—but rather how the junta reacted to the storm or, more precisely, *didn't* react. First, the government largely ignored warnings from the Indian Meteorological Agency, a government institution that has the responsibility for issuing warnings to several countries in the region with lesser forecasting capacity. These warnings included detailed reports and forecasts as well as personal e-mails that were apparently never acknowledged or answered. Of course, the government of Myanmar says it *did* broadcast timely warnings, but there was certainly no attempt to systematically evacuate the area in the path of the storm. In contrast, the Philippine government, well used to the danger of typhoons, evacuated tens of thousands as Haiyan approached in November 2013 and undoubtedly saved countless lives. Evacuation was difficult because that part of the Philippines is made up of numerous small islands, and travel is not easy at any time. The death toll there from the much stronger storm in an equally densely populated area was around 6,000,[13] 20 times fewer than the toll of Cyclone Nargis. Even so, the prime minster of the Philippines grumbled that the figure would have been zero if local government had evacuated more effectively. This recalls the mood of the government officials in Taiwan who viewed deaths from typhoons in their country as embarrassing and avoidable.

Though I wasn't able to go to the delta region in March 2012 due to unanticipated permission issues, I talked to many people who had lived through the cyclone and was able to piece together some sense of how recovery was progressing. The most common answer I received was: not much at all. And what recovery there was came with almost no help from the government.

One thing I found somewhat surprising was that although everyone was very critical of the government for its miserable relief and recovery actions, no one was critical of it for failure to provide a warning. Why would that be? Most likely it was a combination of two things. One was the complete uniqueness of the storm. It was described as a once-in-500-year event by Jeff Masters, cofounder of the US Weather Underground.[14] No one was surprised to be surprised. Such things didn't happen. If you live in London and are told to anticipate a volcanic eruption on the Strand, you would treat the information rather skeptically. The people who lived in the Irrawaddy Delta would have felt the same way about an evacuation order, had they received one, just as people in Port-au-Prince would have been skeptical about a vague earthquake forecast.

The second and probably more important reason is that common people in Myanmar, as in Haiti, have come to expect very little of their government. They are, I heard numerous times, extremely distrustful of anything the government says. If your government does nothing for you, either by intent or by incapacity, and even acts to suppress the ethnic group to which you belong, it is highly unlikely that you would heed a warning for your safety issued by that same government. Lack of trust in the government could, in fact, be part of the reason some people did not try to evacuate New Orleans as Hurricane Katrina approached.

Poverty traps, like the one that the people in the delta of Myanmar live in, are like time traps, where people are locked in ancient settings in a modern world. Their homes or businesses are typically much more fragile and more easily damaged than buildings in richer countries. Few buildings in the delta could withstand a storm like Nargis. Government institutions and emergency management services are equally inadequate. There are few safe places to seek shelter and few workers to help people find shelter. People of the Irrawaddy

Delta in 2008 had little useful information about the approaching storm and few means of escape. Even if they had been warned, many would have died, but the extremely high total—even admitting the uncertainties and distortions—could have been mitigated.

For people in the delta, the government was remote in distance and in caring. As noted, Naypyidaw was almost completely unaffected by Nargis. It is entirely possible that accurate reports of the scale of devastation in the delta did not get to the highest level of government for quite some time. There were no Weather Channel camera crews taking real-time video. Just as the generals don't generally acknowledge that earthquakes happen in Myanmar and very probably understate fatalities from earlier tsunamis, their impulse, like that of Mayor Daley in Chicago in the heat wave discussed in chapter 1, was to understate the extent of the crisis and act as if they could handle the situation by themselves. Chile's president had a similar reaction to the situation in Concepción discussed in chapter 3.

Everything Is Broken: A Tale of Catastrophe in Burma, by Emma Larkin, centers on Cyclone Nargis.[15] In the book, Larkin describes what I heard repeatedly in Myanmar: that the top generals never were told about anything bad occurring in the country, from the economy to domestic unrest to election results to food security to literacy rates. As information is passed up from the lower ranks, from people who typically *do* know the situation on the ground, it is constantly adjusted to put everything in the best light. By the time information about Nargis reached the top general's desk, it was uniformly good news. It's possible that all the generals actually thought the storm was nothing much to worry about.

THE REFORMIST CURRENT PRESIDENT of Myanmar, Thein Sein, was born in a small village in the Irrawaddy Delta, and at the time Cyclone Nargis hit, he was the head of the country's disaster preparedness committee. It is not very clear what Sein's committee actually did in the years prior to Nargis.

An article about Thein Sein in the *New York Times* under the headline "A Most Unlikely Liberator" tells of how he visited the region of his youth after the storm and was appalled at the scale of devastation. According to U Tin Maung Thann, the head of the NGO Myanmar Egress, Nargis "was a mental trigger. It made him [Thein Sein] realize the limitations of the old regime."[16] Thein Sein has not openly admitted this, but I heard it said several times while I was in Myanmar.

The limitations of the operational capacity of the Myanmar government to carry out relief work were starkly evident in the days after Nargis. The inaction stemmed from a deadly mixture of indifference, incapacity, anxiety, and outright cunning. The junta running the government was made up mostly of senior army commanders—the navy and air force are small in comparison to the army and mainly provide support for army actions against insurgents and in securing the country's borders. The Myanmar Police Force, formerly independent of the army, is now an auxiliary military service. Myanmar spends almost 25 percent of its revenues on the military.[17] (The equivalent figure for the United States is 20 percent.[18]) The army has a reputation for being one of the best trained and having the toughest fighters in the region.

The army did not prove to be tough when it came to rescue and relief operations, however. Once the generals found it necessary to act, they did so in what appeared to be an almost random and erratic way. No doubt it was complicated and difficult; the delta region is hard to access at the best of times. There are few roads and transportation is often by small boats, so even a well-organized relief effort would have faced problems. An evacuation would have been difficult and could have achieved only partial success, even if a timely and well-distributed warning had been issued. The situation must have been akin to the fog of war, in which harrowing circumstances make it all but impossible for people, even well-seasoned commanders, to make good decisions. With winds blowing well over 100 mph and water rising, it is surely difficult to make decisions in the fog of disaster.

What I heard from a large number of people was that those in the cyclone-affected region for the most part helped themselves. That included local soldiers based in the region who acted on impulse, without waiting for orders from the top that they may have expected would not come. The local NGOs, often with ethnic roots, were able to provide some measure of relief for their people. In fact, I heard that the ability of these NGOs to act without the usual constraints and oversight by government gave them a sense of empowerment they had not experienced before. Many told me that the storm gave them a way of proving to themselves and to others that they had an important and effective role in Myanmar's civil society.

But the generals seemed to want to do as little as possible for the people of the delta. In fact, they refused offers of aid from foreign nations. The generals sought to give the appearance that they were in control and didn't need help. One way they did this was by trying to diminish the problem to something relatively small scale and manageable. To "prove" this, they went ahead with a national constitutional referendum just eight days after the cyclone hit. Some people in the delta region during or immediately after the cyclone said they never saw any evidence of relief operations from the military. And very little has happened since then.

All one can do is speculate about what was in the minds of the generals in those days. Perhaps in years to come someone will tell the story from the inside. People who make devastatingly bad decisions about the numerical denomination of their currency and move their capital city on a whim should not be expected to make brilliant decisions during a disaster.

THE MORALLY REPREHENSIBLE GENERALS latched onto the opportunity to gain advantage by doing nothing, and they almost got away with it.

But why do nothing? One reason is to hide incompetence. Members of the Myanmar military are not experienced in civil search and rescue. What they do is more or less the opposite. The military controls all economic activity in the country, funneling the benefits to themselves and their cronies. That is not a military action but a political one. Their primary military function is to suppress insurgents so they can hold onto political power. The government's capacity to act in response to the cyclone was weak, and no one in government wanted that weakness to be exposed. In the tortured logic of the generals, doing nothing made it appear as if nothing needed to be done. By the time the cyclone struck, Myanmar's relationship with China had begun to collapse, so the generals could not rely on a capable ally for assistance, and they were on poor terms with all their neighbors to the east and west.

Why thwart others who are trying to help? Part of the reason relates to the first. If you allow people in, it will become clear that something *does* need to be done, and the ruse that things were not so bad and that everything was under control would be exposed. The generals would have had to explain why they did nothing.

But mainly, bizarre as it may seem to people outside Myanmar, the generals did fear an invasion. In a very insightful article in the journal *Contemporary Southeast Asia,* Andrew Selth reminds us that Myanmar had been invaded numerous times in its history.[19] In fact, the three most recent invasions occurred within living memory. Myanmar is subject to severe international sanctions, and those imposing the sanctions couch their rhetoric in terms of the desire for regime change. The generals believed outside influences determined to overthrow the government fueled the riots of 1988, and they earnestly believed that a flood of international aid workers would be nothing more than a pretext for a US invasion. (Selth says they had watched the US invasion of Iraq closely.) They were aware that the French minister for foreign and European affairs, Bernard Kouchner, had called for coercive humanitarian intervention after the cyclone under "the responsibility to protect,"[20] an action that would amount, in the generals' thinking, to invasion under a humanitarian pretext. The arrival of US warships (to lend humanitarian support) off their coast would only have supported that belief.

The generals resisted what they genuinely believed was imminent invasion, and the international community should have realized that would be their reaction. Instead, the international community rebuked the generals, making a difficult situation even worse. Whether a different approach might have been more successful cannot be known, but it now seems to me that the reactions by the international community did nothing but exacerbate the tragedy.

The area damaged in the cyclone was of little importance to the country's economy, and, furthermore, the region supported armed opponents of the government. The generals may have felt that the region just didn't matter very much. Since the people who lived there included their enemies, why help them? We will see this logic emerge again in New Orleans after Hurricane Katrina.

As far as anyone can tell, Cyclone Nargis made no difference at all to the economy of Myanmar. Schumpeter's gale didn't bring creative destruction, at least for most of the delta residents.

IF YOU HAVE READ ANYTHING unbiased about the history of Myanmar, you'd know that grabbing land has been the norm for many decades. In fact, the British colonization of Myanmar was more capture than colonization; it was a blatant land grab. What happened after

Cyclone Nargis was entirely to be expected. Once the winds stopped blowing, the rain stopped falling, the storm surge had retreated, and the sea level was back to normal, a rich opportunity for gain presented itself—and the generals finally became involved. To benefit from the land acquisition that followed, you just needed to be part of the military or closely connected to the military.

And this remains true today, despite the strong move in Myanmar toward democracy. The country is democratic enough that international sanctions have been lifted, and the country is on a strong trajectory toward democratization and growth. What has replaced the old land grab by armed force is a new form of quasi-legal land takeover—"legal land grabs," as Kevin Woods at the University of California, Berkeley, has put it.[21] The new government came to power in 2010 with new laws, some of which—the Farmland Law, for instance—sound as if they are meant to protect farmers. But, in fact, the laws allow land to be expropriated by the state if the property is needed "for the national interest." And it requires no imagination at all to guess who it is who decides what is, or is not, in the national interest. In fact, it is very much the same people who made the decisions before the new form of government came into being.

What has emerged in Myanmar is a sort of elite alliance among military and business interests in a nominal democracy with laws that assist the elite and disengage almost everyone else. I heard on many occasions that nothing is different in terms of who really holds sway in the country; there still exists a deep suspicion of the military. Several people told me that the "democratization" came about because it was in the generals' interests to have it come about. They have lost nothing. In fact, they have gained by selling off state assets, such as land, to foreign businesses that now can operate in Myanmar—businesses to which the generals have very close ties.

After Cyclone Nargis, many in the Irrawaddy Delta fell victim to the Vacant, Fallow and Virgin Lands Management Act. The land that Cyclone Nargis's storm surge inundated could be plausibly declared vacant and fallow by courts working in conjunction with the military-business network that is blossoming in Myanmar and is hungry for land. The Myanmar lands management act operates something like eminent domain in the United States, which grants the government the right to take private land for public use (or for use by a third party in government or civic interest) if the original owners of the land are fairly compensated.[22] Likewise, in Myanmar, people are supposed to be fairly compensated when the government takes land under the management act, but that is not what has happened. Furious complaints and protests claim that compensation, if it happens at all, is trivial and nowhere near the actual value of the land. Displaced farmers are forced to become landless laborers and work for a pittance on other people's farms.

Land is very valuable capital in Myanmar today, and the powerful have no issue with taking it from the weak.

ECHOES OF THE SAME KIND of malfeasance can be heard today in the Philippines following the devastation wrought by Typhoon Haiyan: "Build Back Better is nothing but a legal corporate land grab in the guise of a rehabilitation program." That's the claim of the Philippine youth group Anakbayan in response to the business-led rehabilitation strategy of restoration following Haiyan, known locally as Yolanda. That strategy, under the program name Recovery Assistance for Yolanda (RAY), includes the allocation of state funds and internationally donated resources to establish public-private projects in twenty-four areas devastated by Yolanda that are now described as "development areas or clusters." Nine of the country's largest corporations have claimed sixteen of these areas. Their plans are for tourism, property development, mining, and so on. Their plans are not for the rehabilitation of the livelihoods of those trampled by the storm.

The president of the Philippines, Benigno Simeon Aquino III, claims that everything is going well in the recovery despite noisy "human wave" protests by survivors. He also caused distress and anger by suggesting that the casualty figure should really have been zero and would have been had local officials conducted evacuations properly. Yolanda was well predicted. It made close to a straight-line path into the islands and traveled at high speed across the islands. The speed at which it moved actually helped to limit the damage—if a storm moves slowly, the associated rainfall lasts longer and flooding becomes more likely.

The finger-pointing between the central government and regional and local governments reads so much like that between President George W. Bush, Governor Kathleen Blanco and Mayor Ray Nagin after Hurricane Katrina it is unsettling. Aquino's presidential rehabilitation assistant, Panfilo Lacson, has even described protesting survivors as lazy and leftists—in his view, apparently, the survivors are nuisances because they *should* have evacuated and didn't, making trouble for the government.

It is far too early to say how events will play out in the Philippines. Transparency International ranks the Philippines as a corrupt country—94th out of 177 countries in 2013—but not a completely corrupt country. That level of corruption, combined with the tight intertwining of business interests and government, appears destined to ensure that the beneficiaries of any land redistribution will be the wealthy elite, and the losers will be those already at the bottom of the economic pecking order.

DISASTERS PRESENT TOO MUCH temptation to many in power. Like so much else in society, disasters are to be manipulated for social, political, and/or financial gain. The type of government and stage of development don't appear to matter very much: they just provide different tools for different actors and different methods to achieve gain. And the type of disaster isn't very important either. Whether cyclone or earthquake, expected or unexpected, the aftermath presents the same temptations.

Despite the repressive nature of the Myanmar government and its many bizarre actions, the narrative of Cyclone Nargis is by no means an anomaly. The government's reaction to the storm, while marked by the junta's anxiety, is not unique and can be found in many parts of the world. As we have seen in Haiti and will see again and again, it is all too easy to declare the destruction wrought by a disaster as blight and the blighted areas as vulnerable, as places where people shouldn't be living. Governments and private actors (or the two in partnership) then have the chance to grab land for their own purposes. Nature has unwittingly helped the transfer of property from the poor to the rich.

CHAPTER 6

STRUCK DUMB IN NEW ORLEANS

THE DISASTERS IN MYANMAR AND HAITI ARE SIMILAR TO THOSE IN NEW YORK and New Orleans in that each was worse than it should have been. This chapter discusses why they were so bad and who made them that way.

UNLIKE IN MYANMAR OR HAITI, in New Orleans there *is* a middle class with many vibrant businesses, especially around tourism and entertainment, and some of the people who run them are quite prosperous. Tulane University, Loyola University, and the University of New Orleans are major employers, as are hospitals, the port facility, and the petrochemical industry. But a great majority of those who live in New Orleans are stuck fast in a poverty trap: unemployed, undereducated, and unhealthy, with little hope of progress and mobility. The majority of those who live in New Orleans were born there. For some, evacuation from the city in the face of a hurricane means going somewhere very unfamiliar.

New Orleans is the largest city in the second-poorest state in the United States. (Mississippi, the state immediately adjacent to the east, ranks the poorest.)[1] Household income inequality in New Orleans is also the second highest in the country, behind Atlanta, Georgia.[2] The American Human Development Project calculated a Human Development Index (using a different formula from that used by the United Nations Development Program) that places Louisiana third from the bottom, with Mississippi again coming in last.[3]

Poverty is deeply racial in Louisiana. Twenty-five percent of white families have incomes over $100,000, and only 7 percent have incomes less than $15,000. For African Americans, those figures are exactly reversed—only 7 percent have incomes over $100,000, and 25 percent have incomes below $15,000.[4]

The geographic setting of New Orleans is not unlike that of Yangon in Myanmar. Both lie in the sweeping bend of a river—the Mississippi and Yangon Rivers respectively—that flows in complex meanders into fertile deltas immediately to their south. Both are major centers for shipping, and both export products from their country's interior.

POVERTY REFLECTS GEOGRAPHY in New Orleans. It is quite literally invisible to the tourists on Bourbon Street who are so important to the city's economy, because it is confined to distinct regions where there are no tourist attractions, notably the Lower Ninth Ward and Gentilly. According to Alan Berube and Bruce Katz of the Brookings Institution:

> These neighborhoods did not appear by accident. They emerged in part due to decades of policies that confined poor households, especially poor black ones, to these economically isolated areas. And despite New Orleans' reputation for fine food, these areas are food deserts as well, relying on small bodegas with limited selections. The federal government concentrated public housing in segregated

inner-city neighborhoods, subsidized metropolitan sprawl, and failed to create affordable housing for low-income families and minorities in rapidly developing suburbs, cutting them off from decent housing, educational, and economic opportunities.[5]

The Lower Ninth Ward of New Orleans looks nothing like the Cité Soleil slum of Port-au-Prince, but functionally the two are essentially the same. They are both geographically restricted areas that concentrate the poorest people—who are also the most unhealthy and underserved—and are the most dangerous places in those cities. In Myanmar, the generals don't like to see evidence of poverty so they forcibly evicted millions of inner-city slum dwellers in Yangon and Mandalay to peripheral areas where they would not be seen by the tourists the generals hoped to attract. Motorcycles are also banned in central Yangon. If forcible slum clearing sounds horrifying, remember that the US Housing Act of 1949 permits the use of eminent domain to clear blighted areas and "revitalize" them. Most cities around the world have engaged in slum clearing at some point in their development, usually describing it as "urban renewal."

The wealthy in New Orleans have their enclave too. They are mostly in and around the Garden District, essentially the equivalent of Pétionville in Haiti. Audubon Place, immediately across from the luxuriant Audubon Park, is a private gated community. Tulane's president has a home—a mansion—right on the corner. Audubon Place didn't flood at all. It's in one of the few parts of the city that sits nicely above sea level. So, like Port-au-Prince, the wealthy in New Orleans quite literally occupy the high ground.

This geographic arrangement is far from happenstance. The Mississippi River floods regularly. The floods are the source of fertile soil that made the delta such an ideal place for cotton farming (and the Irrawaddy Delta a fine place for rice growing). Anyone living in the Mississippi Delta before the levee system was constructed (and even after) would have experienced numerous flooding events, and it would not take long to learn which locations remained above the floodwaters. If you are wealthy, that's where you move. Property values quickly rise in those places as they become known for their natural desirability. In very little time, they become enclaves of the rich. But if you are not rich, you stay right where you are, as marginal people in marginal lands.

It would be a significant exaggeration to equate New Orleans with Haiti, but numerous times in print, on television, and in conversations I have had with people in New Orleans, the response to Hurricane Katrina was said to "make us look like a third-world country."[6] Just what people meant by that statement was never quite clear. It was always said with the same sort of embarrassment that came over the government officials I met with in Taiwan. The level of death and destruction was more like what we are used to hearing about in a developing country, such as Haiti or Bangladesh, not a rich country.

So, despite being located in the world's leading economy, New Orleans and the Katrina disaster exhibit many characteristics that echo those of two of the very poorest places on Earth.

AT THE TIME KATRINA STRUCK, corruption was endemic in all levels of government in New Orleans. Louisiana ranked third in the United States in the number of corruption-related convictions relative to total population (following Alaska and Mississippi) in 2005.[7] Two of the most prominent government officials at the time of Hurricane Katrina have since been charged with corruption. In 2014 Mayor Ray Nagin was convicted and sentenced to ten years in prison on 20 counts of various corrupt activities: one overarching conspiracy count, five counts of bribery (he was charged with six), nine counts of wire fraud, one count of money-laundering conspiracy, and four counts of filing false tax returns.[8] Aaron Broussard, the chief executive of Jefferson Parish, which includes a large section of suburban New Orleans, has also pleaded guilty to political corruption charges.

The corrupt activities that Nagin was convicted of were not all directly associated with Katrina. Many were "normal." Nagin has insisted he did nothing wrong, and he may even believe it. The activities were just the way a mayor goes about business in New Orleans. The storm, however, offered a special opportunity for Nagin's corrupt dealings.

Corruption differs little in Haiti, Myanmar, and New Orleans, different though those settings are. Those in power in government, whether through election or by seizure, surround themselves with powerful supporters whom they reward with lucrative contracts or favors to conduct business. In return, they get loyalty, kickbacks, and no scrutiny of their own wealth-generating activities. None of those in power show much care for their people except in times of elections (if they have them), when they must pretend to do so.

DESPITE THE VAST and obvious differences between Myanmar and the United States, it is very hard to read accounts of the official government reaction to Cyclone Nargis in Myanmar and not recall the reaction of the Bush administration to news of Hurricane Katrina in the Louisiana Gulf Coast. Both President George W. Bush and Vice President Dick Cheney were on vacation at the time, and neither thought the situation serious enough to interrupt their leisure time. Days passed before Bush and Cheney returned to Washington. The timing is uncannily similar to the time it took for the Myanmar leaders to take action on Nargis.

We can only speculate about just what Bush understood about the scale of the destruction and the relief operations under way in New Orleans. It is utterly unclear whether Bush, from his vacation home in Crawford, Texas, or from the Oval Office in the White

House, knew more or less about the tragedy unfolding in the Mississippi Delta than Than Shwe, the top general of the armed forces of Myanmar, knew from his office in Naypyidaw about the suffering in the Irrawaddy Delta. Both were informed, but both acted—in very different ways—as if they really didn't know, didn't believe, didn't want to believe, or didn't care. Or couldn't comprehend.

And it wasn't just President Bush who seemed to think Hurricane Katrina wasn't worth worrying about so much. Secretary of Defense Donald Rumsfeld attended a San Diego Padres baseball game the day Katrina made landfall. Two days after, when the massive tragedy unfolding in New Orleans was undeniable and Bush's vacation had ended, Secretary of State Condoleezza Rice went to see a Broadway play, where she was booed by the audience. Undeterred, the next day she attended the US Open and went shoe shopping on Fifth Avenue in New York. Michael Chertoff, the head of Homeland Security, which had absorbed the Federal Emergency Management Agency (FEMA), seemed not to pay much attention for days, claiming afterward to have been unaware of the gravity of the situation. And every statement out of the Bush administration claimed that the relief efforts were going well, just as the generals would claim in Myanmar.

When Than Shwe and George Bush finally began to accept the scope of the disasters in the southern delta reaches of their countries, each acted defensively, concerned more about mitigating political and reputational damage than about the vast damage to life and property. Each had the immediate impulse to assert that everything was under control. Each was eventually persuaded by the media and/or his own staff that he needed to show interest and visit the scene. Bush first flew over the scene in Air Force One on the way back to Washington from his vacation. Although the plane was flying low and relatively slowly, the pass over New Orleans couldn't have taken much time.

Photographs show him staring out the window from his private cabin with a puzzled look on his face. News media were invited into the president's quarters on the plane in the hope that photos would capture the commander in chief looking vexed, concerned but in charge, giving orders. Instead, he looked hopelessly distant from the tragedy below. It earned him the title of the Flyover President[9] from those who felt he was detached from most aspects of life in the United States.

Bush may truly have been unaware of the full scope of the tragedy in New Orleans. After all, the day after the hurricane passed, the central part of the city looked damaged but not devastated, and Mayor Nagin said the city had dodged a bullet. The Lower Ninth had already flooded; he just didn't know it.

Once they finally arrived at the disaster scene, each leader, looking appropriately concerned but now in charge, praised their disaster management agency leaders for their excellent and timely work. President Bush achieved almost instant derision for his infamous statement that Michael Brown, whom he had personally chosen to head FEMA, was doing a "heckofajob [sic]."[10] These words came despite being briefed earlier by Brown and others that New Orleans was 90 percent underwater and that "nothing was working"—according to Brown in a later interview on his 2011 book, *Deadly Indifference: The Perfect (Political) Storm: Hurricane Katrina, The Bush White House, and Beyond.*[11]

Unsurprisingly, in his book Brown attempts rather shamelessly to shift the blame from himself to those above him, especially President Bush. Brown sees himself as the person in the administration who had to take the blame for the botched Katrina response. In US politics, someone always takes the fall when something goes badly wrong, whether they carry any direct blame or not. There were calls for Brown's resignation for days before he was dismissed, and when things go wrong in US responses to natural disasters, FEMA's head is always blamed.

IT IS PARTICULARLY IMPORTANT to recognize just how bad Katrina really was. It was not bad just because the response was dreadful. The finger pointing was not about something trivial or a political squabble; it was about the responsibility for massive death and destruction.

Hurricane Katrina was off the scale in so many ways. While death tolls are surprisingly hard to measure accurately and, as we discussed earlier, don't have very much to do with the long-run social and economic consequences of disasters, one thing we do know with great certainty is that the Katrina mortality figure, whatever it actually is, is appallingly large. The "official" figure is 1,833; the true figure may be as high as twice that.[12]

Until Katrina, even the most massive storms and hurricanes in the United States had not killed many people. Hurricane Andrew made landfall in Dade County, Florida, at category 5 on August 24, 1992. It is notorious in US hurricane history, not because of the number of fatalities it caused but because it resulted in 11 insurance companies being forced out of business by the thousands of claims made by survivors. The death toll was 65. Superstorm Sandy killed 117 people in the United States, the majority of them in New York. Outside the United States, Haiti was hardest hit with 53 deaths.[13] These figures are not trivial, but compared to Katrina, they *are* quite small.

You have to go a lot further back in history than 1992 to find a hurricane with a fatal effect similar to Katrina's. The first you find is in 1928, the Okeechobee hurricane, named for Lake Okeechobee in south Florida. Most reported deaths occurred when levees on the lake were breached, flooding extensive areas of the surrounding farmland. It may be that as many as 2,500 people died (the original official figure was 1,836, remarkably close to the official figure for Hurricane Katrina), but the great majority were black migrant farm-workers, many from the Bahamas, whose numbers were not known before the storm. Hundreds were buried in unmarked mass graves. White people died too, but they were buried in the few caskets that were available. There never was and will never be an accurate count of the dead from the Lake Okeechobee hurricane.

To find a hurricane in the United States with a larger estimated death toll than Katrina's, you have to go back more than a century to the so-called Galveston Flood (actually a hurricane) of September 8, 1900.[14] The death toll there exceeded that of the Lake Okeechobee hurricane and Hurricane Katrina combined by a substantial margin. The *Galveston News* published lists of confirmed dead in the days following the storm and on October 7 made a final tally of 4,263 deaths. The Morrison and Fourmy Company, which published general directories of business and private addresses in many Texas cities in the early 1900s, estimated that Galveston's population dropped by 8,124 but acknowledged that 2,000 or so people may have moved away, so their figure is not a death toll. The most common totals you will see on websites and other sources range from 5,000 to 8,000, the three zeroes a clear giveaway that the figures are not accurate. But even the lowest number, probably derived from the *Galveston News* figure and inflated for good measure, still considerably exceeds the Katrina number.

THE REASON THE SITUATION in New Orleans was so bad physically was not a forecaster's error. The storm track was fairly simple, a minor variation on many storm tracks seen before in the Gulf. Hundreds of storms have passed through the area, and that information is stored and analyzed to assess the possible track of any new storm. Katrina was not a freak event. Forecasters were issuing warnings that New Orleans might be in the path of a major storm for many days before August 29. In fact, three days ahead of Katrina's landfall, the National Hurricane Center was issuing warnings based on projected tracks that were eerily close to Katrina's actual path.[15] It was known that the Gulf of Mexico was unusually warm, so the buildup of hurricane strength was predicted quite well. The information provided to those in authority in the Gulf Coast was more than enough for them to make evacuation plans and protect the people of the region.

Katrina was first and most importantly an urban tragedy. The concentration of people, particularly in the poorer parts of New Orleans, convolved with the force of the storm surge to make Katrina an off-scale tragedy. In other, less urbanized parts of the Gulf Coast, damage was enormous as well, but the death tolls were much smaller. Katrina actually made landfall in Mississippi, in Pass Christian, yet the Mississippi death toll, though high at 238, was not so enormous as the New Orleans figures. Evacuation had been more timely, orderly, and successful in Mississippi. Based on that figure, you could conclude that if New Orleans had been evacuated as well as Mississippi had been, the total Katrina deaths might have been more like 500 to 600. That would keep the storm in the top rankings of hurricane mortality in the United States, and quite significant globally, but it would still be a fraction of what actually happened.

The levees were the central problem for New Orleans. Those that failed were *not* those built to control flooding by the Mississippi River. Those are the only levees visitors to New Orleans are likely to see, and those levees held firm during Katrina.

New Orleans is bordered to the north by Lake Pontchartrain and is protected from the lake waters by an extensive levee system. Those levees, like the Mississippi River levees, were not breached;

still, water did come over their tops as the storm moved inland and the winds changed direction, creating the lake equivalent of a storm surge that pushed south, the opposite direction from the main surge that drowned most of the city.

The levees that failed were those that constrained the waters of man-made shipping canals. The first to breach, and the one that proved the most deadly, was the Industrial Canal that connects Lake Pontchartrain to the Mississippi River. River and lake levels differ, so entry to the Industrial Canal from the Mississippi is through the Inner Harbor Navigation Canal Lock (more commonly, the Industrial Lock). The canal levees that failed were not designed to handle the storm surge that funneled toward New Orleans. They were built to contain the industrial waterways for shipping through the city, not to protect the city from storm surge.

Plans for a canal between Lake Pontchartrain and the Mississippi River were made in the late nineteenth century, and the right-of-way for the original connection gives Canal Street, in the center of New Orleans, its name. That right-of-way was never used, and when the Industrial Canal was built beginning in 1914, the chosen site thrust through the Ninth Ward. Today the Lower Ninth Ward lies to the east of the Industrial Canal and the ward's Bywater section lies to the west. Part of the canal was excavated through uninhabited swamplands, but in the Ninth Ward, houses and businesses and a century-old convent were demolished to make way for it.

The Industrial Canal was the first to serve commercial shipping and provide harbor facilities, including shipyards for vessel maintenance. It was also the first of the levees to be breached when Hurricane Katrina came ashore, flooding the Lower Ninth Ward.

The Mississippi River Gulf Outlet (MRGO) and the Gulf Intracoastal Waterway were built later and connected to Industrial Canal. They were to serve as shortcuts for ships to the Gulf of Mexico.

These canals, constructed to facilitate commerce, cut through what were then and still are today some of the poorest parts of New Orleans. Residents of these areas had little say in where the canals were located, nor did they derive very much benefit from them. At the time they were constructed in the mid-twentieth century, they probably looked very safe. But MRGO was breached in 20 places during Hurricane Katrina, flooding all of Saint Bernard's Parish and parts of Plaquemines Parish. It has subsequently been closed.

Farther to the west in the wealthier section of Lakeview, two more canals suffered levee breaches—the Seventeenth Avenue Canal and the London Avenue Canal. (There is a third canal, the Orleans Avenue Canal, that was not breached.) Both canals head around the middle of the city and exit into Lake Pontchartrain. They are drainage canals used to pump water from the city during heavy (and not so heavy) rainfall. Without them and the many miles of underground drainage systems, New Orleans would flood under even fairly moderate rain. During Katrina, the pumps failed and the pumping stations were flooded. Much of New Orleans is today in a depression, often called the New Orleans Bowl, having subsided to that lower level over the last three centuries. When the French founded New Orleans in 1718, they chose the site because it was strategically located in a defensive position on a sharp bend in the river. It was also a good location for trade and at that time was on high ground above the river. Today the city is mostly below sea level except in a few places, near to the river and the lake.

The canal system in New Orleans is hardly a marvel of modern engineering, but, at the same time, it is hardly ancient. When the shipping canals were built, understanding of hurricane risk was not very sophisticated. Early plans for the Industrial Canal were drawn up about the time of the Galveston hurricane in 1900, when those most knowledgeable about weather systems believed that Galveston could not possibly flood to a depth greater than four feet.[16] That is what the best science of the day indicated.

Those who designed and built the Industrial Canal system in New Orleans didn't have much more knowledge. The now commonly accepted concept of a weather front was not accepted in the United States at that time. (Only after World War II was the concept widely accepted.) Meteorology in the United States was behind developments in Europe. Most people believed, or convinced themselves, that events like the Galveston hurricane were freaks of Nature and unlikely to recur, at least in the lifetime of anyone who was then alive. Katrina, however, was not a freak event. It was a fairly ordinary hurricane, not among the strongest. Many similar hurricanes had passed through the Gulf. In 2005, there was a vast store of meteorological experience of hurricanes much like Katrina.

When the canals were built, quite a bit was known about rivers and river flood control. The river levees were built with good historic information to go on as well as considerable experience with levee engineering. Floods that raise the river level high happen regularly; hurricanes, in contrast, don't occur as often. For that reason, those who designed and constructed the canal levees paid little attention to the possibility of a major hurricane.

All that changed in 1965 with Hurricane Betsy. The storm had a peculiar track and made several tight loops before making landfall in Florida and New Orleans. Unlike Katrina, Betsy posed a very difficult forecasting challenge. The death toll was only 76,[17] even though Betsy was the same strength on the Saffir-Simpson scale as Katrina and it followed a similar path entering New Orleans. Betsy caused extensive flooding in New Orleans from breaches in MRGO and the Industrial Canal and because the pumping system failed, just as happened in Katrina. Betsy was a wake-up call that made clear the fact that the levees needed substantial improvement. The hurricane gave rise to the 1965 Flood Control Act and the Army Corps of Engineers' Greater New Orleans Hurricane Protection project, which was intended to protect the city against the most likely severe storm that would hit the area. Unfortunately, that objective was not fulfilled.

IN ONE OF THE MOST closed governed places on Earth and in one of the most openly governed places, leaders behaved so similarly it is astonishing. Neither Myanmar's top general nor the US commander in chief took command. Each seemed dumbfounded, transfixed, or callously uncaring. Or maybe they were in denial.

Denial is a common reaction to fear. Eliot Aronson, the great behavioral psychologist, analyzes denial in a paper titled "Fear, Denial, and Sensible Actions in the Face of Disaster."[18] He argues, through a set of experiments, that if you scare people but give them no way to deal with the fears that you have induced, denial and inaction will most likely follow. People are not scared into action; they are scared into *inaction*.

Aronson says that people need a concrete, doable, and effective strategy so they know there is a way to deal with what frightens them. The fear of lung cancer can be dealt with by giving up smoking—concrete, doable, and effective—but it may not be so easy for people who have a serious dependence.

President Bush has said, in effect, that he was surprised by the extent of the disaster in New Orleans.[19] He might also have been frightened. He was almost instantly derided for his claim that no one could have anticipated that the levees would break, because he had paid no attention at all to clear warnings. Or maybe the messages just didn't register and he *was* genuinely surprised, even though he ought not to have been.

Most of us living outside of New Orleans were surprised. We had no idea a storm of that size could do so much damage. Who but a few people in New Orleans knew that the levees were in such bad shape? If regular citizens of New Orleans *did* know, what concrete, doable, and effective actions could they have taken? Denial set in, and when the levees broke, people *were* surprised.

Surprise can be deadly. Keren Fraiman from the Massachusetts Institute of Technology, Austin Long from Columbia University, and Caitlin Talmadge from George Washington University, all scholars who research security issues, discussed in the *Washington Post* how Iraqi forces collapsed after a surprise attack by soldiers of the Islamic State of Iraq and Syria, an attack that should have come as no surprise.[20] The authors say that surprise attacks can panic even the best-trained forces and lead to chaos and collapse. Two ingredients for surprise are key, they suggest: poor intelligence and the politicization and corruption of security forces.

Change a few words and you have a description of how Nargis and Katrina were handled. Neither should have been a surprise, but they both were. Michael Brown claims in his book that he told President Bush that "we have lost the city," sounding for all the world like a general reporting a war situation to headquarters.[21] President Bush either didn't listen or didn't want to believe.

Scientists, like me, who are advocates of strong greenhouse gas reduction, are sometimes guilty of this too. We can't resist describing the effects of climate change in anything less than apocalyptic terms. We cast images, inspired by science fiction movies, of cities ablaze and panic in the streets, as massive waves roll through the avenues of Washington and the boulevards of Paris, over statues and monuments in familiar parks, sweeping buildings away in their path, tsunami-like.

And then we don't give people the concrete, doable, and effective strategies they need to deal with the problem of climate change. We tell them that the problem is vast, and so it is, and it requires

coordinated actions by global governments to do anything about it—
and they are so very clearly not coordinating their actions. Climate
change is made to seem beyond any individual's capacity to solve. So
to feel like we have done something, we screw curly light bulbs into
our lamps and recycle everything we possibly can. These actions are
concrete and doable, but they are wholly ineffective. These actions
mostly make us feel better and pay more for lightbulbs.

Were President George W. Bush and Senior General Than Shwe
frightened into denial and inaction that precipitated collapse? Would
Winston Churchill have dithered as well? Looking back at these incidents, I have to believe that fear is the one explanation for their
inaction that seems plausible, and it does have sound psychological
backing. Both men were, I believe, most frightened that they and
their governments would be damaged politically by the disasters, and
neither man knew what to do about it.

FEMA UNDER MICHAEL BROWN was ill prepared and inept. After the
agency was incorporated into the Department of Homeland Security following 9/11, its entire focus was shifted to fighting terrorism,
real or imagined. Bush had appointed Joe Allbaugh as his director of
FEMA, and Allbaugh immediately vowed to downsize the organization, suggesting that it might have grown too large under the Clinton
administration. Bush wanted to privatize much of FEMA's work,
and Allbaugh went along, saying in May 2001 that "many are concerned that federal disaster assistance may have evolved into both an
oversized entitlement program" and that "expectations of when the
federal government should be involved and the degree of involvement
may have ballooned beyond what is an appropriate level."[22]

That lack of relevant experience in disaster management
prompted many scathing editorials, including one in the *Los Angeles
Times* by Ken Silverstein titled "Top FEMA Jobs: No Experience

Required."[23] This sort of blatant cronyism is in every sense the mirror of that practiced by the generals in Myanmar, and the consequences were a mirror as well.

While FEMA was flailing around, utterly failing to perform the function for which it was created by Congress, and officials at all levels were pointing fingers at one another, the news media was busy covering the mistakes and inept response to the crisis. Those "in charge" at FEMA actually turned back offers of aid from the private sector and others. Walmart sent three trailer loads of water to New Orleans that were turned back by FEMA officials, who also prevented the US Coast Guard from delivering much-needed diesel fuel for generators. The issues all concerned who was in charge and who was authorized to do rescue and recovery. Although FEMA was failing completely, it refused to let others help, perhaps out of fear of embarrassment that its own pathetic efforts would be exposed, but certainly not because any of its staff thought they were doing a better job than others could do.

In this, FEMA's actions are no different from the generals in Myanmar who would not let foreign aid into the country for fear of losing control.

One of the most effective agencies during the days of rescue and recovery was the US Coast Guard, despite FEMA's efforts to thwart it.[24] One of the Coast Guard's basic missions is search and recovery of victims stranded by boat accidents, and its troops are trained and well prepared to work in harsh conditions. They had moved 40 percent of their helicopters and other equipment into the vicinity before Katrina arrived, and those helicopters were first to enter the city. Though doing so is very dangerous and typically avoided when possible, the troops were prepared to work at night in the flooded city using night-vision equipment.

Canada sent a first-tier urban search-and-rescue team from Vancouver that arrived the first full day after the storm, well before help from FEMA arrived. Canada also sent three military vessels, a Coast Guard vessel, and several helicopters and coordinated their efforts with the US Coast Guard.

The Louisiana Department of Wildlife and Fisheries (LDWF) also acted quickly and brought scores of small craft to the city, equipment its staff knew would be needed for rescue. Members of the LDWF are skilled boat handlers and carry out many aquatic rescues, often of animals but also of stranded people. One of its agents, Sergeant Rachel Zechenelly, stayed in the New Orleans Convention Center the day before Katrina arrived so that she could be on site as soon as the storm passed, ready to do her duty. She charted routes that enabled LDWF boats and trucks to get into the most difficult areas of the Lower Ninth Ward. In the end, the LDFW made 21,000 rescues.[25]

Professionally trained, serious individuals who had risen through the ranks by fair assessment of skills and demonstrated dedication to duty acted well and saved many lives. No doubt the fog of disaster was dense in New Orleans, but this is no excuse for FEMA's failure. That failure was sealed by the appointment of proxy leaders, Bush administration cronies whose job it was to diminish the scope of the agency so that private actors could move in. They did *that* job very well.

AMID THE CAVALCADE of mistakes and malfeasance in the days after Katrina, a radical switch took place: a shift from underreaction to overreaction.[26] The administration had been caught out. Either it was caught flat-footed because it didn't know or didn't want to know just how bad the situation was, or it was exposed as part of an uncaring elite. Either way, faced with the obvious—that New Orleans was drowning in catastrophe—the administration had to do something. Then a miracle happened.

Just as the crescendo of criticism of FEMA was peaking, the attitude of the press took a sharp turn to a profoundly different focus.

The news media saw the opportunity for framing the disaster in a way that would have the most impact and bolster the standing narrative of disasters, myths and all. "Framing" is an all but essential part of almost all news reporting and was very much a part of the coverage of Katrina.[27]

The framing of disaster coverage is a deadly mix of misunderstandings and prejudices. Many of these misunderstandings are based in persistent myths about how people behave in disaster situations. Anthropologists, such as Enrico Quarantelli of the University of Delaware's Disaster Research Center, have through their disaster studies made a strong case that what our instincts tell us about human behavior in disasters is likely to be largely wrong. First, Quarantelli argues that people don't usually panic, despite the persistent portrayal of panic in almost all disaster movies from the very beginning of the genre. Susan Sontag's brilliant 1965 essay, "The Imagination of Disaster," describes the elements of a typical science fiction movie—which are, she insists, always disaster movies—that inevitably include panicked masses running along highways to get away from some sort of an alien monster.[28]

Likewise, people do not withdraw into fetal positions and await the inevitable. People may be initially stunned and disbelieving, but generally Quarantelli's research shows that they act in a more or less rational way.[29] I was made aware of this fact when reading about the way people evacuated the World Trade Center during the 9/11 terrorist attack. People went down the many, many flights of stairs to get out in a relatively orderly manner. The stairwell was not clogged with bodies of trampled people and others clamoring to climb over them to get out as fast as possible. Instead, people recognized that the best way to get out was to do so in a reasonably systematic and cooperative sort of way. People who work in tall buildings are frequently told that is the most likely way to survive, and at least in this case, that's exactly what they did.

Other myths that Quarantelli describes include "role abandon-ment," in which emergency workers such as nurses will give up their civic duties and opt to stay home and help their families. Quarantelli describes this as "role conflict," the very understandable notion that police officers, say, may feel a stronger duty to stay with their spouse and children and protect them in a disaster situation than to report for duty and try to save others, leaving their family to fend for itself. Although some may yield to this impulse, Quarantelli claims most do not abandon their public responsibility. First they try to make their families as safe as possible (helping them evacuate, for instance) and then they report for duty.[30]

What Quarantelli is saying is that the way we think people will behave in a crisis is an example of Daniel Kahneman's System 1 thinking. It's an instinctive reaction, perhaps fueled by the disaster movies Sontag described, and it is quite wrong.

But the most important and most controversial of the myths is that of rampant antisocial behavior, especially looting. We encoun-tered the issue of looting in our discussion of the earthquake in Haiti and its tragic consequences for one 15-year-old girl. In New Orleans in the days following Katrina's landfall, media reports of looting and other forms of criminal and antisocial behavior were rampant. They overshadowed reporting on FEMA's incompetence and changed the disaster narrative completely. In fact, these reports gave FEMA and the Bush administration the cover they needed to duck discussions of their incompetence.

KATHLEEN TIERNEY—a professor in the Department of Sociology and the Institute of Behavioral Science at the University of Colorado and director of the University of Colorado Natural Hazards Cen-ter—was a student of Quarantelli's. Together with two students, she wrote a very important and insightful analysis of the media coverage of Katrina.[31] They collected newspaper reports on the hurricane from the *New York Times,* the *Washington Post,* and the New Orleans *Times-Picayune.* A few examples, taken directly from their paper with original sources cited in the notes, are quoted next by date.

AUGUST 31

Even as the floodwaters rose, looters roamed the city, sacking department stores and grocery stories and floating their spoils away in plastic garbage cans. . . . Looting began on Canal Street, in the morning, as people carrying plastic garbage pails waded through waist-deep water to break into department stores. In drier areas, looters raced into smashed stores and pharmacies and by nightfall the pillage was widespread.[32]

Officials watched helplessly as looters around the city ransacked stores for food, clothing, appliances, and guns. . . . "The looting is out of control. The French Quarter has been attacked," Councilwoman Jackie Clarkson said.[33]

SEPTEMBER 1

Chaos gripped New Orleans on Wednesday as looters ran wild . . . looters brazenly ripped open gates and ransacked stores for food, clothing, television sets, computers, jewelry, and guns.[34]

Things have spiraled so out of control [in New Orleans] that the city's mayor ordered police officers to focus on looters and give up the search and rescue efforts.[35]

SEPTEMBER 2

Chaos and gunfire hampered efforts to evacuate the Superdome, and, the New Orleans police superintendent said, armed thugs have taken control of the secondary makeshift shelter in the convention center. The thugs repelled eight squads of eleven officers each he sent to secure the place . . . rapes and assaults were occurring unimpeded in the neighborhood streets. . . . Looters set ablaze a shopping center and firefighters, facing guns, abandoned their efforts to extinguish the fires, local radio said.[36]

SEPTEMBER 3

America is once more plunged into a snake pit of anarchy, death, looting, raping, marauding thugs, suffering infrastructure, a gutted police force, insufficient troop levels and criminally negligent government planning.[37]

In just a few days, the narrative had changed from criticism of government inaction to one describing a "war zone."[38] Rescuers, instead of helping victims, became engaged in a counterinsurgency activity akin to the conflict in Iraq from which many of the National Guard soldiers called to New Orleans had recently returned.

Lisa Grow Sun studied the same issue but from a legal standpoint.[39] In her paper, she included a number of the more extreme statements made on TV and by foreign journalists as well. She writes:

New Orleans was, we were told, a city descending into anarchy—a place, according to the New Orleans Police Superintendent, where "little babies [were] getting raped" in the Superdome, a shelter of last resort; a place, as New Orleans Mayor Ray Nagin recounted to Oprah Winfrey, where hurricane survivors had descended into an "almost animalistic state" after days of seeing dead bodies and "watching hooligans killing people, raping people." The mainstream press—including some of the most respected media outlets—built on official accounts of lawlessness to paint an unrelenting picture of bedlam and atrocities in New Orleans. . . . The *Financial Times* of London likewise reported that, at the Convention Center, another shelter of last resort, "girls and boys were raped in the dark and had their throats cut and bodies were stuffed in the kitchens while looters and madmen exchanged fire with weapons they had looted." London's *Evening Standard* took a more literary tack, alluding to *The Lord of the Flies* in its descriptions of New Orleans.

Sun established that at the peak of the deployment, there were 50,116 National Guard troops and 21,408 active-duty federal troops in New Orleans. It has never been very clear how many residents remained in the city. The population at the Superdome, where people who were stranded in New Orleans sought refuge,[40] is thought to have been around 20,000 at its maximum. The total population remaining in the city may have been closer to 100,000. Many were elderly and infirm. Even if you take an absurdly high guess and suggest that 30 percent of the remaining people became looters and rapists, that means there were more than twice as many soldiers as supposed criminals in New Orleans in the days after the storm passed. The ratio is more likely to have been 10 to 1.

Most of the very extreme stories were fictions or gross exaggerations. The *New York Times* acknowledged this in an article one month after the storm headlined "Fear Exceeded Crime's Reality in New Orleans."[41] Stories of murders and the rape of children were found to be unverifiable. Eventually, after autopsies were carried out and despite all the claims that bodies were piling up in the Superdome, only six died there—four from natural causes (though no doubt exacerbated by the awful conditions inside), one drug overdose, and one apparent suicide.[42]

There is absolutely no doubt that serious crime occurred in the flooded city of New Orleans and that it included opportunistic rape. People appropriated food and other provisions but also took advantage of the lack of law enforcement to steal items that were hardly necessities. The image that was published with the *New York Times* article shows an officer inspecting stolen auto parts in the living room of a house used by looters. Looting was real enough. The question is why the reaction was so extreme. Not all the soldiers were in New Orleans to regain control of the city, but many were. How could those in high office conceivably have thought that such a large military presence would be required to get things under control in the city known in better times as the Big Easy?

WHAT HAPPENED IN NEW ORLEANS is best described as "elite panic." The term is usually attributed to Caron Chess and Lee Clarke of Rutgers University, who presented the idea in the journal *Social Forces* in December 2008, although there are antecedents of the idea.[43] Kathleen Tierney, whose work was mentioned earlier, has discussed elite panic in several papers that Chess and Clarke cite. Rebecca Solnit brought the issue to public attention in her popular book *A Paradise Built in Hell* and in interviews.[44] In Chess and Clarke's paper, titled "Elites and Panic: More to Fear than Fear Itself," the notion is simple enough. It is, in fact, the *reverse* of the panic myth that says that regular people panic while a few trusted and well-trained people keep their heads and ensure that order is maintained.

The elite hold power by social, political, economic, and legal force. When their power is threatened, they overreact in what Chess and Clarke see as three distinct modes: elites may fear panic by ordinary people (they panic because they think ordinary people will panic); they may cause panic (by exaggerating what is happening); and they may themselves panic. The three modes are interactive, and all three probably operate simultaneously in many instances. All three operated in New Orleans.

Media coverage of criminal behavior in New Orleans has the hallmarks of pure panic. It no doubt caused panic as well. The brutal suppression of massive riots in Myanmar in 1988 is also an example of elite panic. Sending 70,000 troops to New Orleans is another. Shooting 15-year-old Fabienne in Port-au-Prince for stealing a few cheap pictures is another. Different as these instances are, different as the instruments that the elite had on hand, they are all expressions of the same panic reaction.

In New Orleans, the elite panic was fueled by an intense racialization of the postdisaster narrative. There is no better or more passionate scholar of race in the contrived Katrina narrative than Michael Eric Dyson, whose book *Come Hell or High Water: Hurricane Katrina and the Color of Disaster* came out in 2006, barely a year after the hurricane.[45] The great majority of his writing and deep scholarly analysis has proven to be agonizingly accurate and shamefully so.

The people who were portrayed as making up the mobs of marauding murderers and rapists (baby rapers, no less) were predominantly young black men, the group most feared in the United States by white people of all social ranks. The very language used to describe what was happening has a racial bias. A widely circulated comparison of reporting on people obtaining food shows a young black man wading through chest-deep water with goods that he has "looted" from a grocery store; an essentially identical image of a white couple, just as deep in the floodwater with groceries, has a caption that says they are wading through the water after "finding" bread and water at a grocery store.[46] The implication is obvious—black people are thieves; white people are just trying to survive.

Every negative stereotype of urban blacks was on parade. Stories of vile crimes in the Superdome were readily believed, largely because the supposed perpetrators were almost always black. Almost every face in and around the Superdome and the convention center was black. The faces of those "in charge" of restoring order—Bush, Chertoff, Brown—were all white. Most white people falsely conflated the stories of civil unrest in New Orleans with the unrest in South Central Los Angeles following the Rodney King verdict in 1992. That verdict exonerated several members of the Los Angeles police department who were caught on amateur video severely beating King, who had been pulled over for a traffic violation.

In some ways New Orleans may have seemed visually similar to Los Angeles in 1992, and news commentary made allusions to that fact. The setting was also in a social sense quite similar. While the immediate trigger for the LA riots was the King verdict, the underlying cause of the riots was found by a Special Committee of the California Legislature to be the product of inner-city poverty, discrimination, a poor education system, few job opportunities, and police abuses.[47] You could make the same statement about the poor areas of New Orleans where the purported looters and rapists came from. No wonder so many people conflated them—a black underclass behaving badly. Just what you'd expect! The conflation, while perhaps not wholly intentional, was very effective in making the association.

Another similarity between Katrina and Rodney King riots was the use of federal troops. In 1992, President George H. W. Bush sent federal troops to Los Angeles to quell the riots. Doing so required that he invoke the Insurrection Act of 1807. As the name of the act clearly states, it gives the president the power to command federal troops (and to federalize the command of state national guards) to engage in civilian law enforcement if civil unrest has reached a point where local law enforcement can no longer manage the situation, typically prohibited by the Posse Comitatus Act, the act of 1878 that limits the power of the federal government to use the US military for civilian law enforcement. The act has been called upon rarely and cautiously. Presidents Eisenhower and Kennedy had used it against the will of state governors to enforce civil rights laws in the South in the late 1950s and early 1960s. During the LA riots, the governor of California asked the president to send federal troops. Each use of the Insurrection Act has had a deeply racial context.

George W. Bush did not invoke the Insurrection Act in 2005, although he tried to put the Louisiana National Guard under federal authority. Governor Kathleen Blanco resisted that plan, however, and Bush relented largely for political expediency, not wishing to overrule the governor's authority. He did send federal troops to help with the humanitarian mission, as is sanctioned under the Stafford Act. But such apparent consideration of use of the Insurrection Act suggests to me that the Bush administration believed that the situation in New Orleans was akin to that in Los Angeles in 1992—an uprising of black outrage against a white elite and a situation that required military intervention to get things back to order.

South Central LA in 1992 *was* out of control. A large number of poor black and Hispanic people vented their anger and frustration at store owners who, by and large, were not residents of their community. Many stores were ransacked. Over 1,000 buildings were set on fire. Fifty-three people were killed.[48] News helicopters flew over the scenes, and commentators—largely white—described the unrest graphically, imploring people (white people) not to go near the areas where the riots were happening.

The aftermath of Katrina was never analogous to the Rodney King riots, but many people appear to have, consciously or unconsciously, perceived it as such. The King riots were the only incident in recent history that "looked" like the Katrina aftermath. Mostly these biases are deeply unconscious, built up from years of biased reporting by the media and other cultural influences that assign and reinforce stereotypes and prejudices. They are not biases you can get rid of very easily. The only thing a right-minded person can do is be aware and fight against them.

Almost every image of a person said to be involved in antisocial behavior in the media coverage after Katrina was a black person. Often it was a photo of a young male or a group of males, just like in South Central LA. The thousands of troops on the ground gave the impression that martial law had been declared. In other words, civil law enforcement had been suspended, and the military was in charge. In fact, however, Governor Blanco did not declare martial law. She called the looters "hoodlums" and seemed to have declared martial law (which she is not empowered to do) after troops arrived in New Orleans by stating to a BBC reporter that "[troops] have M-16s and are locked and loaded. These troops know how to shoot and kill and I expect they will."[49]

Improper declarations of martial law are well known throughout history. For example, the army took control of Lisbon after the earthquake of 1755 and erected gallows at high points in the city to deter looters. Over 30 people were hanged without trial. Philip Fradkin's work on the 1906 earthquake in San Francisco describes panic among those in authority there and a scene of chaos with unclear lines of authority.[50] Federal troops stationed in the area were ordered into the city, not at the request of the governor or the mayor of San Francisco but by their battalion commander, acting with the best of intentions to assist in the rescue mission that overwhelmed the city's police. The city's mayor, Eugene Schmitz, anticipating widespread looting, ordered looters to be shot on sight—by the military. In effect, Schmitz declared martial law, though he had no authority to do so. As Fradkin writes, "Schmitz set in motion one of the most infamous and illegal orders ever issued by a civil authority in this country's history." Almost 100 years later, Governor Blanco made a good imitation of Schmitz's order.

And, of course, poor people and ethnic minorities were singled out for summary execution in San Francisco while upper-class people who sifted through rubble for valuables other than their own (just like the poorest did) were dispersed but not shot at. No doubt there are many other instances where this sort of overreach by panicked authorities has occurred.

IN FACT, AS TIME HAS PASSED and more has emerged about what really happened in New Orleans, it is likely that white vigilante groups and the New Orleans police (about a third of whom did not report for duty) themselves were responsible for some of the most callous violence. At the time, the police force was roughly 50 percent African American, in a city that was nearly 70 percent African American. The strongest and most thoroughly engaged voice on white vigilante actions is that of investigative reporter A. C. Thompson. His article in *The Nation* titled "Katrina's Hidden Race War" came from a year and a half of researching and interviewing numerous people who lived through Katrina's aftermath.[51] What Thompson shows is that many white groups, especially those in a white enclave across the Mississippi in Algiers Point, who harbored deep prejudices toward black people, used the diminished law enforcement as an opportunity to harass and even kill black citizens for essentially no reason other than their race. Thompson thinks that white vigilante groups were responsible for as many as 11 killings of black people. The groups exploited the chaos, the lack of police officers, and irrational fear of looting and other forms of lawlessness that they attached to the black stereotype to unleash their long-standing contempt for the black community, and they expressed that contempt with deadly weapons.

No one would be foolish enough to say that race relations in the US South are free of tensions. In fact, the South is where race relations are probably at their worst, inherited from the history of slavery and civil war. It is the region where school desegregation had to be enacted forcibly against the will of most people in state government. It was the home ground of the Ku Klux Klan and a variety of other racist organizations. But could anyone have imagined what actually took place after Katrina?

The white vigilantes of Algiers Point engaged in acts of revenge and reprisal made possible by a law-absent postdisaster setting. Through their actions, they got even for deeply felt injustices. Many of the most bigoted whites in the US South do not believe black people merit social equality and do believe they achieved it illegitimately. Many of the people Thompson interviewed—as seen in YouTube videos—sounded bitter and vengeful yet at the same time thrilled that they had been given a chance to take out their built-up hostilities on black people. They saw blacks as the source of most of the troubles the South experiences—troubles such as the high crime rates and high poverty and unemployment that give the Southern states an overall low ranking in most comparisons.

Like so much else about disasters, history can provide precedent for this sort of revenge. In the aftermath of the Kanto earthquake of 1923 that all but obliterated Tokyo and Yokohama, local Japanese massacred Koreans and Japanese socialists by the hundreds, perhaps the thousands.[52] A false rumor was started that Koreans had used the opportunity of the chaos to set fires, loot, poison wells, and place bombs. At the time, Koreans in Japan had been agitating for an independent state and were responsible for terrorist acts in Tokyo and Yokohama. Native Japanese had a great deal of ill feeling toward the Koreans, and the disaster proved an irresistible opportunity to punish them. Accounts of the massacre make clear that the attacks were tantamount to ethnic cleansing. A Korean's crime was nothing more than to be Korean. They were beaten by mobs, stabbed to death with swords, and killed in horrifying numbers without any evidence that they had committed a crime of any sort. The police themselves abducted and killed leaders of socialist and anarchist groups. No one knows the true total killed, but it may have been as many as 10,000.[53]

After the 1906 earthquake in San Francisco, city officials attempted to remove Chinatown from the city in order to claim the valuable downtown property for redevelopment. Chinatown was popular with white people, but the Chinese people themselves risked beatings by white vigilantes if they strayed outside the ethnic community. Most Chinese had gone to San Francisco after the California Gold Rush ended and set up their own district. Very restrictive immigration laws prevented the population from expanding. (An active group known as the Japanese and Korean Exclusion League worked vigorously to ensure these very tough laws existed.) After the quake, Chinatown was effectively purged of its inhabitants, who were moved to Oakland and to the Presidio area, well out of San Francisco itself. That plan, really an exercise in social engineering, failed. City planners woke up when they realized they would lose considerable tax revenues and a flourishing trade with China and Japan if they moved Chinatown and its residents out of the city: hardly an act of generosity toward its Asian residents, but the Chinese population was allowed to return.

The Japanese in 1923 came close to blaming Koreans for the damage to Tokyo—the damage caused by the fires, at least. Americans did not blame the Chinese for the destruction of San Francisco. But in both cases the chaos of the disasters gave cover and opportunity to settle old grievances in grim ways. The opportunity a disaster presents can be to provide the greater good to all people, to take good for just a few, or simply to give free rein to act on prejudices.

In New Orleans, poor black people were not accused of causing the natural disaster of Hurricane Katrina, but they *were* accused and summarily punished for causing a disaster of social unrest. The fact that the accusation was largely false has not penetrated the public mind and still resonates today. The accusation was all that was needed to give permission for those in power to act to change the social order, as we will see in the following chapter.

CHAPTER 7

REBUILDING AS SOCIAL ENGINEERING

DISASTER SEEN AS AN OPPORTUNITY FOR ENGINEERING SOCIAL CHANGE IS
not a new idea.

The Great Kanto Earthquake of 1923 occurred simultaneously with a typhoon, the only occurrence of such a double disaster
on record. The earthquake, and more so the subsequent fires, destroyed 45 percent of Tokyo and 90 percent of Yokohama, killing
well over 100,000 people. (As always, estimates vary.)[1] The fires no
doubt killed more people than the quake itself as the quake occurred
around midday, when many people were cooking outdoors on open
fires. Descriptions of the conflagration sound like scenes from a fi-
ery hell. Some 38,000 people were incinerated together when they
sought refuge in a huge former army clothing warehouse; it was instantly engulfed in the inferno of a massive fire tornado created by
the typhoon winds and the roaring fires.[2]

Like so many other disasters at that time and even today, the
Kanto earthquake was seen as a divine message. In this case, it was
said to be a clear statement to the people of Tokyo that they were
being punished for living a profligate lifestyle of luxury and excess.

The ruin of Tokyo was seen as an opportunity for retrospection and reevaluation of morals.

A certain elite also saw the earthquake as an opportunity to rebuild the city in a more modern and efficient way, similar to Georges-Eugene Haussmann's renewal of Paris, with wide boulevards and grand architecture, at the behest of Napoleon III in the 1850s. (Tellingly, Haussmann's plans have been criticized for creating an overly grandiose city meant for tourists, the wealthy, and the bourgeoisie, with working-class people effectively ignored and marginalized to the periphery of the city.) In its layout and architecture, the new Tokyo was meant to somehow reflect new moral values as well. Haussmann used military cannons to demolish Paris, but for Tokyo, there was no need for cannons: Nature had razed the city.

In fact, the grand plan for heroic and moral reconstruction of Tokyo never came to fruition. James Schencking, a professor of history at Melbourne's Asia Institute, outlines several reasons, not the least of which was the vast cost involved.[3]

But the driving force was business interests and the demands of commerce. Business owners had no interest in waiting while elaborate plans were drawn up and debated and rebuilding was executed according to plan. They wanted their businesses back and running as soon as possible, and that meant more or less re-erecting what they had before, perhaps with some minor improvements. They had no interest in a Haussmann-like Tokyo; that might take too long. And they prevailed. Tokyo was rebuilt quickly and with few improvements.

After the Tokyo disaster in 1923, there was no chance for Schumpeter's gale to bring creative destruction, and this is the norm rather than the exception. Even when new materials and technologies are available, there is a very strong impulse to get things back on track quickly.

Makeover planning was also contemplated for San Francisco after the 1906 earthquake. In the nineteenth century, fires in Boston and New York had damaged large tracts of land in both cities and had been viewed as, and had effectively become, opportunities for renewal, for expansion, and, of course, for profit. Kevin Rozario, in *Culture of Calamity: Disasters and the Making of Modern America*, describes how property values rose steeply in New York after the fire of 1835.[4] In some instances, the values rose almost tenfold, and property owners who may have been of the middle class before the fire were suddenly propelled into the wealthy class. The wealthy became even more so.

San Francisco had a Haussmann-like plan too—the Burnham Plan—on the table before the earthquake, but it had stalled for many of the same reasons the Kanto renewal plan would not get enacted. The 1906 earthquake achieved the first part of the plan, which was the razing of large parts of the city. Like those who backed plans for renewal in Tokyo, those who backed the Burnham Plan tried to use the opportunity the disaster presented to make improvements. But as would happen in Tokyo, businessmen in San Francisco wanted their businesses to come back quickly so they used financing, largely from outside the city and the state, to start rebuilding quickly. San Francisco's strategic location and central port/trading facilities were too important to regions outside the city to let them die. Non-San Franciscans "needed" San Francisco, and it was largely rebuilt with money that came from elsewhere in the United States.

The external private capital for rebuilding acted then much like foreign aid for disaster relief does today. The affected area was relieved of the need to fully fund the reconstruction. It was similar in that way to the rebuilding of Lisbon after the earthquake of 1755. The city and port of Lisbon were critical for trade at that time, and much of the financing for reconstruction came from Portugal's trading partners.

As in New York, property values in San Francisco increased quickly, and businesses boomed. In his book, Rozario includes a photo of the San Francisco business district taken in 1906 and one from the same location in 1909. The first shows utter destruction, while in the second you cannot tell that the destruction had ever happened.

WHEN EVERYTHING HAD QUIETED DOWN in New Orleans after Katrina, there were plenty of people itching to use the opportunity presented by the razing of the city to give New Orleans a makeover. A makeover plan that was included in a report from the Committee for a Better New Orleans became a starting point. For most of the planners, a New Orleans makeover meant changing the demographics as much as the architecture and city layout. That is, in fact, what has happened.

One person who anticipated demographic change was John Logan, a professor of sociology at Brown University. He used the assessment of damage categories by the Federal Emergency Management Agency (FEMA) in New Orleans to correlate the extent of damage with socioeconomic indicators, asking, in effect, who suffered the most.[5] Logan's conclusions: "The storm's impact was disproportionately borne by the region's African American community, by people who rented their homes, and by the poor and unemployed." In many instances, the most affected people fell into all four categories simultaneously. The greatest single disparity was by race. Logan's analysis showed that the populations of the most damaged areas "were 45.8 percent black, compared to 26.4 percent in undamaged areas." In other words, being African American made it almost twice as likely that your dwelling would be seriously damaged.

Less than a year after the storm, in May 2006, Logan speculated about what the "new" New Orleans might look like. He reasoned that if repopulation was not permitted in regions that were heavily damaged (something that was being talked about at the time and advocated by many of my colleagues in the natural sciences), the city would lose 50 percent of its white residents and more than 80 percent of its black population. The final sentence of his paper reads: "This is why the continuing question about the hurricane is this: whose city will be rebuilt?"

As it turned out, Logan wasn't quite right about the percentages, but he had the right idea. What happened in New Orleans mirrors what the generals did in Myanmar because it involved, in part, being strategic about doing nothing. The first attempt to reshape New Orleans came soon after the storm. Called Bring New Orleans Back, or BNOB, it was the product of an advisory panel handpicked by Mayor Ray Nagin. The most influential person on the panel was the real estate mogul Joseph Canizaro. Like many of his colleagues high up in the New Orleans elite, he viewed the damage to the city caused by Katrina as an opportunity. He expressed it this way: "I think we have a clean sheet to start again, and with that clean sheet we have some very big opportunities."[6] Others were not as tactful. Richard H. Baker, the ten-term Republican representative from Baton Rouge, was quoted by the *Wall Street Journal* as saying, "We finally cleaned up public housing in New Orleans. We couldn't do it, but God did."[7] Soon after, he posted a sort of retraction and rewording, saying that he was misquoted and what he "remembered expressing" was "we have been trying for decades to clean up New Orleans public housing to provide decent housing for residents, and now it looks like God is finally making us do it."[8]

I wonder if Joe Canizaro knew of Haussmann or the postdisaster master planners in Tokyo and San Francisco. I doubt it, but he was following in their path. The logic is, in brief, that the most damaged areas are the most likely to be damaged again (for the same reasons they were so badly damaged in the first place) so the best thing to do is strip people out of those areas. That will keep people safe. Even though they might not want to be moved out, it's for their own good.

In an article in *Mother Jones,* Mike Davis argued that the New Orleans elite had long been anxious to purge the "problem people" from the city and tells us that one French Quarter landowner, speaking to *Der Spiegel,* said, "The hurricane drove poor people and criminals out of the city and we hope they don't come back."[9] You can only imagine what was said behind closed doors on New Orleans' tony Audubon Drive. US housing secretary Alphonso Jackson predicted that the city was "not going to be as black as it was for a long time, if ever again."[10] It seemed more like a wish than a prediction.

The *Washington Post* quoted then Republican House Speaker J. Dennis Hastert advocating bulldozing part of New Orleans and Republican senator Rick Santorum suggesting that people should be punished for "ignoring" pre-storm evacuation orders, as if being flushed out of their homes and into the Superdome were not punishment enough.[11]

In New Orleans, race played a defining role in hurricane mortality as well, though it did not look that way at first. What stood out most strongly in the initial statistics of deaths from Katrina was that the elderly were particularly at risk. In retrospect, that hardly sounds novel, but it did catch people by surprise, mainly because the proportions were so high—about 75 percent of the deceased were over 60 and nearly half were over 75. That's very different from the representation of that 60-plus age group in the population.

What was more surprising from the initial impression was that black people were underrepresented in the deaths relative to their numbers in the New Orleans population overall. This seemed especially so given the racial makeup of those suffering from heat and hardship after fleeing to the Superdome. This fact led some commentators to gleefully suggest that race was not an issue in Katrina's lethal blow. Freelance journalist Cathy Young even wrote an article titled "Everything You Knew about Hurricane Katrina Was Wrong."[12]

But victims of disasters and survivors of disasters are not likely to have the same demographics. In fact, you might well expect them to be different—survivors should be younger and stronger, able to swim or climb to a rooftop. Those who could not would become victims. But why were black residents underrepresented in the death toll?

These two observations are actually linked. First, if elderly people are overrepresented among the deceased victims, you have to ask about the racial mix of the elderly. That's what I did when I first looked at the death statistics and what Patrick Sharkey noted in the *Journal of Black Studies* in 2007.[13] It doesn't take long to realize that among the elderly, white people are *over*represented, particularly elderly women. In general, women outlive men, and white people outlive black people. So there simply were more elderly white people for Katrina to seek out than elderly black people. Sharkey made the adjustment for the initial population figures and found what most people suspected, that "race was deeply implicated in the tragedy of Katrina."

THE FIRST VERSION OF BNOB was described by Marc Morial, the New Orleans mayor who preceded Ray Nagin, as "a massive redlining exercise wrapped around a land grab."[14] Basically, it proposed that some areas not be rebuilt at all. And no prize for guessing which areas would not be rebuilt—those where the "problem people" lived. The most damaged areas would be turned into greenways, pleasant places for the on-average whiter residents to enjoy biking and other leisure activities on weekends. Joseph Canizaro was the main architect of the plan, and it was instantly viewed as a master plan for the business elite, an exercise that Mike Davis dubbed "ethnic cleansing GOP style."[15] And who was in a better position to benefit from such a plan than a real estate mogul? So the answer to John Logan's question, "Whose city will be rebuilt?" began to emerge soon after the hurricane had carried out its first phase and a wealthy elite saw how to take advantage of the opportunity.

Not surprisingly, the advisory panel's plan was met with hostility when it was presented at a packed town hall meeting in January 2006. The presentation drew an oft-quoted remark from Harvey Bender, a resident of New Orleans East (a place that might have ended up as a nice golf course in BNOB), when he stood up in the meeting during the time for public remarks to say, "Mr. Canizaro, I don't know you, but I hate you. You've been in the background scheming to take our land."[16] Who could blame him?

Canizaro and the mayor and the advisory panel really *did* seem surprised at the hostility to the plan, just as President George W. Bush and his coterie apparently had been by the damage Hurricane Katrina had caused. And the problem is the same in each instance. Decisions were made by an elite group focused entirely on their own self-interest, distant from those for whom they had responsibility, oblivious and uncaring of the needs and the lives of anyone but themselves and their close-knit group of associates.

I VISITED BREEZY POINT on Long Island, where Superstorm Sandy had come ashore and caused vast amounts of damage, including a fire that destroyed scores of homes. I was asked by CBS television to do a last-minute interview. CBS had, as it turned out, never intended to include hurricane disasters in its series on climate. The arrival of Superstorm Sandy changed network officials' minds very quickly.

I had never been to that part of New York before and had little idea what I would see. Breezy Point and much of the region called the Far Rockaways is more or less a large pile of sand. And it is anything but static. The US Geological Survey's online publication, "Geology of National Parks," begins its description of Breezy Point with this cheery observation: "Had you planned a visit to Breezy Point before the Civil War you would have been in for a surprise. It did not exist!"[17] Most of it is, in fact, less than a century old and came into existence when structures known as groins were built to protect Fort Tilden, a US Army installation with cannons that acted as a defense for New York during World War I and World War II. The groins disrupted the ocean currents that run parallel to shore, causing sand to pile up into what is now Breezy Point. If you live in Breezy Point you live in the sand, and you live very close to sea level. The highest ground is perhaps ten feet above sea level. Storm surges commonly exceed ten feet.

For me, just being there felt dangerous, though the day was completely calm. The jumble of collapsed and burned-out houses only reinforced my sense of danger. But I know that had I lived through several previous storms there that caused some flooding and some damage but were not devastating or deadly, I would have gained the sense that Breezy Point was a safe and pleasant place to live. And I wouldn't want to move because a scientist or anyone else told me, against all my experience, that it was a dangerous place to live.

You could say—and many people did—much the same about the people who lived in the areas of New Orleans that lay well below sea level: Are these people crazy? What do they think they are doing, living in a hole in a delta right by the ocean? Don't they understand the danger?

But how could they understand the danger? It's not like they were living below sea level for the vicarious pleasure of it, laughing in the face of danger. Generation after generation had lived there, far longer than the residents of Breezy Point, and they suffered periodic flooding, even quite severe flooding, as Hurricane Betsy brought in 1965. But that had led to the construction of hurricane protections. Surely those protections made them safe.

The people who lived below sea level in New Orleans were no more aware of the danger they were in than people living in Breezy Point or the residents of Port-au-Prince. They wanted to rebuild in place, right where they were born, even though each disaster had shown that they did indeed live in a dangerous place. But BNOB wasn't about to let that happen.

ONE PART OF THE BNOB PLAN did have quasi-logic to it. The argument was made that there should be a moratorium on reconstruction until it was clear how many people would return. There is no point, it was argued, in starting to rebuild a neighborhood if hardly anyone was going to return to it. If the total returnees to New Orleans were a small fraction of the original population, then there would not be the tax base, it was argued, to provide services to communities with just a few houses scattered among the desolation of Katrina's ruins.

The authors of BNOB either missed the catch-22 logic of this or knew it and pretended they didn't. People couldn't return to nothing and no promise of rebuilding. If there is a serious question as to whether your neighborhood will get services, why would you return? So the whole plan becomes self-fulfilling. Few people would return because few people *could* return, having nothing to return to. Anyway, the places to which they would return were deemed unsafe, and hence on the bottom of the list for reconstruction and with no real plan to make them safe. To a lot of people, it read like a trick to keep certain people—the "problem people"—from returning; a way of having Housing secretary Alphonso Jackson make good on his prediction that New Orleans was "not going to be as black as it was for a long time, if ever again."

And in the first year, the plan worked. Narayan Sastry and Jesse Gregory from the University of Michigan used data from the US Census Bureau's American Community Survey to show that blacks were significantly less likely to return to New Orleans than whites.[18] They tested for socioeconomic status, using education as a proxy, asking whether the higher-status people were more able to return, but found that race was the strongest determinant of the probability of return.

And these return-rate differences persist today. The least-repopulated areas today are exactly those that Sastry and Gregory found to be the most underpopulated in the year following Katrina. The lights did not come back on for everyone, just for some.

AS ONE MIGHT HAVE PREDICTED and has been written about compellingly by Naomi Klein in particular,[19] cronies of the Bush administration benefited hugely in the reconstruction of New Orleans. Kellogg Brown & Root (KBR), a subsidiary of Halliburton, which was run by Dick Cheney from 1995 to 2000 (but not at the time of Katrina), received tens of millions of dollars in no-bid contracts for reconstruction work at US Navy and other facilities. KBR is the largest non-union engineering company in the United States and has provided large-scale engineering services globally, including during times of conflict. It was part of a group that provided infrastructure for the military in Vietnam during the war, and it received the contract for cleanup after the 9/11 attack on the World Trade Center towers.

An extremely capable and effective company, KBR has few competitors, and although it has benefited from huge no-bid federal contracts, it has also won many open-bid contracts. It is perfectly possible that KBR would have won the no-bid contracts it was awarded, had they been openly bid. That was more or less the logic, combined with the imperative to move quickly after the disaster—bidding takes a long time, KBR has a proven record in what needs to be done, it will probably win the bid anyway, so why not give it the contract?

The problem, of course, is that under that scenario, no one has any idea if the price of the contract is fair or inflated. The opportunity to overcharge is enormous.

Two scholars, Peter Leeson from George Mason University and Russell Sobel from West Virginia University, found that there is a very strong association between the level of corruption and the number of disasters experienced by a state.[20] Disasters are always followed quickly by FEMA relief money and the need to get things moving again by cutting red tape, awarding no-bid contracts, and the like. The opportunity for misappropriation is obvious, and the researchers cite several instances when charges of corruption have been made in connection with the alleged misuse of FEMA or other disaster relief funds.

Through very careful statistical analyses, they were able to show that the correlation of disaster frequency to corruption is robust. Leeson and Sobel's conclusion reads: "Our findings suggest that notoriously corrupt regions of the United States, such as the Gulf Coast, are in part notoriously corrupt because disasters frequently strike them. They attract more disaster relief, which makes them more corrupt." It is important to note that they say that disasters are "in part" the cause of corruption, not wholly responsible. Their wording is cautious, but there is a strong logic to their argument.

HOW IS NEW ORLEANS DOING these days? The answer remains the same as when John Logan asked the question almost ten years ago. It depends on whom you ask.

In 2015, New Orleans *is* indeed looking better by some measures, but it depends very much where you look. Many of the poorest black people who were swept out of the Lower Ninth and other poor neighborhoods did not—could not—return. If you take a large group of unemployed poor people and move them out of town, then the unemployment rate in the town will improve, as will the average wage, and the poverty rate will drop. Even so, in 2011, only 53 percent of black males in New Orleans were employed.[21] As always, things can look better or worse depending on where you look and how you measure.

What is truly striking about the regrowth of New Orleans is the spatial pattern. The *New York Times* produced an interactive map of the recovery of New Orleans that shows how the city has repopulated in the years following Hurricane Katrina.[22] The *Times* used data from a local New Orleans private research group, GCR & Associates, which analyzed utility, sanitation, mail, and voter activity statistics to obtain a fine-grained estimate of repopulation trends. It shows where the most aggressive and weakest regrowth has taken place.

Another excellent source is the New Orleans Index, a joint project of the Greater New Orleans Community Data Center (GNOCDC) and the Brookings Institution's Metropolitan Policy Program. The most recent index is from 2013, eight years after Katrina.[23] The index is the most comprehensive tracking of postdisaster regrowth that has been done anywhere in the world and is a model for how it should be done. The reports are dense with information on housing, wages, employment, productivity, and a great deal more.

What you learn quickly from these data is that regrowth has been very uneven spatially. Some parts of the city have rebounded much faster than others. Why should that be the case? At first you might think it's not so unreasonable to suppose that the more damaged areas would take longer to recover. Parts of the French Quarter were hardly damaged at all, no more than you might expect in a fairly commonplace storm. They could be back in business in no time at all.

So the lights would come on in the French Quarter first, as well as in other places that were on high ground and were only moderately damaged. But you would expect the lights to come on everywhere at some point, even if it took a year or even more.

That's not what has happened. The *New York Times* map takes you to 2010, five years on, and the GNOCDC data take us eight years on. The lights are still out in many places while they shine brightly in others.

ACCORDING TO THE 2012 CENSUS, there are about 100,000 fewer African American residents in the New Orleans metro area than before Katrina and only about 15,000 fewer white people.[24] That means that almost seven times as many African Americans as whites have never returned. While African Americans remain a majority, the city is whiter, as Housing secretary Jackson had predicted. Logan calculated, based on damage estimates, that the black population would be reduced by 80 percent while the white population would drop by 50 percent. Those large drops did not come to pass, but the disparity in outcomes for the white and black residents was actually much more dramatic.

With so many black residents located somewhere other than where they used to live, the neighborhoods that once were their homes are now the bleakest and most underpopulated. A New Orleans *Times-Picayune* article by Michelle Krupa in 2011 revealed that parishes that showed the biggest population drops are also repopulating least well and recovering the least.[25] A study published by Elizabeth Fussell and her colleagues in 2014 noted that many of those who did return had not gone very far.[26] An earlier study showed that white residents were clearly more likely to return, in large part because they had something to return to, as their properties were generally much less damaged than those of the black population.[27]

Seven thousand of those who are no longer in New Orleans may be the public school teachers, mostly black, who were fired in the wake of Katrina to make way for an education system makeover. They were replaced by mostly white, nonunionized Teach for America teachers from out of state. The fired teachers did win a lawsuit for wrongful termination, and damages awarded in that suit could total more than $1 billion, but the school makeover has largely been achieved. New schools have risen in the place of the old ones. The school system has been largely privatized while still receiving public funding in what is known as charter schools. And the plan seems to be working— creative destruction? High school graduation rates are up 23 percent.[28]

But here's the problem, and it's not a new one. White students are the predominant attendees at the best of the charter schools, and they do well at those schools. An activist group in New Orleans has joined with Detroit and Newark to file a federal civil rights complaint, backed by the teachers' union, charging that the best schools have admissions policies that discriminate against African Americans. They also rarely have programs for children with special educational challenges. Even the state superintendent for schools in Louisiana, John White, admitted that "conversion to charters" is "never easy" but promises "the best outcome for most students." In other words, it does not produce the best outcome for some. White has nevertheless described the civil rights complaint as a farce.[29]

Those people with the best chances at success in New Orleans today are young, highly skilled professionals from somewhere else, entrepreneurs who have come in following Katrina to create something new. In fact, the GNOCDC data show that almost nothing has grown faster than new business start-ups, with a total upsurge of 129 percent.[30]

What has grown faster than start-ups are cultural and arts non-profit organizations, mostly owned by white people. There are now almost three times as many of these per 100,000 people in New Orleans than in the United States as a whole.[31] The aftermath of Katrina has somehow opened up a space that has proven ideal for these organizations. No doubt the very strong cultural traditions in New Orleans proved conducive and encouraging, but that hardly is a complete explanation.

At the same time, the size of the black middle and upper class has dropped 4 percent and that of the white upper and middle class has grown 8 percent. New Orleans has a higher share of minority-owned businesses relative to the size of the black population than US averages, but the receipts from those businesses amount to only 2 percent of the city's business.

And the essentials of living in New Orleans have become harder for some. The percentage of those renting apartments at an unaffordable rate (considered to be more than 35 percent of income) rose by 10 percent following Katrina. Now more than half of the city's renters are making unaffordable rent payments, a figure that is well above the national average.

The only place where the state pays for your accommodation is prison, and if that's your home in New Orleans, you have fewer roommates. The rate of incarcerations has fallen there after initially spiking immediately after Katrina, but it still remains well above the national average, especially for violent crime.[32]

To Richard Campanella, a geographer at the Tulane School of Architecture, New Orleans is becoming gentrified. The mode of gentrification follows that of places like Austin, Texas; Portland, Oregon; and parts of Brooklyn, New York. Young urban rebuilding professionals (YURPs), or, alternatively, the creative class, are attracted to the very rundown and grimy aspect of these areas that make some people want to leave. They start upscale businesses like specialty coffee shops and yoga studios and go to the inevitable Saturday farmers' market where they talk about "tactical urbanism, the Klezmer music scene and every conceivable permutation of sustainability and resilience."[33] Christchurch, New Zealand, experienced the same sort of regeneration following the 2011 earthquake, with young people from out of town starting cultural organizations and businesses in areas that were damaged and saw land prices fall.[34]

In the American Midwest, the disaster that Detroit suffered was economic, due to the decline of manufacturing industries, especially the big US automakers that were the city's main employers, but post-disaster gentrification has much the same signature as that in New Orleans. The extent of urban blight is huge. Detroit has lost more than a million residents since its peak, and that has meant a vast number of abandoned houses and businesses. Detroit filed for municipal bankruptcy in 2013, the largest such case in US history. Public services are minimal. Most of the streetlights don't work. Firehouses and schools are closing all over the city.[35]

But, just as in New Orleans, new businesses are starting up, launched by young urban professionals. Detroit even has a new Whole Foods (as does New Orleans), a beacon of gentrification. Some large businesses are growing in Detroit too. Quicken Loans has its headquarters in downtown Detroit. Its owner, Dan Gilbert, has purchased or has long-term leases on 60 buildings in the central business area.[36] Cheap real estate is the reason why you see so many businesses started by young out-of-towners like those Richard Campanella describes starting up businesses in New Orleans. The similarities are striking. And the situations are very different from the sort of reconstruction we saw in San Francisco in 1906 and after the Kanto earthquake.

This sort of revitalization is highly isolated, with pockets of progress amid a sea of stagnation. It is not the sort of development that can bring a whole community forward. It doesn't create many jobs and interacts only with a few of the more well-to-do people. In Detroit, it has been called a private boom among public blight.[37]

HOW DID NEW YORKERS BEHAVE and how has recovery been after Superstorm Sandy? For most people in New York, Superstorm Sandy was a huge supernuisance. The city was without power for a few days, gasoline was hard to come by, public transportation was badly disrupted, and there was no cell-phone service. But the storm's death toll was not very high, given the number of people who were affected. The storm was forecast well—New Yorkers heard about it for days before it came ashore. The storm snaked up the Atlantic seaboard, then made a sharp turn left toward New York, but all this was predicted and quite accurately. Areas that anticipated flooding were evacuated.

Many of those who died were found in areas where people were supposed to have evacuated but didn't, either by choice or lack of means or knowledge. (This also happened on the Mississippi Gulf Coast during Katrina; the number of deaths there was also relatively small for a storm so large in an area so densely populated.) There were only two deaths in Manhattan. A typical cause of death for those who died farther inland was a tree falling on them or their home or electrocution by fallen power lines. Many people suffered fatal injuries in falls in their darkened homes, which happen in regular storms as well. Some people were asphyxiated when they ran backup generators inside their homes.

But some people were a lot more than inconvenienced. Some people on Breezy Point and in very similar locations on Staten Island and in New Jersey lost their homes.

Although there was no crime reported in Manhattan or in many other areas, including Newark, New Jersey, which is known for its high crime rate, that was not true for other parts of the city, especially South Brooklyn and Queens. Some looting did happen.

Rebuilding and renewal have proceeded differently in New York as well. A state buyout program allows owners of damaged or destroyed homes to sell their property at a reasonable price and start anew in another location. Those areas will be returned to Nature and will never be developed for housing in the future.

Some people don't want to leave. They want to rebuild, but to do that, they have to raise their houses to a safe level so they will not be flooded again. Doing that costs about $100,000, and FEMA will cover only $30,000. Because most people have no way of financing the rebuilding, some people are selling their properties for a song, and the new owners are razing and rebuilding them. The price of flood insurance has become astronomical.[38]

What most people from outside the region don't realize is that these beachfront areas in New York are not the playgrounds of the wealthy. They are very much working-class neighborhoods and include low-income project housing in the Far Rockaways. At the same time, the neighborhoods are not enclaves of "problem people" whom the elite are itching to move out to improve the city. No one had a master plan at the ready that would erase the communities from the map of New York. Planners realized rather belatedly that these areas probably should never have been developed for housing in the first place. But no one had aspirations to reimagine New York without these areas.

For certain, some parts of the shoreline devastated by Sandy are not rebounding very quickly, and some people are in limbo, not knowing whether they will or will not be able to rebuild or move. The wealthy are not trying to remove the lower-income people to build seaside palaces on high stilts. There have been no land grabs.

For most New Yorkers, Sandy is a thing of the past; for others, it drags on in contested insurance claims and temporary housing. In 2015, there are still places you can't get to on the subway, but in most of the city, especially Manhattan, you'd never know that the storm had happened. As noted, for most New Yorkers, Sandy was a transient inconvenience. New Yorkers don't much like to be inconvenienced and complain about it a lot, but there is a world of difference between a few days without a cell phone and loss of home and livelihood.

What protected most New Yorkers was their relative wealth as well as the efficient functioning of city institutions. What made those who suffered end up in bad situations was the danger of the places they lived. But, like those in the Lower Ninth Ward of New Orleans and the rice farmers of the Irrawaddy Delta, they did not live there out of hubris, thumbing their noses at the dangers of their chosen life. They were there because that is where they could afford to be, where they could make a living, and where generations lived before without experiencing anything of the dangers that others know are present. They lived in dangerous situations because they didn't know they were doing so, because their financial situations forced them there, or both.

Was New York's rebuilding after Sandy a form of profiteering by those who had suffered little? The term *profiteering* has an ugly ring to it. *Profit*, from which *profiteering* is derived, means the advantage or benefit that is gained from doing something.[39] The gain can be and most often is money, but it need not be. A profiteer is someone who makes an unreasonable gain by taking advantage of a situation. And profiteering is, of course, what profiteers do. In New Orleans, the racial disparities among returnees indicate that there has been social profiteering by an elite, a reinforcing and exaggerating of conditions that give advantage to a small group. A few powerful New Orleans planners tried a land grab as blatant as any that happened in Myanmar, under guises that seemed to be little different. But is a Teach for America volunteer in New Orleans aptly described as a profiteer? That seems unfair. What about business interests in and around Kanto and San Francisco that ensured that their needs trumped more inclusive visions for those cities? Or Haussmann's disregard for lower-class Parisians? All, to varying degrees, are forms of profiteering, but what is gained, what advantage is taken, differs from case to case. What all these cases do reflect is an ordering of society and a geography of poverty and wealth that increasingly put physical and financial distance between the classes. And every disaster, because it harms the lower ranks and merely inconveniences the upper, separates us more and more.

CHAPTER 8

DISASTERS AS CASUS BELLI

DIVIDED SOCIETIES CAN RESPOND EXPLOSIVELY WHEN UNDER STRESS. DIVIsions provide an undercurrent of tension that adds energy to the system, and, as we see with climate change, added energy can cause explosive changes out of proportion to their proximate causes. If natural disasters continue to add to, rather than diminish, the growing distances between classes and races, we are likely to continue to see more upheavals—even those not related to natural disasters at all. We are seeing these already, and it is surprising how similar their narratives are to those of natural disasters.

The tragedy in Ferguson, Missouri continues. A grand jury has determined that the policeman who shot an unarmed African American youth, Michael Brown, in August 2014 will not be indicted. The policeman responsible has resigned. More rioting after that decision has further deepened the analogy with the Rodney King riots in Los Angeles in 1992. Three weeks earlier another, older black man, Eric Garner, had died at the hands of the police in Staten Island, New York. Again the policeman was not indicted. In December 2014, a deranged young black man first shot and wounded his ex-girlfriend in Baltimore, Maryland, then went to New York where he shot two policemen at close range while they were sitting in their patrol car in Brooklyn. He then ran off, descended into a subway station, and killed himself with the same weapon. He had posted his intentions on social media, citing motivations of revenge for the killings by police. All the police officers involved in these alleged incidents of misconduct were white, though the young man's victims were not. Months later, when things seemed to be calming down, two more policemen were shot and wounded in Ferguson, and a young black man was arrested.

The governor of Missouri first replaced the local Ferguson police with the highway patrol, then brought in the National Guard to maintain order. The local police were replaced because they had overreacted to the initial protests—they immediately donned riot gear, fired tear gas, threw flash grenades, and, in camouflage gear, pointed heavy assault weapons (not standard police issue) at peaceful protestors from atop roaming armored vehicles (also camouflaged). But that didn't stop the escalation of protests and an increase in violence. The police prevented reporters from going into some areas and detained but did not charge them. The police just didn't want reporters to see what was going on. Most recently, the Justice Department found that police officers and city officials in Ferguson routinely violated the constitutional rights of the city's African American residents and made racist jokes in their city e-mail accounts, including one about President Barack Obama.[1]

Armored vehicles carrying soldiers with powerful weapons at the ready and patrolling city streets belong in countries at war. We see them, too, in places where large crowds have gathered to protest the actions of authoritarian governments, as in the Ukraine and Venezuela, hoping to dislodge the government and change the regime. But the soldiers who roamed the suburban streets of Ferguson and

New Orleans were indistinguishable from those deployed in conflict settings. This is due to a disturbing and increasing militarization of policing in the United States. Who would even have guessed that a small-town police force in Ferguson, Missouri, would even have such equipment? Apparently, it is widely available and widely used. In his 2013 book *Rise of the Warrior Cop: The Militarization of America's Police Forces,* Radley Balko, a *Washington Post* reporter, describes this trend.[2] He also details its very negative consequences for civilian law enforcement, including mission creep among SWAT teams, where more and more force is used for fairly minor infractions. The normally strong separation between military activities and civilian police work is made vague and porous if the police themselves obtain military equipment and take actions indistinguishable from military ones.

Police departments across the United States have become paramilitary units.[3] And this assertion is especially true in places like Ferguson and New Orleans, where a majority black and poor population is policed by a majority white police force that does not come from the community it serves and sees its work as containing the "problem people."

THIS MIND-SET—that a "problem people" majority must be contained for the sake of the privileged minority who live among them—is all too common around the world. From it we can discern a narrative common to most natural disasters almost regardless of where they happen and how citizens are governed. First, a terrible event happens. Nature has a tantrum, everything seems terribly wrong, outside the norm. A massive fire erupts on an oil rig. A riot breaks out. The ground shakes violently where no one could remember it ever having shaken before. A massive storm arrives out of nowhere. This is analogous to stage 1 in Susan Sontag's[4] brilliantly satirical description of science fiction movies of the 1950s—it's the arrival of the Thing. In the movies Sontag discusses, the Thing almost always arrives in the United States or Japan, often from outer space but sometimes from deep inside Earth. The terrible event of a disaster can arrive anywhere.

The authorities are the most surprised, or act as if they are, even though they should be the least surprised. The class, race, or ethnic group of those who form the authorities, whether a military junta, a major company, or an elected governor, does not reflect that of the majority of the people most affected by the event. The authorities consist of a small, perhaps tiny elite that holds almost all the wealth and political power. They don't care very much about those most affected by the event. They have to say they care and sometimes they do initially, but that soon fades. The Thing doesn't care about any humans, either.

Scientists say they are not surprised. They say "I told you so," and then are not heard from again. Sometimes a smug scientist is interviewed on television. When the Thing emerges, the press is initially delighted. They describe it in apocalyptic terms and rush to see it for themselves and report back from the field, breathless and harried. Scientists do the same.

The authorities downplay the scale of the event, wanting us to think it's not as bad as reporters and scientists are saying. You can't believe those reports, the authorities tell us. We all know how they exaggerate. Don't worry; everything is under control. You can trust those in authority. New Orleans is over 80 percent submerged—no problem, we've got it, we'll send KBR, the private security firm that was made infamous when a group of Blackwater guards was involved in the killing of seventeen Iraqi civilians.[5] A no-bid contract to KBR would get things moving along the fastest.

An attempt is made to deal with the event that is in proportion to its advertised, downscaled magnitude. In Sontag's science fiction movies, for example, police are sent in to deal with the Thing and are slaughtered. The head of Homeland Security pays no attention to Katrina and trusts Michael Brown to deal with the problem. At least in science fiction, or figuratively, Brown will be slaughtered soon enough. In Myanmar, the generals ask, Cyclone? What cyclone are you talking about? Everyone in the elite stands flat-footed for days, hoping that the Thing will go away. Incompetent people in government who are political appointees with little to no experience make pathetic efforts to deal with it. People in the affected area try to help each other because no help has arrived. Lying and finger-pointing begin. All attempts to kill the Thing are failing badly.

The elite start to panic while regular people don't, although the media says they do. But soon the regular people start to realize they do not have the capacity to gain control of the situation and no one has come to their assistance. People who have been bravely helping each other realize that food and water are running out. They can't produce either out of thin air. Because no one has come to help, the people take what they need from stores. The media sometimes call these actions provisioning (if performed by members of the elite's racial group) and sometimes call it looting (if performed by those outside the elite's group).

Frustration mounts among the affected population. They are angry but not panicked and are starting to feel hostile. Members of the elite class in the affected area are long gone, having left at the first news of the Thing. If they made the mistake of staying, they are rescued by the first of the rescuers to arrive on the scene and are treated for any injuries they might have sustained.

Looting, whether real or imagined, extensive or trivial, begins in earnest and is a game changer. Looting is a godsend for the elite. It's a way out, a way to deflect attention from their incompetence. Looting is a godsend for the media, too, and where earlier the elite wanted everyone to ignore the media, now they want everyone to believe the media. No more downplaying. The media are showing things as they really are, they tell us. By this time, the Thing that arrived to start all the trouble is gone, and it's hard to keep the public's attention. The story has moved back a few pages in the newspapers and is no longer the first item discussed on the nightly news. Then, luckily, looting "breaks out," and there is something to exaggerate and moralize about, a way to frame a story that the public will accept—a framing adapted from movies mixed with racial and class bias. The event is back on the front page again. When there are no reports of looting—as in Japan after the Tohoku earthquake and tsunami—media focus remains on government incompetence and inconsistent reporting from authorities.

The elite who supposedly struggled to quell the Thing are able to say that the very people they were trying to save from the monster are actually monsters themselves. They are problem people behaving badly, rejecting the elite's valiant, not to mention expensive, efforts to help them. They are criminals, bad people, not only stealing luxury goods from stores owned by good people but raping and killing each other, even children. It doesn't matter that few if any of the stories of rape and murder are substantiated; it's just what you would expect these non-elites to do. What next? Soon they will start killing and raping members of the elite. They must be suppressed at all costs. We need curfews, martial law, the military, and shoot-to-kill orders. That's the only hope.

By this time in the disaster event, the Thing re-emerges; it had not gone away at all. But it has changed. It is no longer an act of Nature; it's a group of people. The military is brought in. In some countries, the military is already there. Looting and crime, real or manufactured by the media, become the reason to wage war on the people.

The elite win. How can they not? They command the military. "Peace" is restored.

Scientists give advice. Sontag's young hero scientist, having built a device to kill the Thing in his lab, stands cheek to cheek with his beautiful girlfriend, looks into the sky, and asks, "But will they return?"

Today's scientists say the Thing *will* return, and it will be bigger and more aggressive than ever. They recommend abandoning places where the Thing might appear next and creating massive fortifications against it everywhere that matters to them. Members of the elite consider protecting themselves but hardly anyone else. Plans are being considered for a storm barrier to protect lower Manhattan, for example, but not much can be done about the Rockaways. That's too bad, but what were those people doing there in the first place? What were people doing in the Lower Ninth Ward? Didn't those problem people know it was dangerous?

Now the second opportunity opens wide: The winners can plunder the vanquished. It's their turn to loot, but they would never call it that. Money is needed and needed quickly. No time for lengthy bidding processes, review, and oversight. "Dangerous" lands must be taken and used for better purposes. Scientists agree. In rich countries, that means gentrification or "urban renewal"—euphemisms for property development that benefits the elite and enriches them. In poorer countries, it means land grabs under bizarre laws made by the elite that typically ensure that regular people either do not own land or can be easily displaced from areas they have been farming and living on for generations. Or rebuilding in a damaged area becomes so expensive and so regulation-restricted that those who lived there earlier (in the Lower Ninth of New Orleans, for instance) can't possibly afford to return. The losers also lose what capital assets they might have had, and the winners gain them. Capital is key to gaining wealth. If winners already had private capital assets, and they usually do, those assets become more valuable. The winners can control who gets the lucrative contracts for reconstruction of public infrastructure and ensure that they go to members of the elite.

The rich win; the poor lose.

It's completely expected in a world of great inequality that the outcome of a natural disaster will also be unequal. Disasters may well affect everybody, rich or poor, in some way, and they are never pleasant for anyone. We want to believe that a disaster is a moment when everyone pulls together—but it is not. It is a moment of pulling apart because the effect on each group is so different, and the way each group can cope is vastly different. The way each group can *capitalize* on a disaster is incomparably different—the rich can, the poor can't. Schumpeter's gale puts wind in the sails of the rich's yachts but sinks the fragile craft of the poor. The rich can move further up; the poor can only stay in their poverty trap or slide down the slope back into the trap—descending from having land and a meager income to no land and no income, for example.

Thomas Piketty, the French economist who recently rose to international stardom with his book *Capital in the Twenty-First Century*,[6] has argued that the only time inequality decreases is in times of catastrophe, after which inequality inexorably rises again as returns on capital outpace the overall economy (r > g). Piketty is referring to financial crises; the opposite is true for natural disaster crises, where owners of capital see the value of that capital actually increase rapidly in the immediate postdisaster period. Disasters make the owners of capital even more wealthy; those lacking capital are made poorer, and inequality becomes greater.

WHAT IS THERE TO BE DONE? Disaster risk reduction (DRR) is extraordinarily important. That hardly needs to be said. But DRR might better be called DLR—disaster *loss* reduction—because it focuses mostly on the initial loss from whatever has happened, be it storm or quake or flood. It is important to help ensure that the poor don't suffer and can be helped back to as good a condition as possible, as quickly as possible. The less the loss, the quicker the recovery: this appears to be the logic. But we know this isn't the case except in the extremely unlikely situation where all losses have been reduced to zero.

But it is what happens before and after that tormented moment of loss that is the most important. One death occurred in Ferguson, Missouri. What happened after that death is, one could say, out of proportion to the death itself. There may be more deaths in Ferguson. But the turmoil that followed has no scaling relationship to the number of lives lost. It is the result of inequality. Ferguson is not a disaster because of the number of deaths. The shooting of a 15-year-old Haitian girl, the abandonment of people in the Irrawaddy Delta, the crushing of schoolchildren in China, and the events in Ferguson are all social disasters, and all should have been avoidable.

Ferguson was fairly prosperous and mostly white in 2000 and has changed rapidly to become mostly black, with areas of intense concentrated poverty. The source of the strife in Ferguson is that all forms of the city's governance have remained overwhelmingly white, though recent elections have tripled the number of African Americans on the city council.[7] Nonetheless, governance in general has not changed, even though the city's demographics and economic prospects have changed. It is as out of touch with those it governs as the generals in Myanmar were out of touch with the average citizens there or the elite in Pétionville, Haiti were with the majority of Haitians. People in the Ferguson city government don't like the way their town has changed, and they are afraid of the people who are now the majority. Why else would the police in a small town in Missouri have armored vehicles, riot gear, and assault weapons? In a moral sense, their fortifications are no different from the high walls and barbed wire enclosing the elite of Haiti; no different from the suppression of ethnic minorities in Myanmar or the isolation of the poor in the Lower Ninth Ward of New Orleans. To have acquired such equipment, they must have believed they would come under assault at some time, by someone, and the "someone" could only be the black community. Were they anticipating an attack or spoiling for a fight, like the white vigilantes in New Orleans?

It's not fatalistic to say that we will never stop natural disasters from happening. It may be somewhat fatalistic to suggest they are going to increase. What is very likely to happen is that the true injustices of disasters will increase. As the gap between the wealthy elite and the 99 percent grows and grows, it will become easier and easier for the elite to control the outcomes of the disasters amid the chaos. And that is no accident. It is not only because of existing inequalities—that's an excuse; it is because inequalities can be made greater still by the actions of those who have power. The disaster itself provides a cover, a sort of shield to hide behind, a distraction. Most people will believe that what is going on really *is* natural, but the natural part of the drama of disaster is over fairly quickly.

Many natural scientists believe that burgeoning climate change will increase the frequency of extreme weather disasters, including prolonged droughts, intense rainfall, and strong storms. Even if that does not occur per se, climate change will progressively increase the area of our planet on which we cannot successfully grow food crops. A smaller and smaller habitable planet will be asked to serve the needs of a much larger number of people. As the years pass and change continues slowly but inexorably, the elite will grab more and more habitable land for themselves, leaving the majority in the badlands. If there is anything certain about climate change, it is that it will send us further apart than we already are. Natural disasters teach us how it will be done.

MOST IMPORTANT OF ALL is to recognize that disasters are economic and political in nature as much as, perhaps more than, they are natural events. They are briefly natural, in the horrifying minutes and hours of the first attack of Nature. In that moment, Nature is in charge. Before and after that, however, disasters are pure social phenomena. Returning to some form of normality after a disaster requires economic stimulus, good planning and discipline, and other actions similar to what was needed following the financial crisis of 2008 and 2009. The two kinds of events are different, but we can learn from the errors and the successes of the financial crisis to help us think about the road to recovery for all of those who endure Nature's wrath. We have to be very hard on any form of profiteering, not just because it might bring a quick gain for some at the expense of others but also because it can do permanent damage by enhancing existing inequalities.

In planning for disaster risk reduction, the focus is on the prelude (phase 1) and the event itself (phase 2). Governments think about preparations, strengthening, protecting. After the event, a build-back-better approach is invoked to repair the physical damage as a way of being better prepared for the next disaster. But planning must include realistic approaches to post-disaster social risk reduction. Militarization is not the answer. Allowing the elites to control the post-disaster period is not the answer, either, and will do little more than allow the elites to profit and exclude. Reconstruction must be an inclusive process. Rather than sending in the military for disasters that occur in states and countries known to be poorly governed and corrupt, we should send in neutral parties to help ensure that relief money is spent to restore and improve society. That means more than treating people for posttraumatic stress or helping them with the grieving process. It means understanding the social dynamics before disasters happen so that societies don't become disordered after.

Rather than turn our attention elsewhere when phase 2 has ended, phrase 3 of the disaster must be carefully scrutinized. The New Orleans Index provides a model for how this might be done. Recovery can't be properly measured by the number of buildings restored; it should be measured by the number of lives restored. Every disaster presents an example of how we cannot work from only one side of the Feynman line or the other.

Extreme and growing social inequality is the source of countless social ills and of financial disaster. It is one of the great challenges of our time. Removing the opportunities for profiteering from disasters will not only right an injustice but also help to bring us closer together.

SIMPLIFIED SOCIOECONOMICS OF NATURAL DISASTER SHOCKS AND THEIR CONSEQUENCES

THIS APPENDIX AMPLIFIES SOME OF THE ISSUES RAISED IN CHAPTER 1. CONSIDER Figure 1.[1]

Figure 1. The transformation of a physical shock into a social shock.

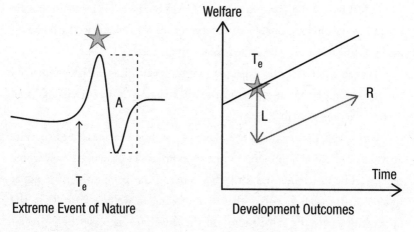

Extreme Event of Nature   Development Outcomes

On the left is a generic natural shock represented in diagram form. It could be an earthquake because it looks a little like the swing of a seismograph needle, but it doesn't have to be. It is characterized by the time of onset of the event, T_e (when the event starts), and its magnitude, A.

On the right is a diagram of the social consequence of the shock. The horizontal axis is time, and the vertical is some measure of welfare. It could be gross domestic product (GDP), but it could be any one of many others discussed in chapter 1, such as the Human Development Index (HDI) or Gross National Income (GNI).

The disaster event occurs at the time designated T_e, the same as on the left. The heavy line is the growth in welfare that we assume would have occurred had the disaster not happened. It is constructed by taking the growth before the disaster and simply extrapolating on past T_e. We can think of it as the growth rate unperturbed by disasters.

At T_e there is an immediate loss of *something* by the amount L. What it usually means is the replacement cost of losses of capital stocks such as homes and businesses, roads and airports. It may be people, but what it usually refers to is some sort of loss of a manufactured capital. Remember that this sort of built capital isn't directly included in the GDP formula in chapter 1, so GDP might not show an immediate drop.

What follows is the recovery, designated R. It is shown in the diagram as if the social welfare resumes growing immediately after the disaster at the same rate as it did before, but starting from the lower level (the level it was at just before the disaster, minus L). Although that is quite unrealistic because you would reasonably expect the economy to do less well after being hit by a disaster, it sets the stage for our discussion.

Two things about the expected rate of growth in a disaster-impacted society are important and are illustrated in Figure 2. The horizontal and vertical axes are as before.

One important factor is the slope of the line that describes the rate at which welfare is improving. Some economies are growing slowly, some quickly. The lower line has a much steeper upward slope than the upper line, so it describes a society that is improving in welfare faster than the upper line—over the same period of time, welfare increases by a greater amount for the lower line.

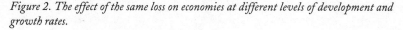

Figure 2. The effect of the same loss on economies at different levels of development and growth rates.

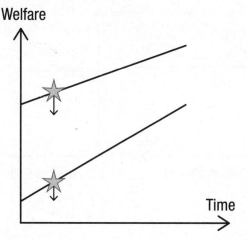

The other thing to note is that the absolute level of welfare is different in the two cases as well. The upper line lies in a higher part of the graph, so the absolute level of welfare at all places along that line is greater than for the lower line. So the lower line describes a fast-growing economy but one that has yet to achieve a high absolute level of welfare. The upper line might represent a country more developed than the lower one. These differences are consistent with empirical evidence that developed economies tend to grow more slowly than economies of developing nations, such as China and India, which have seen double-digit growth.

The amount of the disaster loss (the downward arrow) is shown as the same absolute amount in both cases, and it is fairly obvious that the same loss in these two economies might have different effects. For the upper line, the loss is a smaller *percentage* of the total welfare than for the lower case.

What constitutes recovery? Figure 3 shows two cases; the one to the left is for a relatively fast-growing economy and the one to the right is for a relatively slow-growing economy. Each experienced the same absolute loss. The times denoted T_1 and T_2 are the times at which welfare has returned to the level it was at before the disaster.

T_2 is clearly much greater than T_1, so the expectation is that the faster-growing country will recover to its predisaster level more quickly than the

Figure 3. The effect on recovery time due to growth rate.

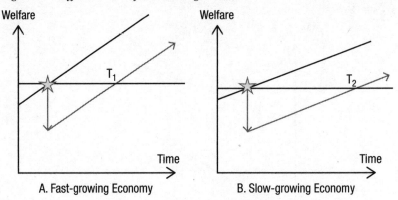

A. Fast-growing Economy

B. Slow-growing Economy

slow-growing country. The absolute level from which the disaster fell is not important here. This slow recovery time is something that greatly concerns the World Bank when it considers what sort of actions to take after a major disaster in poor countries that are not growing very rapidly. What is also clear from this simple diagram is that the larger the drop, the longer the recovery time will be and that even a small drop in a slow-growing country can require a very long time for recovery, just because the natural growth rate is slow.

As measured in GDP, the US economy has returned to where it was before the recession. If the vertical axis was employment, things would not look different.

It is very reasonable to suppose that there would be a period of slow or zero growth after the disaster, and perhaps even a period of negative growth, meaning continued losses and retraction of the economy. That is illustrated in Figure 4.

The period of stagnation is designated S. The natural growth rate and the size of the loss, L, are the same in both diagrams. What is intuitively clear is that any period of stagnation lengthens the time to recovery by the length of the stagnation period—in other words, T_1 is extended by S_1, and T_2 is extended by S_2. What is perhaps less obvious is that stagnation periods, in effect, increase losses—L_2 and L_3 are larger than the original loss, L.

Figure 4. *The effect of a period of post–disaster stagnation on recovery time.*

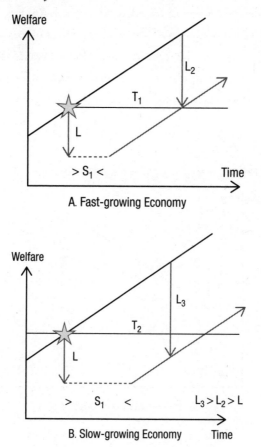

A. Fast-growing Economy

B. Slow-growing Economy

Not only capital is destroyed; also destroyed is the welfare that would have accrued during that period had the disaster not happened.

You can think about these graphs describing disaster losses and recovery in much the same way as you think about the 2008 financial crisis and recession and the recovery after it. In June 2014, the *New York Times* published a figure very similar to Figure 4, soon after the US government declared that the economy had finally reached its prerecession level.[2] The drop in GDP wasn't as precipitous as shown in the disaster graphs because the recession, although evolving alarmingly quickly, took time to fully develop.

Another way to extend the recovery time, though it may seem counter-intuitive, is to make use of national reserves, as shown in Figure 5. These reserves are denoted R and r in the diagrams, where R is larger than r.

The use of national reserves can have the effect of *increasing* the loss. In doing so, it increases the recovery time. That is because the initial loss, L, as well as the amount of reserve that has been drawn on to help effect recovery also have to be regained. The capital that is represented by R or r is

Figure 5. The effect of the use of capital reserves.

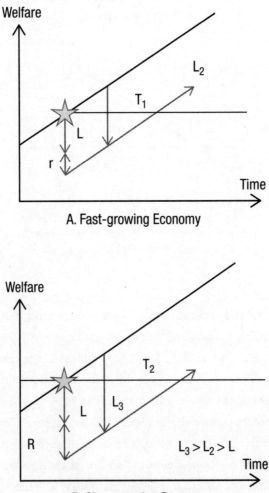

financial capital. It is not the same as the capital lost in L, which is built or manufactured capital, so it's really not correct to just add it on to L as I have done, but it illustrates the point. Financial capital will always be needed for recovery, but it is much better for many countries, especially poorer ones, if that capital comes from outside in the form of direct aid or a grant than if it has to come from the countries' reserve funds or loans because using reserves or loans also adds to a country's debt and hence requires repayment.

Drawing on reserves might be thought of as reducing losses, something that would make L smaller by shaving some losses off the bottom. But what is lost is lost. Expenditures to counter those losses are also lost in the sense that they are no longer available for other, more productive uses, and they also have to be replenished.

Whether the use of capital reserves has a positive or negative effect very much depends on what the reserve capital is spent on. If it is spent on temporary housing, cleaning up debris, or emergency health care, it is really lost. If it can be used to restore infrastructure, it could have a positive effect on economic recovery. One of the best uses of reserves is to reduce the stagnation period by getting things moving again quickly after a disaster.

Returning to an earlier question: What do we mean by a *disaster loss?* Figure 6 repeats one that we used earlier. The only difference is that we have filled in a triangular area.

The shaded area is the time integration of the losses accumulated from the disaster instant until the point at which recovery to the predisaster level of welfare has been achieved—T_1 in the faster-growing case, or T_2 in the slower setting. This integration of losses is much closer to expressing the true economic loss than the initial loss, L, described earlier.

The area of the lower triangle is larger than the area in the upper one even though the initial losses are the same.[3] That means that a slow-growing country could lose as much as a fast-growing country, even if it suffered smaller initial losses. So the slow-growing country could take longer to recover and have greater overall losses.

But the points on the recovery line are still below the counterfactual line—the line where the economy *would* have been had the disaster not happened. What recovery should mean is a return to the initial growth line, not the predisaster level of welfare. Figure 6 shows this.

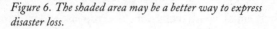

*Figure 6. The shaded area may be a better way to express
disaster loss.*

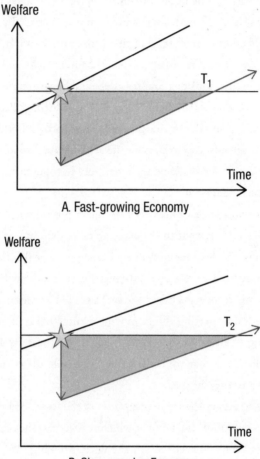

The economy was at point *A* before the disaster. At point *A'*, the economy has returned to the initial level *A*. But, had the disaster *not* happened, the economy, *ceteris paribus*, would have grown to be at *B*.

Thinking back to the US economy and its recovery from recession, in June 2014, the US Labor Department announced that the economy was finally employing as many people as it had been before the recession in 2007. So in this diagram, you can think of the vertical axis as jobs. In the US economy, we are at *A'*. What the Labor Department announced was, in

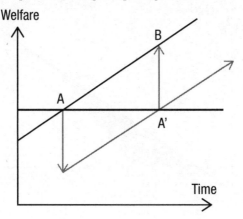

Figure 7. Illustration of recovery to predisaster level and predisaster level plus expected growth.

essence, that there has actually been *no* growth in employment in six years; catching up the amount lost cannot be thought of as growth.

The economy is growing again and has more or less reached its 2007 level, but it is nowhere near a projection of where it would have been had pre-2007 growth continued.

On the day of the announcement, the *New York Times* online edition produced an analysis of the recovery in 255 interactive graphs.[4] The purpose of the graphs was to show that the recovery has been very heterogeneous as measured in employment. The oil and gas sector has recovered to where it would have been had the recession not occurred—back to point *B* on our stylized plot in Figure 7. This may have been helped by the shale gas revolution.

Furniture stores, however, were not doing particularly well before the recession. They were hit very hard in the crisis and have not recovered their losses at all. The business, environment, and other consulting area has recovered to its prerecession level but not to where it would have been without the recession. So the businesses growth trajectory has recovered but not the absolute level of jobs.

The graphs in the *New York Times* show clearly that different sectors of the economy have experienced job recovery at different rates, including

Figure 8. Full recovery occurs when the line representing recovery meets the line on which the economy would have grown had the disaster not happened.

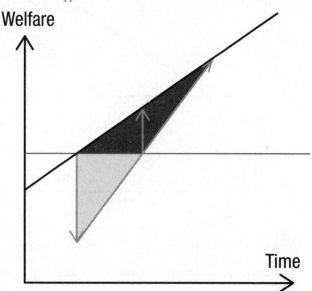

what might be called a negative rate. Natural disasters will affect different businesses and different people differently. In a very broad analogy, perhaps we could think of Haiti after the 2010 earthquake as the furniture business. Perhaps the consulting business is like New Orleans after Hurricane Katrina. It's harder to find an example to match the oil and gas industry.

So, in a stylized way, what we really want to achieve is shown in Figure 8.

Now the postdisaster growth line has met the expected growth trajectory and a different, larger triangular area is involved. What you notice right away about this is diagram that in order to meet the predisaster growth trajectory, the recovery growth line has to slope upward more steeply than the natural growth trajectory. That means that if an economy is ever to return to where it would have been without the disaster, it has to grow *faster* in the postdisaster recovery period than it did before.

In Figure 9, the two counterfactual growth lines are the same.

What is different is that the initial loss in the upper example is greater than in the lower example, but the rate of recovery is faster in the upper

Figure 9. Full recovery at different recovery rates.

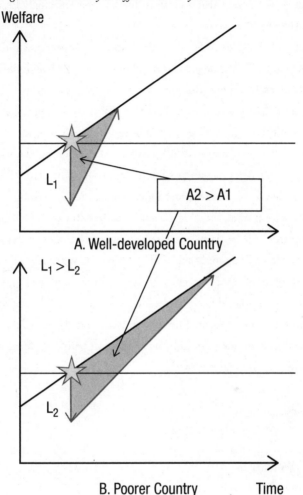

A. Well-developed Country

B. Poorer Country   Time

one than in the lower one. The area in the upper example is clearly smaller than in the lower example. The upper case can be thought of as an economy capable of rapid response even in the face of large absolute losses. It more likely represents a well-developed country; the lower line represents a poorer situation.

Could there be a silver lining? Imagine that postdisaster growth was somehow made faster than in the predisaster period. A massive infusion of capital from outside the economy with no debt obligation and spent exceedingly well might achieve that. Then why should that slope of high growth stop when the natural growth line has been reached? Figure 10 illustrates the idea.[5]

What you have to imagine is the following scenario. In almost any urban setting, there will be old and new homes, new and old buildings, new and old bridges and roads and ports and other critical facilities. Images of cities in developing countries often show slums on the periphery, luxury high-rises in the center, and perhaps a beautiful beach behind.

In almost any type of natural disaster in a developing country, practically everything is damaged to some extent, but some structures remain fairly intact because, by intent or happenstance, they are stronger. It is reasonable to expect that the older, weaker capital stocks, including critical infrastructure, will be damaged far more severely than the newer capital stock. The old capital would normally be replaced with new capital that is better and more efficient in every way, if only because it's newer. Old roads and bridges are replaced with new wider, stronger roads and bridges. New schools and hospitals appear. The economy with newly replaced infrastructure critical to commerce should run faster than before. A forced technology upgrade led to greater growth.

Figure 10. Recovery overshoot.

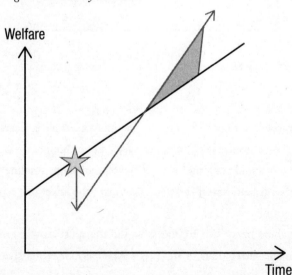

Figure 11. Full recovery in two sectors of society and the growth of inequality.

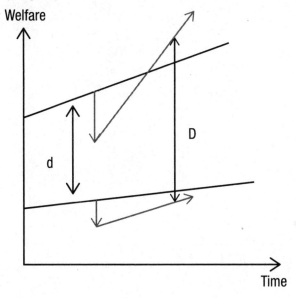

Figure 11 illustrates how a two-component economy might be affected by disaster.

Everything is as before except that there are two lines of predisaster growth, the upper one representing wealth and strong growth, the lower one representing the lower overall assets and slower growth. The growth rate on the lower line is smaller and the absolute level is lower. Just before the disaster, the inequality between the two is *d* and is widening. A disaster strikes as before. Now we see that the drop from the upper curve is much greater than that from the lower curve, but recovery is much faster. The lower sector loses less, but the recovery is much slower or perhaps not at all.

Now it is easy to see that after a short time, the gap between the two new growth curves has increased—*D* is now greater than *d* and is greater than what the gap would have widened to without the disaster. Inequality was sure to have increased anyway, but now it has increased all the more. The disaster has exacerbated inequality. But it's not the immediate effect of the disaster that matters, it's the effect of differing recoveries: A rich, capital-owning group appears to have lost a lot more than the poorer group, but in the end it gains at the expense of the poorer group.

DISASTERS IN NEOCLASSICAL GROWTH THEORY

NEOCLASSICAL GROWTH THEORY IS ATTRIBUTED TO ROBERT SOLOW, AND THE IDEAS are often referred to as the Solow model, or the Solow-Swan model.[1] (Swan refers to T. S. Swan, who came up with almost the same model independently of Solow, both in 1956.) The ideas are contained in Figure 1.

The vertical axis is the output per person, usually designated q, but other letters also are used (y is common). Output per person is created by a so-called production function,[2] here written as $Af(k)$, where A is the total factor productivity and k is the capital-labor ratio. So the horizontal axis is capital, and the curve shows how output depends on capital. That means that output is driven by capital (strictly, capital in relation to available labor). The upper curve that plots that function sometimes is called an L-curve for its shape. Near the origin (lower left corner), the curve is steep, meaning that for small additions of capital, large increases in production occur. It is almost flat in the upper right so that additions of capital achieve less; there is a diminishing return on marginal capital investment.

The lower curve, which is very similar, is the same function with s as the factor modifying the first curve, $sAf(k)$, where s denotes the savings rate. Because no one ever saves everything, s is less than 1, and the second curve will always sit below the first. Then there is a straight line $(n + d)k$.

Figure 1. A standard depiction of the Solow–Swan exogenous growth model. All symbols are explained in the text. Reference 1 gives citations for the model.

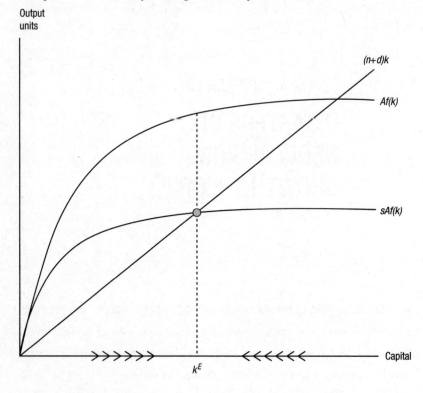

Here k is the same as before, n is population growth rate, and d is the rate of depreciation of capital.

The term $(n + d)k$ is called capital widening; it is the amount of savings necessary to keep the capital-labor ratio the same despite depreciation and population growth. Those latter two elements can be thought of as having similar effects on growth—if the population increases greatly but the capital stock stays the same, then production per capita will drop because the model regards capital as the source of growth. In the opposite case, where the capital depreciates and the population is the same, productivity decreases as well. There is a point where this straight line meets the savings curve, $sAf(k)$; that is the point when the economy is in equilibrium. At that point, per person capital is designated k^E. We could associate k^E with an equilibrium output q^E. In the standard theory, when the capital-widening line is below the savings curve (perhaps a more realistic way to say it is that the savings curve exceeds capital widening), the economy grows. That is, output grows.

Using the graph and adding the effect of a capital shock, we see in Figure 2 that the capital shifted left to k^D, the amount remaining after the disaster. We could say the capital loss is the difference between the equilibrium and the new capital, $\Delta k = k^D - k^E$. The same could be achieved by making the capital-widening line steeper by increasing depreciation of the capital stock. That would push the dot that is the point of intersection of the savings function with the capital-widening line to the left as well and have the same effect on production. Here we can say it was lowered by an amount Δq to q^D.

Figure 2. The effect of a capital shock Δk on output Δq. Output has dropped by the amount Δq, an amount that is determined by the shape of the growth curve that is governed by the utility function, explained above.

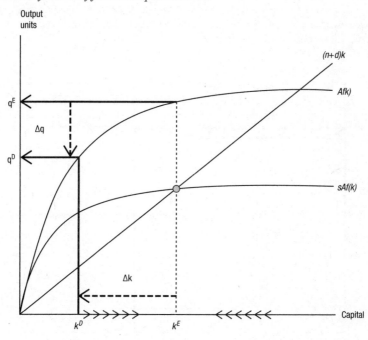

So the disaster does lower economic output, at least in the short run. It is fairly obvious also that the loss of output will be greater in this model for greater capital losses. Your position on the upper curve when a disaster happens matters a great deal. Imagine that the capital-widening line was less steep, caused, for instance, by a reduction in population growth rate, n. (Other things could cause the line to be less steep, of course.) The black dot in the center of the diagram would then move to the right and be on a flatter part of the curve. The amount of output loss is a direct function of the shape of the curve. If I moved everything to the right, the same Δk will have much less effect on output. That's shown in Figure 3. What the figure expresses is that the loss of capital matters a lot less when an economy already has a lot of capital; the same point that was made in Appendix I using different graphics. And it is essentially the opposite of the effect of additions of capital in the Solow-Swan system: The marginal return on capital is smaller when you start with a great deal of capital; the marginal loss also is small when you have a great deal of capital to start.

Figure 3. The same amount of capital loss occurs in this depiction, but the drop in output is much less because returns to capital are much more modeled on where the utility function is very flat.

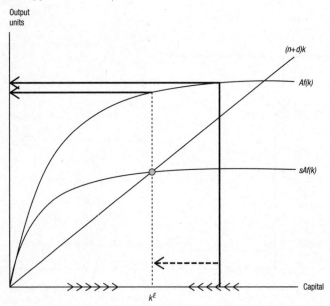

If you look at Figure 2, which shows the first way we considered production loss resulting from capital loss, you see how this might come about. Although you have fallen to a lower position on the production curve, that

Figure 4. The effect of output on capital loss is the same as in Figure 2. Note that the slope of the utility function designated by the dash–dot line is actually steeper where output is, in an absolute sense lower.

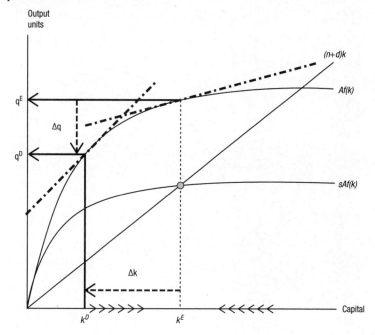

part of the curve actually has a steeper upward slope. The slopes are the dot-dash lines.

Even though you have dropped to a position of lower production, you are now at a place on the growth function where output growth is more rapid for a given capital input, just as capital additions should be more effective in poorer economies. So capital was lost, but growth rate increased. That increase means you will experience a growth spurt from any new additions of capital (from disaster recovery assistance, say) and quickly get back to where you were. That quick recovery matches the thinking about getting back to the predisaster growth trajectory discussed before. In Figure 4 we see it is because the economy has moved to a state where returns to growth from capital input are greater.

The Solow-Swan growth model predicts that poor countries should be growing very rapidly; many, however, simply are not. In fact, many are mired in stagnation, and some are even going backward. Jeffrey Sachs, the

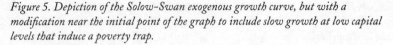

Figure 5. Depiction of the Solow–Swan exogenous growth curve, but with a modification near the initial point of the graph to include slow growth at low capital levels that induce a poverty trap.

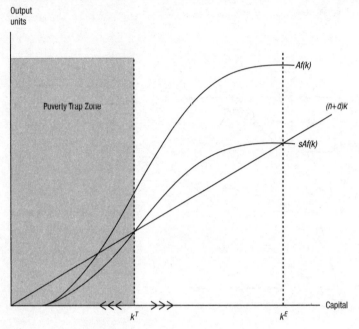

outspoken economist and director of Columbia's Earth Institute, thinks that it is because at extremely low levels of capital accumulation, capital-based growth doesn't work anymore. For additions of capital to be utilized effectively, a country needs some basic infrastructure of roads and ports and factories and a minimally literate, reasonably healthy population of workers. Sachs suggests there is a threshold of capital below which returns to capital may be low. Figure 5 is from the same study by Sachs and others. This curve is now S-shaped instead of L-shaped, with a very steep high-growth section in the middle and regions of low growth at the beginning and the end.

The critical capital threshold is k^T. Below that level, individual savings are *below* the capital-widening line, which means the economy is going nowhere, even with positive (but not high enough) capital investments. Sachs (and he is not alone) argues that economies on the wrong side of the critical capital threshold k^T will experience poverty traps, which generally are defined as "any self-reinforcing mechanism that causes poverty to persist."[3]

Many mechanisms can cause poverty traps. The health trap is perhaps easiest to grasp. People who are ill cannot work to earn income; if they are young, they cannot go to school to gain skills. That means that illness will likely lead to income reduction. But if you live in a poor country, you are much more likely to become ill because of poor levels of sanitation and low levels of health services. So poverty will cause you to be ill, but then your illness will cause you to be poorer still. The gray area on the diagram is the region of the poverty trap. Sachs's argument is that, in this region, savings rates are just too low relative to population growth for places in this condition to get ahead.

Now we finally can add the effect of disaster capital losses in this scheme. Look at the next graph. Three things are evident. One is that there is a dramatic drop in production for the same loss of capital, Δ*k,* because the loss happens across the threshold on the steepest part of the production

Figure 6. The same magnitude of capital shock Δk *is shown in poverty trap scenario. The output loss is now very large and has the potential effect of sending an economy from outside a poverty trap into such a trap.*

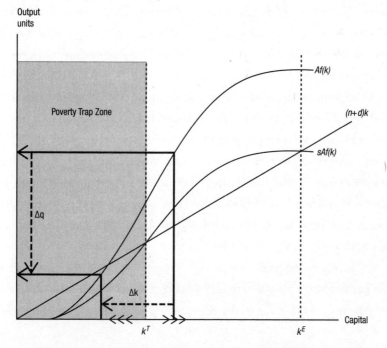

curve. Second is that because returns to capital are negligible in the poverty trap setting, loss of capital has little effect. This finding might explain why it sometimes seems that poor countries don't suffer development setbacks as a result of disasters. Again, these invisible setbacks are like development in reverse. Because additions of capital don't help a great deal in a poverty trap, losing a great deal of capital doesn't matter much either.

This finding gels with an idea put forward by Stéphane Hallegatte and Michael Ghil, but not about poor countries.[4] They analyzed the effects that disasters have at different stages within the business cycle that is common in developed economies. It often is observed that businesses typically go through cycles in which good times follow low times follow good times, and so on. The cycle doesn't have to be boom and bust exactly, but a cycle is evident all the same. So you can ask: Would you rather have a disaster happen during a good time or a low time? Almost everyone, including me, would answer in the good time. But Hallegatte and Ghil suggest that the opposite is true.

They suggest that in good times, when things are going well, the economy is at full capacity and there is no excess capacity available. But in poor times, there *is* excess capacity. That may mean unemployed people sitting around waiting for work, idle machinery, empty retail stores, and the like. In boom times, the economy is already working at full tilt, and there is no one available to deal with a disaster. If a disaster happens in low times, there is capacity to deal with it.

The third and possibly most important insight the last graph gives us is that capital losses that would have little effect on a highly developed country well to the right of the threshold can throw a country near the threshold from a growth situation into a poverty trap. The steeper and more precarious the middle part of the S-shaped curve is, the more dangerous it is to be near it. If you have just been able to claw your way out of the poverty trap, you want to get as far away from the edge as you possibly can. Even a small step backward can send you down into the trap again.

The important point here is the difference between the factors that can put you into a poverty trap and those that can keep you there. A disaster can throw a society into the chasm of a poverty trap. Once there, the mechanism by which individuals are kept from climbing out may have little to do with the disaster itself.

Of course, this same S-curve can apply to different people in the same country or different economic sectors in the same overall aggregate economy. Everywhere countries contain both poor people and rich people. Rich people live well to the right of the threshold; poor people live near the threshold or to the left of it. The poor experience losses from a disaster very differently from how the rich experience them.

ACKNOWLEDGMENTS

THIS WORK WOULD NOT HAVE BEEN POSSIBLE WITHOUT THE PERSISTENT, almost relentless encouragement from my agent, Elizabeth Evans. I probably never would have begun the project at all were it not for discussions with her, and I certainly would not have finished it without her support.

I have been deeply informed by discussions on the subject of natural disasters with Sonali Deraliyagala, author of *The Wave*, with whom I teach and do research at Columbia University, and with whom I traveled to Myanmar to understand the effects of Cyclone Nargis on that country. I worked with Elisabeth King, now at New York University, on a project comparing natural disasters and civil conflicts from which—including many deeply meaningful conversations—I learned how similar yet different these two events can be. Before beginning this project I worked with Kye Borang on a project that looked at disasters along a human rights axis, and that work was the opening for thoughts about disasters and injustice that salted many themes in this book.

I benefited tremendously from extensive discussions and travel to New Orleans with Richard Garfield, currently at the Center for Disease Control, but formerly at Columbia's Mailman School of Public Health. I know no one more dedicated to understanding how to respond to the trauma of the disaster moment and minimizing the threat to life that it poses.

I particularly want to acknowledge Stacy Parker LeMelle, with whom I traveled to New Orleans several times, and who, through her network of local friends and her skill and diligence at discovering key actors in the Katrina drama, gave me insight into that city and the trials of its people; it was an indispensable education to me. One person we met, Pastor Joe Cull of the New Orleans Police Department, who ministers to police officers in distress and alerted me to the high incidence of police officer suicides following Katrina, was a true inspiration.

Many students and others helped me assemble thoughts and words for this book. I particularly want to acknowledge Solomon Hsiang, Amir Jinar, Jesse Antilla-Hughs, Stephanie Lackner, Epsita Kumar, Valentina Mara, Svetlana Maronova, Leila Wisdom, Marissa Brodney, Semee Yoon, Belinda Archibong, Erin Stahmer, Brenden Kline, Elizabeth Thornton, Jessica Rosen, Meran Killackey, Saira Qureshi, and Phoebe Leung.

NOTES

INTRODUCTION. CROSSING THE FEYNMAN LINE

1. One example is Social Science Research Council, "Understanding Katrina: Perspectives from the Social Sciences," June 2006, http://under standingkatrina.ssrc.org/.
2. Daniel Kahneman, *Thinking, Fast and Slow* (New York: Farrar, Straus and Giroux, 2011).
3. Daniel Kahneman and Amos Tversky, "Prospect Theory: An Analysis of Decision under Risk," *Econometrica* 47, no. 2 (1979): 263.
4. Daniel Mendelsohn, "Unsinkable: Why We Can't Let Go of the *Titanic*," *New Yorker*, April 16, 2012, http://www.newyorker.com/magazine /2012/04/16/unsinkable-3.

CHAPTER 1. NATURAL DISASTERS: AGENTS OF SOCIAL GOOD AND EVIL

1. The way in which this might come about is described in chapter 2.
2. The best work done using these approaches is that of Amir Jina and Solomon Hsiang, and their study considers only tropical cyclones. Still, it is very compelling. See S. M. Hsiang and A. S. Jina, "The Causal Effect of Environmental Catastrophe on Long-Run Economic Growth: Evidence from 6,700 Cyclones," working paper NBER 20352, National Bureau of Economic Research, Cambridge, MA, 2014.
3. "Japan's Demography: The incredible Shrinking Country," *The Economist*, March 25, 2014, http://www.economist.com/blogs/banyan/2014/03/jap ans-demography.
4. The San Juan earthquake of 1944 destroyed essentially the entire city and took an estimated 10,000 lives.
5. Mark Skidmore and Hideki Toya, "Do Natural Disasters Promote Long-Run Growth?" *Economic Inquiry* 40 (2002): 664–687, doi:10.1093/ei/40. 4.664.
6. To be accurate, Schumpeter was born in what was at the time the Austro-Hungarian Empire and is now the Czech Republic.

7. Joseph Schumpeter, *Capitalism, Socialism and Democracy* (New York: Harper, 1947).

8. Drake Bennett, "Do Natural Disasters Stimulate Economic Growth?" *New York Times,* July 8, 2008, http://www.nytimes.com/2008/07/08/bus iness/worldbusiness/08iht-disasters.4.14335899.html?pagewanted=all.

9. Douglas C. Dacy and Howard Kunreuther, *The Economics of Natural Disasters: Implications for Federal Policy* (New York: Free Press, 1969), 270.

10. Betty Hearn Morrow, "Stretching the Bonds: The Families of Andrew," in *Hurricane Andrew: Ethnicity, Gender and the Sociology of Disaster,* eds. Walter Peacock, Betty Hearn Morrow, and Hugh Gladwin (New York: Routledge, 1997), 141–69.

11. *Online Etymology Dictionary,* http://www.etymonline.com/index.php?te rm=disaster.

12. John Stuart Mill, *Principles of Political Economy with Some of Their Applications to Social Philosophy* (1848; London: Longmans, Green, 1909), http://www.econlib.org/library/Mill/mlP5.html#I.5.19.html.

13. See, for instance, Philip Brickman, Dan Coates, and Ronnie Janoff-Bulman, "Lottery Winners and Accident Victims: Is Happiness Relative?" *Journal of Personality and Social Psychology* 36, no. 8 (1978): 917–27.

14. An article in *Time* magazine describes Bonanno's work and that of others in the new field of bereavement research by suggesting that the new studies debunk a series of grief myths. Ruth David Konigsberg, "New Ways to Think about Grief," *Time,* January 29, 2011, http://content.time.com /time/magazine/article/0,9171,2042372-1,00.html. The book was published as *The Other Side of Sadness: What the New Science of Bereavement Tells Us About Life after Loss* (New York: Basic Books, 2009).

15. W. G. Sebold, *The Natural History of Destruction* (Munich: Carl Hanser Verlag, 1999).

16. The *Economist* magazine defines *moral hazard* as "one of two main sorts of market failure often associated with the provision of insurance. The other is adverse selection. Moral hazard means that people with insurance may take greater risks than they would do without it because they know they are protected, so the insurer may get more claims than it bargained for." The definition is available at http://www.economist.com /economics-a-to-z/m#node-21529763.

17. Charles Percy Snow, *The Two Cultures* (1959; repr., London: Cambridge University Press, 2001).

18. Public Religion Research Institute, "Believers, Sympathizers, and Skeptics: Why Americans Are Conflicted about Climate Change, Environmental Policy, and Science," report, November 21, 2014, Washington, DC, http://publicreligion.org/research/2014/11/believers-sympathizers -skeptics-americans-conflicted-climate-change-environmental-policy -science/.

19. CRED's web address is http://www.cred.be/.

20. David Stromberg, "Natural Disasters, Economic Development, and Humanitarian Aid," *Journal of Economic Perspectives* 21, no. 3 (Summer 2007): 199–222.

21. "Counting the Cost of Calamities," *Economist*, January 14, 2012, http://www.economist.com/node/21542755.

22. Geoffrey Ward, review of *This Republic of Suffering: Death and the American Civil War* by Drew Gilpin Faust, *New York Times*, January 27, 2008, http://www.nytimes.com/2008/01/27/books/review/Ward-t.html?_r=0,

23. His son was killed by Confederate soldiers who were stranded behind Union lines after a battle and had disguised themselves as Union soldiers by wearing the uniforms of dead soldiers.

24. Eric Klinenberg, *Heat Wave: A Social Autopsy of Disaster in Chicago* (Chicago: University of Chicago Press, 2002). See also "Dying Alone: An interview with Eric Klinenberg, author of *Heat Wave: A Social Autopsy of Disaster in Chicago*," University of Chicago Press website, 2002, http://www.press.uchicago.edu/Misc/Chicago/443213in.html.

25. David Laskin, *The Children's Blizzard* (New York: HarperCollins, 2004).

26. William Bronson, *The Earth Shook, the Sky Burned* (San Francisco: Chronicle Books, 1996).

27. National Oceanic and Atmospheric Administration, *A Study of Earthquake Losses in the San Francisco Bay Area–Data and Analysis*, report prepared for the Office of Emergency Preparedness (Washington, DC: U.S. Department of Commerce, 1972).

28. Gladys Hansen and Emmit Condon, *Denial of Disaster: The Untold Story and Photographs of the San Francisco Earthquake and Fire of 1906* (San Francisco: Cameron, 1989).

29. Centers for Disease Control, "Deaths in World Trade Center Terrorist Attacks—New York City, 2001," *Morbidity and Mortality Weekly Report* 51, Special Issue (September 11, 2002):16-18, http://www.cdc.gov/MMWR/preview/mmwrhtml/mm51SPa6.htm.

30. Diane Coyle, *GDP: A Brief but Affectionate History* (Princeton, NJ: Princeton University Press, 2014).

31. Thomas Piketty, *Capital in the Twenty-First Century*, trans. Arthur Goldhammer (Cambridge, MA: Belknap Press, 2014).

32. Joseph Stiglitz, Amartya Sen, and Jean-Paul Fitoussi, *Mismeasuring Our Lives: Why GDP Doesn't Add Up* (New York: New Press, 2010).

33. Friedrich Schneider, "Size and Measurement of the Informal Economy in 110 Countries around the World," paper presented at a Workshop of Australian National Tax Centre, Australian National University, Canberra, July 2002, http://www.amnet.co.il/attachments/informal_economy110.pdf.

34. "Sex, Drugs and GDP: Italy's Inclusion of Illicit Activities in Its Figures Excites Much Interest," *Economist*, May 31, 2014, http://www.economist.com/news/finance-and-economics/21603073-italys-inclusion

-illicit-activities-its-figures-excites-much-interest-sex; Sarah O'Connor, "Sex, Drugs and GDP—How Did the ONSZ Do It?" *Financial Times*, May 2014, http://blogs.ft.com/money-supply/2014/05/29/sex-drugs-and -gdp-how-did-the-ons-do-it/; Angela Monaghan, "Drugs and Prostitution to Be Included in UK National Accounts," *Guardian*, May 29, 2014, http://www.theguardian.com/society/2014/may/29/drugs-prostitution -uk-national-accounts.

35. *The Big Mac Index*, http://bigmacindex.org/.

CHAPTER 2. THE GEOGRAPHY OF WEALTH AND POVERTY: KNOWLEDGE AND NATURAL DISASTERS

1. John L. Gallup, Jeffrey D. Sachs, and Andrew D. Mellinger, "Geography and Economic Development," *International Regional Science Review* 22, 2 (1999): 179–232.

2. Daron Acemoglu and James A. Robinson, *Why Nations Fail: The Origins of Power, Prosperity, and Poverty* (New York: Crown Business, 2013).

3. C. Mayhew and R. Simmon, *Earth's City Lights*, October 23, 2000. Retrieved from National Aeronautics and Space Administration (NASA) Visible Earth: http://visibleearth.nasa.gov/view.php?id=55167.

4. By *proxy* we mean a factor that can be measured that is directly related to something of interest that cannot be measured directly. The properties of tree rings, for instance, are used to obtain information about past temperatures but do not measure temperature directly.

5. William Spence, Stuart A. Sipkin, and George L. Choy, "Measuring the Size of an Earthquake," *Earthquakes and Volcanoes* 21, no. 1 (1989): 58–63, http://earthquake.usgs.gov/learn/topics/measure.php.

6. Many basic textbooks describe plate tectonics. A good college-level book with excellent illustrations is Stephen Marshak, *Earth: Portrait of a Planet* (New York: W. W. Norton, 2014). The Wikipedia site at http:// en.wikipedia.org/wiki/Plate_tectonics is quite comprehensive and cites many good references.

7. R. A. Rohde, "Saffir-Simpson Hurricane Intensity Scale," NASA Earth Observatory, November 2, 2006, http://earthobservatory.nasa.gov/IOTD /view.php?id=7079.

8. *Flood* means the result of heavy rains inland, sometimes called freshwater flooding, as distinct from flooding due to storm surge from the ocean.

9. The explosion of Krakatoa Island killed about 36,000 people in the tsunami that followed its eruption; that explosion was the loudest sound made on Earth in modern times and was heard as far as 3,000 miles away.

10. Incorporated Institutes for Seismology, Education and Outreach, http:// www.iris.edu/hq/programs/education_and_outreach.

11. The Coriolis force (strictly an effect, not a force) operates on any rotating body. On Earth, it causes anything moving across the face of the planet in any direction other than exactly east or exactly west to be deflected from its intended path. So if a small, not-so-fast airplane were to start

off in London heading due south to Accra, the capital of Ghana (on the same line of longitude), it would probably land in Senegal on the coast of West Africa. Accra moved east as the airplane made its journey due south. In a frame of reference in which the Earth is fixed, the airplane appears to be deflected westward. The exact opposite happens in the Southern Hemisphere. Consider the same airplane trying to fly north from Johannesburg to Cairo. More details can be found at HyperPhysics, *Coriolis Force,* a resource hosted by the Department of Physics and Astronomy at Georgia State University, http://hyperphysics.phy-astr.gsu.edu/hbase /corf.html.

12. No cyclones form at the equator or for about five degrees of latitude (300 miles) on either side. The reasons for these two blank zones differ. In the equatorial belt, the Coriolis effect is too small to cause rotation of the disorganized "stormlettes" that initiate cyclones. In the South Atlantic, sea surface temperatures are a little too low for cyclone formation, and high-level vertical wind shear is too strong to permit the formation of cyclones (the top more or less blows off), and the inter-tropical convergence zone of strong evaporation and cloud formation doesn't come far enough south there.

13. National Oceanic and Atmospheric Administration (NOAA)/National Weather Service, "Saffir-Simpson Hurricane Wind Scale," May 24, 2013; http://www.nhc.noaa.gov/aboutsshws.php.

14. Another common way to describe this is through the idea of an *observation window.* You can think of it as the period of time during which a phenomenon has been observed. So, for instance, we need to observe the weather in Paris for only a few years to know that it commonly rains there, but to know how the El Niño affects how much it rains, we would need to observe for many decades because the El Niño recurs every three to seven years and we would want to have observed its effect several times.

15. Ross S. Stein, "Earthquake Conversations," *Scientific American* 288 (2003): 72–79. Also published in *Our Ever Changing Earth, Scientific American, Special Edition* 15, no. 2 (2005): 82–89.

16. Tokuji Utsu, Yoshihiko Ogata, Ritsuko S. Matsu'ura, "The Centenary of the Omori Formula for a Decay Law of Aftershock Activity," *Journal of the Physics of the Earth* 43 (1995): 1–33.

17. John C. Mutter, "Voices: Italian Seismologists: What Should They Have Said?" *Earth Magazine,* July 1, 2010, http://www.earthmagazine.org /article/voices-italian-seismologists-what-should-they-have-said.

18. Tia Ghose, "L'Aquila Earthquake Forces Geologists to Rethink Risk," *Live Science,* December 11, 2012, http://www.livescience.com/25420 -laquila-earthquake-lessons.html.

19. For more on fault creep, see United States Geological Survey, "Haywood—Creeping Fault," geomaps.wr.usgs.gov/sfgeo/quaternary/stories /hayward_creep.html.

20. Roger Bilham, "The Seismic Future of Cities," *Bulletin of Earthquake Engineering* 7, no. 4 (November 2009): 839–87. See also an interview with

Bilham at World Bank, "Seismic Future of Cities. Interview with Dr. Roger Bilham," February 22, 2011, http://go.worldbank.org/GTQ1A L0AG0.

21. Travis Daub, "China's War on Illegal Buildings," *The Rundown* (blog), PBS Newshour, August 17, 2010, http://www.pbs.org/newshour/run down/chinas-war-on-illegal-buildings/.

22. "Workers Forced to Join Work," *Daily Star,* April 25, 2013, http://archive .thedailystar.net/beta2/news/workers-forced-to-join-work.

23. Mark Lincoln, "New Christchurch Earthquake Photos," *NZ Raw* (blog), February 24, 2011, http://www.nzraw.co.nz/news/new-christ church-earthquake-photos/.

24. A good basic introduction to this material can be found at Charles J. Ammon, "Earthquake Effects," Department of Geosciences, Penn State University, n.d., http://eqseis.geosc.psu.edu/~cammon/HTML/Classes /IntroQuakes/Notes/earthquake_effects.html.

25. The reason is that the speed at which earthquake waves travel depends on the material properties of the rocks through which they travel. More rigid rocks propagate energy at higher velocity. Loose soil is not rigid and prop- agates energy quite slowly. When a seismic wave that has been traveling through strong rocks encounters loose soil, it slows down, but because the wave carries the same amount of energy, the energy is concentrated in a smaller region, causing greater shaking. The energy piles up and increases the amplitude of shaking. The effect is quite like the way the height of a tsunami wave increases as the wave enters shallow water near a coast. Areas of infill within solid rock regions can amplify shaking considerably. Because of this fact, considerable effort is put into seismic microzona- tion, in which soil properties are measured and maps are produced that show where the greatest shaking is likely to occur. Such measurements can guide first responders to areas most likely to be damaged in an earthquake and help planners in fortifying existing public structures and siting new ones.

26. Suzanne Snively, "New Zealand Tops 2013 Corruption Perceptions In- dex," Transparency International, December 3, 2013, http://www.trans parency.org/news/pressrelease/new_zealand_tops_2013_corruption _perceptions_index.

27. This needs to be qualified a little. The polar regions are also not very pro- ductive because of the harsh environment. As in the tropics, wealth can be generated in such regions, but typically only through resource extraction.

28. The latest annual report (2012–13) of the Institute of Seismologi- cal Research can be found at http://www.isr.gujarat.gov.in/images/pdf /APR%202012-13.pdf. I traveled with a colleague, Arthur Lerner-Lam, to Gujarat several times to advise the government on how to structure the institute in the two years before it was established.

29. Generally, poor countries have much better systems in place to monitor the weather than to monitor earthquakes. Basic meteorological mea- surements are easier to make than seismic measurements and much less

costly. As with the mapping of faults, colonial powers, especially Britain, installed weather stations and operated meteorological services in their colonies, because they knew local weather was important to the crops they wanted to produce and export. Typically colonial systems were established as replicas of systems that operated in the home country. Some British colonies, especially India, experienced devastating droughts and famines that were egregiously mismanaged by the colonizers, in part, one can suppose, because they had no experience of droughts of such massive scales. (An arresting account of the massive mismanagement and catastrophic death toll in Indian droughts can be found in *Late Victorian Holocausts* by Mike Davis.)

In many instances, when and if postcolonial countries established seismometer networks, they used the sites established for meteorological observations, and very often they attached their operations to whatever meteorological service existed. This made perfectly good sense from a management perspective. The sites were already prepared and visited routinely, and the same personnel could be trained to ensure the seismometers operated correctly. Unfortunately, an ideal site for a meteorological station may not be very suitable for seismic observations. In fact, the two have nothing at all to do with one another, and many seismometers that exist in poorer countries are less than ideally located.

Today, extensive satellite observation systems available throughout the world are openly available to practically everyone, and there is little reason to be surprised by a bad weather event. Countries have very different capacities to receive and analyze this sort of information and rely on local readings from ground-based instruments. Those with high-level capacity often share information with regional neighbors that have less capability, although data sharing can be difficult with isolated states, such as Myanmar and North Korea. The meteorological office in India is quite sophisticated and has its own satellites. Bad weather scenarios, such as failure of the monsoon or droughts associated with El Niño, have devastating effects on the Indian economy, and weather forecasting has been of the highest priority in the country for more than a century. Although adjacent countries are equally affected by the weather, their capabilities are not as advanced as India's.

CHAPTER 3. CARNAGE IN THE CARIBBEAN, CHAOS IN CONCEPCIÓN

1. Jonathan M. Katz, *The Big Truck That Went By: How the World Came to Save Haiti and Left Behind a Disaster* (New York: Palgrave Macmillan, 2013).
2. P. Cockburn, "Haiti's Elite Haunted by Fear of Revenge: Supporters of the Embattled Military Regime Dread a Bloody Repeat of 1791 When Tormented Slaves Massacred Their Rich Masters," *The Independent*, July 18, 1994.
3. Mike Davis, "Planet of Slums," *New Left Review* 26 (2004): 5–34.

4. Pure Water for the World, "Transforming the Lives of Children & Families Struggling in Cité Soleil, Haiti," 2015, http://purewaterfortheworld .org/our-projects-cite-soleil-1000-homes.html.

5. CIA, *The World Factbook: Haiti*, March 11, 2015, https://www.cia.gov /library/publications/the-world-factbook/geos/ha.html.

6. Ibid.

7. Several sources say Haiti is the most violent place on Earth. See Sudhir Muralidhar, "Gangs of Port-au-Prince," *The American Prospect*, March 11, 2015, http://prospect.org/article/gangs-port-au-prince. The article quotes the UN as the source of that assessment without being specific about the UN agency that makes the assessment. Asger Leth's documentary film *Ghosts of Cité Soleil* (A. Leth and M. Loncarevic, directors, 2007), documents life and death in the gangs of Port-au-Prince.

8. Richard Sanders, "Chimère, the 'N' Word of Haiti," *Press for Conversion!* no. 61 (2007): 50–51, http://coat.ncf.ca/our_magazine/links/61/50-51 .pdf.

9. Athena R. Kolbe, "Revisiting Haiti's Gangs and Organized Violence," *Humanitarian Action in Situations Other than War Discussion Paper* 5 (2013): 1–36, http://hasow.org/uploads/trabalhos/101/doc/449921257 .pdf; United Nations Stabilization Mission in Haiti, "MINUSTAH Facts and Figures," October 14, 2014, http://www.un.org/en/peacekeeping /missions/minustah/facts.shtml.

10. UN Stabilization Mission in Haiti, "MINUSTAH Facts and Figures."

11. Daniele Lantagne, G. Balakrish Nair, Claaudio F. Lanata, and Alejando Cravioto, "The Cholera in Haiti: Where and How Did It Begin?" *Current Topics in Microbiology and Immunology,* 2013. A good summary can be found at http://www.cepr.net/index.php/blogs/relief-and-reconstruc tion-watch/uns-own-independent-experts-now-say-minustah-troops -most-likely-caused-cholera-epidemic.

12. One measurement of inequality is Gini. Evans Jardotte has estimated that Haiti's Gini coefficient is 0.6457. This coefficient runs from 0, which indicates perfect equality, to 1.0, representing maximum inequality. Only Namibia is more unequal than Haiti, according to Jardotte, although other sources place South Africa and several other African countries higher. The Gini is a statistical measure of income inequality derived by taking the difference between the actual distribution of incomes (modeled by a Lorenz function) and a hypothetical perfect equality, meaning that, for instance, 5 percent of the population holds 5 percent of the wealth, 20 percent holds 20 percent wealth, et cetera. Evans Jardotte, "Income Distribution and Poverty in the Republic of Haiti," Partnership for Economic Policy—Poverty Monitoring, Measurement and Analysis, paper provided by PEP-PMMA in its series *Working Papers PMMA* with number 2006-13.

13. Oxfam, "Working for the Few: Political Capture and Economic Inequality," Oxfam Briefing Paper 178 (2014): 1–6, https://www.oxfam.org

/sites/www.oxfam.org/files/bp-working-for-few-political-capture-econo
mic-inequality-200114-summ-en.pdf.

14. World Bank, "Investing in People to Fight Poverty in Haiti," Washington, DC, 2015, http://www.worldbank.org/content/dam/Worldbank/doc
ument/Poverty%20documents/Haiti_PA_overview_web_EN.pdf.

15. Deborah Sontag, "Years after Haiti Quake, Safe Housing Is a Dream
for Many," *New York Times,* August 15, 2012, http://www.nytimes.com
/2012/08/16/world/americas/years-after-haiti-quake-safe-housing-is
-dream-for-multitudes.html?_r=1.

16. Manuel Roig-Franzia, Mary Beth Sheridan, and Michael E. Ruane, "Haitians Struggle to Find the Dead and Keep Survivors Alive after Earthquake," *Washington Post,* January 15, 2010, http://www.washingtonpost
.com/wp-dyn/content/article/2010/01/14/AR2010011401013.html.

17. Maura R. O'Connor, "Two Years Later, Haitian Earthquake Death Toll in
Dispute," *Columbia Journalism Review,* January 12, 2012, http://www.cjr
.org/behind_the_news/one_year_later_haitian_earthqu.php?page=all.

18. Hans Jaap Melissen, "Haiti Quake Death Toll Well under 100,000,"
Radio Netherlands Worldwide, February 23, 2010, http://www.rnw.nl
/english/article/haiti-quake-death-toll-well-under-100,000.

19. Global Agriculture and Food Security Program, "Haiti Earthquake
PDNA: Assessment of Damage, Losses, General and Sectoral Needs,"
World Bank, Washington, DC, March 24, 2010.

20. World Health Organization, Division of Mental Health, *Psychological
Consequences of Disasters: Prevention and Management* (Geneva: World
Health Organization, 1992).

21. Timothy T. Schwartz, Yves-François Pierre, and Eric Calpas for LTL
Strategies, *Building Assessments and Rubble Removal in Quake-Affected
Neighborhoods in Haiti* (Washington, DC: USAID, 2011).

22. Claude de Ville de Goyet, Juan Pablo Sarmiento, and François Grünewald,
*Health Response to the Earthquake in Haiti January 2010: Lessons to Be
Learned for the Next Massive Sudden-Onset Disaster* (Washington, DC:
Pan American Health Organization, 2011).

23. Financial Tracking Service, "Haiti in 2013—Related Emergencies. List
of Outstanding Pledges and Funding In 2013," United Nations Office for
the Coordination of Humanitarian Affairs, 2013.

24. Elizabeth Ferris, "Earthquakes and Floods: Comparing Haiti and Pakistan," Brookings Institute, August 26, 2010, http://www.brookings
.edu/~/media/research/files/papers/2010/8/26-earthquakes-floods-ferris
/0826_earthquakes_floods_ferris.pdf.

25. For more on this, see the paper I co-authored: Elisabeth King and John
C. Mutter, "Violent Conflicts and Natural Disasters: The Growing Case
for Cross-Disciplinary Dialogue," *Third World Quarterly* 35, no. 7 (2014):
1239–55. It is rare for faults to exist in isolation. Typically, one main fault,
such as the San Andreas, will be associated with numerous splays that
originate from the main fault but cause dislocations far from it.

26. Katz, *The Big Truck That Went By.* May 5, 2012.

27. Vivian A. Bernal, and Paul Procee, "Four Years On: What China Got Right When Rebuilding after the Sichuan Earthquake," *East Asia & Pacific on the Rise* (blog), World Bank, May 11, 2012, http://blogs.world bank.org/eastasiapacific/four-years-on-what-china-got-right-when-rebui lding-after-the-sichuan-earthquake 5/11/2012.

28. Louisa Lim, "Five Years after a Quake, Chinese Cite Shoddy Reconstruction," *All Things Considered,* NPR, May 13, 2013, http://www.npr.org /blogs/parallels/2013/05/14/183635289/Five-Years-After-A-Quake -Chinese-Cite-Shoddy-Reconstruction.

29. Sarah Chayes, *Thieves of State: Why Corruption Threatens Global Security* (New York: W. W. Norton, 2015).

30. Nicholas Ambraseys and Roger Bilham, "Corruption Kills," *Nature* 469 (2011): 153–55.

31. Haiti is 161st out of 175 countries ranked; China is at 100. "Corruption Measurement Tools: Haiti," Transparency International, 2014, http:// www.transparency.org/country#HTI.

32. Geotechnical engineering is a branch of civil engineering that deals with the properties of natural earth materials and the effects of man-made interventions in the landscape. A branch of this field focuses on the effects of earthquakes on different Earth formations. The field differs from geology in that it studies mechanical properties specifically and not the origin and history of the formations.

33. When the towers of the World Trade Center collapsed, they each generated ground motion equivalent to a magnitude 2 earthquake.

34. National Science Foundation, "Collaborative Research: Geoengineering Extreme Events Reconnaissance (GEER) Association: Turning Disaster into Knowledge," July 17, 2012, http://www.nsf.gov/awardsearch/show Award?AWD_ID=0825507; http://www.geerassociation.org/GEER_Po st%20EQ%20Reports/Haiti_2010/Cover_Haiti10.html.

35. United Nations Institute for Research and Training, "Haiti Earthquake 2010: Remote Sensing Based Building Damage Assessment Data," 2010, http://www.unitar.org/unosat/haiti-earthquake-2010-remote-sensing -based-building-damage-assessment-data.

36. Ellen Rathje et al., "Geotechnical Engineering Reconnaissance of the 2010 Haiti Earthquake," Version1, February 22, 2010, http://www.geer association.org/GEER_Post%20EQ%20Reports/Haiti_2010/0-GEER %20Web%20Report%20Version%201/Haiti%20Report%202010.pdf.

37. For more about the UNISAT Operational Satellite, see http://www.uni tar.org/unosat/.

38. Rathje et al., "Geotechnical Engineering," 11.

39. Mac McClelland, "Rebuilding Haiti for the Rich," *Mother Jones,* January 11, 2011, http://www.motherjones.com/rights-stuff/2011/01/rebuilding -haiti-rich.

40. Sonoma County Permit and Resource Management Department, Sonoma County Hazard Mitigation Map, Sonoma, CA, 2011.

41. Strictly, a refugee is someone who, "owing to a well-founded fear of being persecuted for reasons of race, religion, nationality, membership of a particular social group or political opinion, is outside the country of his nationality, and is unable to, or owing to such fear, is unwilling to avail himself of the protection of that country." See UN High Commission for Refugees, "Refugees: Flowing across Borders," March 11, 2015, http://www.unhcr.org/pages/49c3646c125.html.

42. Megan Bradley, "Four Years after the Haiti Earthquake, the Search for Solutions to Displacement Continues," Brookings Institute, January 13, 2014, http://www.brookings.edu/blogs/up-front/posts/2014/01/13-haiti-earthquake-anniversary-bradley.

43. Executive Office of the President, *2014 Native Youth Report*, Washington, DC, 2014.

44. Amanda Ripley, "The Gangs of New Orleans," *Time*, May 14, 2006, http://content.time.com/time/magazine/article/0,9171,1194016,00.html.

45. Athena Kolbe and Robert Muggah, "Haiti's Silenced Victims," *New York Times*, December 8, 2012, http://www.nytimes.com/2012/12/09/opinion/sunday/haitis-silenced-victims.html?_r=0.

46. Mary A. Renda, *Taking Haiti: Military Occupation and the Culture of U.S. Imperialism, 1915–1940* (Chapel Hill: University of North Carolina Press, 2001).

47. Alisa Klein, *Sexual Violence in Disasters: A Planning Guide for Prevention and Response* (Enola, LA: Louisiana Foundation Against Sexual Assault and National Sexual Violence Resource Center, 2008).

48. Athena R. Kolbe and Royce A. Hutson, "Human Rights Abuses and Other Criminal Violations in Port-au-Prince, Haiti: A Random Survey of Households," *Lancet* 368, no. 9538 (2006): 864–73.

49. Ibid.

50. Enrico L. Quarantelli, "Conventional Beliefs and Counterintuitive Realities," *Social Research: An International Quarterly of the Social Sciences* 75, no. 3, (2008): 873–904.

51. Melissa Lyttle, "Yet More on Fabienne Cherisma," *Prison Photography*, February 10, 2010, http://prisonphotography.org/2010/02/10/yet-more-on-fabienne-cherisma/.

52. James Oatway, "Haiti Earthquake Aftermath," 2010, http://www.jamesoatway.com/haiti-earthquake-aftermath/.

53. Jan Granup, "This Is 15-Year-Old Fabienne Cherisma, Shot Dead by Policeman after Looting Three Picture Frames," *Colors Magazine* no. 86 (April 9, 2013), http://www.colorsmagazine.com/stories/magazine/86/story/this-is-15-year-old-fabienne-cherisma-shot-dead-by-a-policeman-after-lootin.

54. In some accounts of this shooting, the death is described as accidental. Policemen may have been shooting over the heads of a crowd in order to restore order, and Fabienne was hit by a stray bullet. If that is the case, no one actually took aim at her and deliberately killed her. I am not sure

there is really much difference in the end. Certainly not for Fabienne's family.

55. Frank Bajak, "Chile-Haiti Earthquake Comparison: Chile Was More Prepared," *Huffington Post*, April 29, 2010, http://www.huffingtonpost.com/2010/02/27/chile-haiti-earthquake-co_n_479705.html.

56. Transparency International, "Corruption Perception Index," 2014, http://www.transparency.org/cpi2014/results#myAnchor1.

57. World Bank, "Gini Index (World Bank Estimate)," March 11, 2015, http://data.worldbank.org/indicator/SI.POV.GINI.

58. UN Development Programme, *Human Development Reports*, March 11, 2015, http://hdr.undp.org/en/countries/profiles/CHL.

59. Cristián Larroulet, "Chile's Path to Development: Key Reforms to Become the First Developed Country in Latin America," Heritage Foundation, October 15, 2013, http://www.heritage.org/research/reports/2013/10/chiles-path-to-development-key-reforms-to-become-the-first-developed-country-in-latin-america.

60. Council on Hemispheric Affairs, "The Inequality behind Chile's Prosperity," November 23, 2011, http://www.coha.org/the-inequality-behind-chiles-prosperity/.

61. CIA, *The World Factbook: Chile*, March 11, 2015, https://www.cia.gov/library/publications/the-world-factbook/geos/ci.html.

62. Sara M. Llana, "Chile Earthquake: President Bachelet Opens Up to Foreign Aid," *Christian Science Monitor*, March 10, 2010, http://www.csmonitor.com/World/Americas/2010/0301/Chile-earthquake-President-Bachelet-opens-up-to-foreign-aid.

63. Patrick J. McDonnell, "Chile Sends Army into Post-Quake Chaos," *Los Angeles Times*, March 3, 2010, http://articles.latimes.com/2010/mar/03/world/la-fg-chile-quake3-2010mar03.

64. J. Busby, "Feeding Insecurity," in S. E. Rice, C. Graff, and C. Pascua, *Confronting Poverty: Weak States and U.S. National Security* (Washington, DC: Brookings Institute, 2010), 140.

65. Juan Forero, "Post-Quake Looting Challenges Chile's Perceptions of Social Progress," *Washington Post*, March 5, 2010, http://www.washingtonpost.com/wp-dyn/content/article/2010/03/03/AR2010030304595.html.

66. Felipe Cordero, "Chile: Earthquake Reveals Social Inequalities," *Global Voices*, March 10, 2010, http://globalvoicesonline.org/2010/03/10/chile-earthquake-reveals-social-inequalities/; Felipe Cordero, "Chile: Army Deployments to Streets of Concepción," *Global Voices*, March 2, 2010, http://globalvoicesonline.org/2010/03/02/chile-army-deployed-to-streets-of-concepcion/.

67. Ibid.

68. Ibid.

69. Ibid.

70. Ibid.

71. Useem Michael, Howard Kunreuther, and Erwann Michel-Kerjan. *Leadership Dispatches: Chile's Extraordinary Comeback from Disaster.* Stanford University Press, 2015.

72. Paul Collier, *The Bottom Billion: Why the Poorest Countries Are Failing and What Can Be Done About It* (New York: Oxford University Press, 2007).

73. Paul Collier, "Haiti: From Natural Catastrophe to Economic Security: A Report for the Secretary-General of the United Nations," United Nations Secretary-General's Office, 2009, http://www.focal.ca/pdf/haiticollier .pdf.

74. Center for Economic and Policy Research, "Haitian Companies Still Sidelined from Reconstruction Contracts," April 19, 2011, http://www .cepr.net/index.php/blogs/relief-and-reconstruction-watch/haitian-comp anies-still-sidelined-from-reconstruction-contracts.

75. Ibid.

76. For more information about the Caracol Industrial Park, see US Agency for International Development, "Caracol Industrial Park," January 28, 2015, http://www.usaid.gov/haiti/caracol-industrial-park; and "Clinton Foundation in Haiti: Caracol Industrial Park," https://www.clinton foundation.org/our-work/clinton-foundation-haiti/programs/caracol-ind ustrial-park.

77. Jonathan M. Katz, "A Glittering Industrial Park in Haiti Falls Short," *Al Jazeera America,* September 10, 2013, http://america.aljazeera.com /articles/2013/9/10/a-glittering-industrialparkfallsshortinhaiti.html.

78. C. S. Prentice et al., "Seismic Hazard of the Enriquillo–Plantain Garden Fault in Haiti Inferred from Palaeoseismology," *Nature Geoscience* 3 (2010): 789–93.

79. CIA, "Distribution of Family Income—Gini Index," *The World Factbook,* 2015, https://www.cia.gov/library/publications/the-world-factbook/rank order/2172rank.html.

80. "Black swan event" is from a book by Nassin Taleb in a book by the same name, subtitled *The Impact of the Highly Unlikely* (New York: Random House, 2007). It is used to describe extremely rare events. Taleb apparently does not know that there are thousands of black swans native to southwestern Australia. In Perth, people think white swans are rare.

CHAPTER 4. WALLS OF WATER, OCEANS OF DEATH

1. International Tsunami Information Center, "10 Years Since Dec. 26, 2004 Indian Ocean Tsunami," 2014, http://itic.ioc-unesco.org/index.php.

2. Peter Symonds, "The Asian Tsunami: Why There Were No Warnings," World Socialist Web Site, International Committee of the Fourth International, January 3, 2005, https://www.wsws.org/en/articles/2005/01 /warn-j03.html.

3. Maryann Mott, "Did Animals Sense Tsunami Was Coming?" *National Geographic,* January 4, 2005, http://news.nationalgeographic.com/news

/2005/01/0104_050104_tsunami_animals.html; Charles Sabine, "Senses Helped Animals Survive the Tsunami," NBC News, January 6, 2005, http://www.nbcnews.com/id/6795562/ns/nbc_nightly_news_with_br ian_williams/t/senses-helped-animals-survive-tsunami/%20-%20.U— P7EgfmHk#.VQcG6Y7F So.

4. World Bank, "Sri Lanka Overview," February 2015, http://www.world bank.org/en/country/srilanka/overview#1.

5. A. K. Jayawardane, "Recent Tsunami Disaster Stricken to Sri Lanka and Recovery," International Seminar on Risk Management for Roads, Vietnam, April 26–28, 2006.

6. Harvard University, "What Did Sri Lanka Export in 2012?" *Atlas of Economic Complexity*, March 2015, http://atlas.cid.harvard.edu/explore /tree_map/export/lka/all/show/2012/. The clever diagram of exports in the *Harvard Atlas* doesn't even include fish products, which means they must represent less than 1 percent of Sri Lanka's gross domestic product (GDP).

7. Sisira Jayasuriya and Peter McCawley, *The Asian Tsunami: Aid and Reconstruction after a Disaster* (Cheltenham, UK: Asian Development Bank, Edward Elgar, 2010), http://www.e-elgar.co.uk/bookentry_main .lasso?id=13668.

8. World Bank, "Data: GDP Growth (Annual %)," 2015, http://data.world bank.org/indicator/NY.GDP.MKTP.KD.ZG?page=1.

9. Nishara Fernando, "Forced Relocation after the Indian Ocean Tsunami. Case Study of Vulnerable Populations in Three Relocation Settlements in Galle, Sri Lanka," UNU-EHS Graduate Research Series, Bonn, 2010, http://www.ehs.unu.edu/file/get/10660.pdf.

10. Ibid.

11. World Bank, "Sri Lanka: Country Snapshot," 2014, http://documents .worldbank.org/curated/en/2014/10/20305899/sri-lanka-country-snap shot.

12. National Police Agency of Japan, "Damage Situation and Police Countermeasures Associated with 2011 Tohoku District—Off the Pacific Ocean Earthquake," 2015, https://www.npa.go.jp/archive/keibi/biki/hi gaijokyo_e.pdf.

13. Kazuhiro Morimoto, "The Tohoku Economy Three Years After the Great East Japan Earthquake," April 30, 2014, http://www.iist.or.jp /en-m/2014/0230-0927/.

14. Molly Schnell is now in a doctoral program at Princeton. See Molly K. Schnell David E. Weinstein, "Evaluating the Economic Response to Japan's Earthquake," Research Institute of Economy, Trade and Industry Policy Discussion Paper Series 12-P-003, 2012, http://www.rieti.go.jp /jp/publications/pdp/12p003.pdf.

15. Preston Phro, "Nearly 290,000 People Still Living in Shelters 2 1/2 Years after Tohoku Disaster," *Japan Today*, September 18, 2013, http://www .japantoday.com/category/national/view/nearly-290000-people-still-liv ing-in-shelters-2-12-years-after-tohoku-disaster.

16. Tim Stephens, "Slippery Fault Unleashed Destructive Tohoku-Oki Earthquake and Tsunami," *University of California, Santa Cruz Newscenter,* December 5, 2013, http://news.ucsc.edu/2013/12/slippery-fault.html.

17. David Funkhouser, "Lessons from the Japan Earthquake," *State of the Planet: Blogs from the Earth Institute,* March 31, 2011, http://blogs.ei.columbia.edu/2011/03/31/lessons-from-the-tohoku-earthquake/.

18. Dambisa Moyo, *Dead Aid: Why Aid Is Not Working and How There Is a Better Way for Africa* (New York: Farrar, Straus Giroux, 2009); William Easterly, *The White Man's Burden: Why the West's Efforts to Aid the Rest Have Done So Much Ill and So Little Good* (New York: Oxford University Press, 2006).

CHAPTER 5. MALEVOLENCE BY NEGLECT IN MYANMAR

1. CIA, *The World Factbook: Myanmar,* March 11, 2015, https://www.cia.gov/library/publications/the-world-factbook/geos/bm.html.

2. T. T. Win, "Composition of the Different Ethnic Groups under the 8 Major National Ethnic Races in Myanmar," 2008, http://www.embassyofmyanmar.be/ABOUT/ethnicgroups.htm.

3. CIA, *World Factbook: Myanmar.*

4. Emma Larkin, *Everything Is Broken: A Tale of Catastrophe in Burma* (New York: Penguin Books, 2010).

5. Win, "Composition of the Different Ethnic Groups."

6. For instance, Kallie Szczepanski, "The 8888 Uprising in Myanmar (Burma)," March 2015, http://asianhistory.about.com/od/burmamyanmar/fl/The-8888-Uprising-in-Myanmar-Myanmar.htm.

7. Barbara Crossette, "Burma's Eroding Isolation," *New York Times,* November 24, 1985, http://www.nytimes.com/1985/11/24/magazine/burma-s-eroding-isolation.html.

8. Arakan Oil Watch "Burma's Resource Curse: The Case for Revenue Transparency in the Oil and Gas Sector," March 2012, http://www.burmalibrary.org/docs13/Burmas_Resource_Curse%28en%29-red.pdf.

9. The resource curse occurs as a country begins to focus all of its energies on an extractive industry, such as mining or oil. The nation becomes overly dependent on the price of that commodity, exchange rates become tied to commodity prices and other exports such as agriculture suffer. "Resource Curse," *Investopedia,* n.d., http://www.investopedia.com/terms/r/resource-curse.asp#ixzz3X1ITJ4bF.

10. National Oceanic and Atmospheric Administration, National Weather Service, "Saffir-Simpson Hurricane Wind Scale," May 24, 2013, http://www.nhc.noaa.gov/aboutsshws.php.

11. For estimated death toll, see International Federation of Red Cross and Red Crescent Societies, "Myanmar: Cyclone Nargis 2008 Facts and Figures," May 3, 2011, http://www.ifrc.org/en/news-and-media/news-stories/asia-pacific/myanmar/myanmar-cyclone-nargis-2008-facts-and-figures/#sthash.3vTxw4sW.dpuf: 8.

12. Swiss Reinsurance Company, *Natural Catastrophes and Man-Made Disasters in 2008: North America and Asia Suffer Heavy Losses* (Zurich: Swiss Reinsurance Company, 2009).

13. National Disaster Risk Reduction and Management Council, "NDRRMC Update: Updates re the Effects of Typhoon 'Yolanda' (Haiyan)," April 17, 2014, https://web.archive.org/web/20141006091212/http://www.ndr rmc.gov.ph/attachments/article/1177/Update%20Effects%20TY%20 YOLANDA%2017%20April%202014.pdf.

14. Michael Casey, "Cyclone Nargis Had All the Makings of a Perfect Storm," *Washington Post,* May 8, 2008, http://www.washingtonpost.com /wp-dyn/content/article/2008/05/08/AR2008050801931_pf.html.

15. Larkin, *Everything Is Broken.*

16. Thomas Fuller, "A Most Unlikely Liberator in Myanmar," *New York Times,* March 14, 2012, http://www.nytimes.com/2012/03/15/world/asia /a-most-unlikely-liberator-in-myanmar.html.

17. "Myanmar—Defense Spending," GlobalSecurity.org, February 1, 2015, http://www.globalsecurity.org/military/world/myanmar/budget.htm.

18. Peter G. Peterson Foundation, "The U.S. Spends More on Defense Than the Next Eight Countries Combined," April 13, 2014, http://pgpf.org /Chart-Archive/0053_defense-comparison.

19. Andrew Selth, "Even Paranoids Have Enemies: Cyclone Nargis and Myanmar's Fears of Invasion," *Contemporary Southeast Asia* 30, no. 3 (2008): 379–402.

20. Gareth Evans, "Facing Up to Our Responsibilities," International Crisis Group, May 12, 2008, http://www.crisisgroup.org/en/regions/asia/south -east-asia/myanmar/evans-facing-up-to-our-responsibilities.aspx.

21. Kevin Woods, "A Political Anatomy of Land Grabs," *Myanmar Times,* March 3, 2014, http://www.mmtimes.com/index.php/national-news/97 40-a-political-anatomy-of-land-grabs.html.

22. "Eminent Domain," Cornell University Law School, Legal Information Institute, March 12, 2015, https://www.law.cornell.edu/wex/eminent _domain.

CHAPTER 6. STRUCK DUMB IN NEW ORLEANS

1. "Louisiana, Worldmark Encyclopedia of the States," Encyclopedia.com, 2007; http://www.encyclopedia.com/doc/1G2-2661700031.html.

2. Daniel H. Weinberg, "U.S. Neighborhood Income Inequality in the 2005–2009 Period," *American Community Survey Reports,* Census Bureau, US Department of Commerce, Washington, DC, October 2011, 12, http://www.census.gov/prod/2011pubs/acs-16.pdf.

3. Sarah Burd-Sharps, Kristen Lewis, and Eduardo B. Martins, *A Portrait of Louisiana. Louisiana Human Development Report 2009,* American Human Development Project of the Social Science Research Council, 2009, http://ssrc-static.s3.amazonaws.com/moa/A_Portrait_of_Louisiana.pdf.

4. Ibid.

5. Alan Berube and Bruce Katz, "Katrina's Window: Confronting Concentrated Poverty Across America" *Brookings,* October 2005, http://www .brookings.edu/research/reports/2005/10/poverty-berube.

6. Kris Macomber, Sarah E. Rusche, and Delmar Wright, "After the Levees Broke: Reaction of College Students to the Aftermeth of Hurricane Katrina," in David L. Brunsma, David Overfelt, and J. Stephen Picou, *The Sociology of Katrina: Perspectives on a Modern Catastrophe* (Lanham, MD: Rowman and Littlefield, 2010), 166.

7. Edward L. Glaeser and Raven E. Saks, "Corruption in America," *Journal of Public Economics* 90 (2006): 1053–72.

8. "Ex-New Orleans Mayor Ray Nagin Gets 10 Years in Prison," CNN, July 9, 2014, http://www.cnn.com/2014/07/09/justice/ray-nagin-sentencing/.

9. Arianna Huffington, "The Flyover Presidency of George W. Bush," *Huffington Post,* May 25, 2011, http://www.huffingtonpost.com/arianna -huffington/the-flyover-presidency-of_b_6566.html.

10. Stephen C. Webster, "Bush's Disgraced FEMA Director Stunned at Sandy Response: 'Why Was This So Quick?'" *Raw Story,* October 30, 2012, http://www.rawstory.com/rs/2012/10/bushs-disgraced-fema-direc tor-stunned-at-sandy-response-why-was-this-so-quick/.

11. Michael D. Brown and Ted Schwarz, *Deadly Indifference: The Perfect (Political) Storm: Hurricane Katrina, the Bush White House, and Beyond* (Plymouth, MA: Taylor Trade, 2011).

12. Richard D. Knabb, Jamie R. Rhome, and Daniel P. Brown, "Tropical Cyclone Report: Hurricane Katrina," National Oceanic and Atmospheric Administration (NOAA) National Hurricane Center, 2005, http://www .nhc.noaa.gov/pdf/TCR-AL122005_Katrina.pdf.

13. Eric S. Blake, Todd B. Kimberlain, Robert J. Berg, John P. Cangialosi, and John L. Beven II, "Tropical Cyclone Report Hurricane Sandy (AL182012) 22–29 October 2012," NOAA National Hurricane Center, http://www.nhc.noaa.gov/data/tcr/AL182012_Sandy.pdf.

14. Erik Larson, *Isaac's Storm: A Man, a Time, and the Deadliest Hurricane in History* (New York: Crown, 2000).

15. David L. Johnson, "Service Assessment: Hurricane Katrina August 23–31, 2005," NOAA, National Weather Service, 2006, http://www.nws .noaa.gov/om/assessments/pdfs/Katrina.pdf.

16. Isaac M. Cline, "Special Report on the Galveston Hurricane of September 8, 1900," NOAA History, February 4, 2004, http://www.history .noaa.gov/stories_tales/cline2.html.

17. Julian Gavaghan, "On This Day: Hurricane Betsy Kills 76 in New Orleans in Deadliest Storm Before Katrina," September 24, 2013, https:// uk.news.yahoo.com/on-this-day—hurricane-betsy-kills-76-in-new-orle ans-in-deadliest-storm-before-katrina-152855522.html.

18. Elliot Aronson, "Fear, Denial, and Sensible Action in the Face of Disasters," *Social Research* 75, no. 3 (2008): 855–72.

19. Eric Lipton, "White House Knew of Levee's Failure on Night of Storm," *New York Times,* February 10, 2006, http://www.nytimes.com /2006/02/10/politics/10katrina.html?pagewanted=all&_r=0.

20. Keren Fraiman, Austin Long, and Caitlin Talmadge, "Why the Iraqi Army Collapsed (and What Can Be Done about It)," *Washington Post,* June 13, 2014, http://www.washingtonpost.com/blogs/monkey-cage/wp /2014/06/13/why-the-iraqi-army-collapsed-and-what-can-be-done-abo ut-it/.

21. Brown and Schwarz, *Deadly Indifference.*

22. Kevin Drum, "Bush and Katrina," *Political Animal* (blog), *Washington Monthly,* September 1, 2005, http://www.washingtonmonthly.com/arch ives/individual/2005_09/007023.php.

23. Ken Silverstein, "Top FEMA Jobs: No Experience Required," *Los Angeles Times,* September 9, 2005, http://articles.latimes.com/2005/sep/09 /nation/na-fema9.

24. Scott Price, "The Coast Guard's Katrina Documentation Project," *The U.S. Coast Guard & Hurricane Katrina,* November 17, 2014, http://www .uscg.mil/history/katrina/docs/karthistory.asp. Originally published in *The Federalist: Newsletter for the Society for History in the Federal Government,* 2nd series, no. 12 (Winter 2006-2007): 1, 3-5.

25. Kathleen B. Blanco, "Taskforce Pelican," September 30, 2005, http:// www.blancogovernor.com/index.cfm?md=newsroom&tmp=detail&cat ID=1&articleID=532&navID=3&printer=1.

26. Douglas Brinkley, *The Great Deluge: Hurricane Katrina, New Orleans, and the Mississippi Gulf Coast* (New York: Harper Perennial, 2007); Jed Horne, *Breach of Faith: Hurricane Katrina and the Near Death of a Great American City* (New York: Random House, 2006).

27. Thomas E. Nelson, Zoe M. Oxley, and Rosalee A. Clawson, "Toward a Psychology of Framing Effects," *Political Behavior* 19, no. 3 (1997): 221–246.

28. Susan Sontag, "The Imagination of Disaster," *Commentary* (October 1965), https://www.commentarymagazine.com/article/the-imagination -of-disaster/; see also https://americanfuturesiup.files.wordpress.com/20 13/01/sontag-the-imagination-of-disaster.pdf.

29. E. L. Quarantelli, "Conventional Beliefs and Counterintuitive Realities," *Social Research: An International Quarterly of the Social Sciences* 75, no. 3 (2008): 873–904, http://dspace.udel.edu/bitstream/handle/19716/4242 /Article%20450%20for%20DSpace.pdf?sequence=1.

30. Ibid.

31. Kathleen Tierney, Christine Bevc, and Erica Kuligowski, "Metaphors Matter: Disaster Myths, Media Frames, and Their Consequences in Hurricane Katrina," *Annals of the American Academy of Political and Social Science* 604, no. 1 (2006): 57–81.

32. Guy Gugliotta and Peter Whoriskey, "Floods Ravage New Orleans; Two Levees Give Way," *Washington Post,* August 31, 2005, http://truth-out .org/archive/component/k2/item/56907:floods-ravage-new-orleans.

33. Kevin McGill, "Officials Throw Up Hands as Looters Ransack City," *San Diego Union-Tribune,* August 31, 2005, http://legacy.utsandiego.com /news/nation/20050831-0839-katrina-looting.html.

34. Robert McFadden and Ralph Blumenthal, "Higher Death Toll Seen; Police Ordered to Stop Looters," *New York Times,* September 1, 2005, http:// www.nytimes.com/2005/09/01/national/nationalspecial/01storm.html ?pagewanted=print&_r=0.

35. Sam Coates and Dan Eggen, "In New Orleans, a Desperate Exodus," *Washington Post,* September 1, 2005, http://www.washingtonpost.com /wp-dyn/content/article/2005/08/31/AR2005083101804.html.

36. Joseph B. Treaster and Deborah Sontag, "Local Officials Criticize Federal Government over Response," *New York Times,* September 2, 2005, http:// www.nytimes.com/2005/09/02/national/nationalspecial/02storm.html ?pagewanted=all.

37. Maureen Dowd, "United States of Shame," *New York Times,* September 3, 2005, http://www.nytimes.com/2005/09/03/opinion/03dowd.html.

38. Anderson Cooper et al., "New Orleans Shelters to Be Evacuated. Floodwaters Rising, Devastation Widespread in Katrina's Wake," CNN, August 31, 2005, http://www.cnn.com/2005/WEATHER/08/30/katrina /index.html?PHPSESSID=80205969dd4db592b10a3c325fb0e01c.

39. Lisa G. Sun, "Disaster Mythology and the Law," *Cornell Law Review* 96, no. 5 (2011): 1132.

40. The stadium had been used twice before—in 1998 and 2004—as a "refuge of last resort" so that people who had been flooded out of their homes knew to seek shelter in the stadium, where they expected food and drink to be supplied as in the past.

41. Jim Dwyver and Christopher Drew, "Fear Exceeded Crime's Reality in New Orleans," *New York Times,* September 29, 2005, http://www.ny times.com/2005/09/29/national/nationalspecial/29crime.html?adxnnl =1&fta=y&pagewanted=1&adxnnlx=1406477443-FbnkdjkU0QyYWci0LqBcpA; Astra Taylor, "Rebecca Solnit by Astra Taylor," *BOMB* (Fall 2009), http://bombmagazine.org/article/3327/rebecca-solnit.

42. Brian Thevenot, "Reports of Anarchy at Superdome Overstated," *Seattle Times,* September 26, 2005, http://www.seattletimes.com/nation-world /reports-of-anarchy-at-superdome-overstated/.

43. Lee Clarke and Caron Chess, "Elites and Panic: More to Fear Than Fear Itself," *Social Forces* 87, no. 2 (2008): 993–1014.

44. Rebecca Solnit, *A Paradise Built in Hell: The Extraordinary Communities That Arise in Disaster* (New York: Penguin Books, 2009). Taylor, "Rebecca Solnit by Astra Taylor."

45. Michael E. Dyson, *Come Hell or High Water: Hurricane Katrina and the Color of Disaster* (New York: Basic Civitas, 2005).

46. Van Jones, "Black People 'Loot' Food . . . White People 'Find' Food," *Huffington Post,* May 25, 2011, http://www.huffingtonpost.com/van -jones/black-people-loot-food-wh_b_6614.html.

47. Webster Commission, *The City in Crisis: A Report by the Special Advisor to the Board of Police Commissioners on the Civil Disorder in Los Angeles,* UCLA, Institute for Government and Public Affairs, 1992.

48. Federal Emergency Management Agency, *Report of the Joint Fire/Police Task Force on Civil Unrest,* February 1994, http://www.usfa.fema.gov /downloads/pdf/publications/fa-142.pdf.

49. "New Orleans Rocked by Huge Blasts," BBC, September 2, 2005, http:// news.bbc.co.uk/2/hi/americas/4207202.stm.

50. Philip L. Fradkin, *The Great Earthquake and Firestorms of 1906: How San Francisco Nearly Destroyed Itself* (Berkeley: University of California Press, 2006).

51. A. C. Thompson, "Katrina's Hidden Race War," *The Nation,* December 17, 2008, http://www.thenation.com/article/katrinas-hidden-race-war.

52. Mai Denawa, "Behind the Accounts of the Great Kanto Earthquake of 1923," Brown University Library Center for Digital Scholarship, 2005, http://library.brown.edu/cds/kanto/denewa.html

53. Robert Neff, "The Great Kanto Earthquake Massacre," *Ohmy News,* September 29, 2006, http://english.ohmynews.com/articleview/article_view .asp?at_code=363496.

CHAPTER 7. REBUILDING AS SOCIAL ENGINEERING

1. Mai Denawa, "Behind the Accounts of the Great Kanto Earthquake of 1923," Brown University Library Center for Digital Scholarship, 2005, http://library.brown.edu/cds/kanto/denewa.html; Joshua Hammer, "The Great Japan Earthquake of 1923," *Smithsonian Magazine* (May 2011), http://www.smithsonianmag.com/history/the-great-japan-earthquake -of-1923-1764539/?no-ist; US Geological Survey, "Earthquakes with 1,000 or More Deaths 1900–2014," USGS Earthquakes Hazard Program, February 19, 2015, http://earthquake.usgs.gov/earthquakes/world /world_deaths.php.

2. C. D. James, "The 1923 Tokyo Earthquake and Fire," 2002, http://nisee .berkeley.edu/kanto/tokyo1923.pdf.

3. J. Charles Schencking, *The Great Kanto Earthquake and the Chimera of National Reconstruction in Japan* (New York: Columbia University Press, 2013).

4. Kevin Rozario, *The Culture of Calamity: Disaster and the Making of Modern America* (Chicago: University of Chicago Press, 2007).

5. John R. Logan, "The Impact of Katrina: Race and Class in Storm-Damaged Neighborhoods," Brown University, 2006, http://www.s4.brown .edu/katrina/report.pdf.

6. Gary Rivlin, "A Mogul Who Would Rebuild New Orleans," *New York Times,* September 29, 2005, http://www.nytimes.com/2005/09/29/busi ness/29mogul.html?pagewanted=all&_r=0.

7. John Harwood, "Louisiana Lawmakers Aim to Cope with Political Fallout," *Wall Street Journal,* September 9, 2005, http://www.wsj.com/art icles/SB112622923108136137.

8. Charles Babington, "Some GOP Legislators Hit Jarring Notes in Addressing Katrina," *Washington Post*, September 10, 2005, http://www.washingtonpost.com/wp-dyn/content/article/2005/09/09/AR2005090901930.html.

9. Mike Davis, "Gentrifying Disaster," *Mother Jones*, October 25, 2005, http://www.motherjones.com/politics/2005/10/gentrifying-disaster.

10. Lori Rodriguez and Zeke Minaya, "HUD Chief Doubts New Orleans Will Be As Black," *Houston Chronicle*, September 29, 2005, http://www.chron.com/news/hurricanes/article/HUD-chief-doubts-New-Orleans-will-be-as-black-1919882.php.

11. Babington, "Some GOP Legislators Hit Jarring Notes in Addressing Katrina."

12. Cathy Young, "Everything You Knew about Hurricane Katrina Was Wrong," *Y-Files* (blog), January 6, 2006, http://cathyyoung.blogspot.com/2006/01/everything-you-knew-about-hurricane.html.

13. Patrick Sharkey, "Survival and Death in New Orleans: An Empirical Look at the Human Impact of Katrina," *Journal of Black Studies* 37, no. 4 (2007): 482–501, http://jbs.sagepub.com/content/37/4/482. See also Patrick Sharkey, *Were Whites Really More Likely to Die in Katrina? A Reanalysis of Data on Race and the Casualties of Katrina* (Cambridge, MA: New Vision, 2006).

14. Gary Rivlin, "Anger Meets New Orleans Renewal Plan," *New York Times*, January 12, 2006, http://www.nytimes.com/2006/01/12/national/nationalspecial/12plan.html.

15. Davis, "Gentrifying Disaster."

16. Ben Margot, "Plans to Rebuild New Orleans Spark Controversy," *USA Today*, January 11, 2006, http://usatoday30.usatoday.com/news/nation/2006-01-11-neworleansrebuilding_x.htm.

17. "Geology of National Parks, 3D and Photographic Tours: Breezy Point (Gateway National Recreation Area)," US Geological Survey, January 20, 2015, http://3dparks.wr.usgs.gov/nyc/parks/loc69.htm.

18. Narayan Sastry and Jesse Gregory, *Spatial Dislocation and Return Migration Among New Orleans Residents After Hurricane Katrina* (Ann Arbor, MI: University of Michigan Institute for Social Research, 2009), http://paa2010.princeton.edu/papers/101643.

19. Naomi Klein, *The Shock Doctrine: The Rise of Disaster Capitalism* (New York: Metropolitan Books, 2007).

20. Peter T. Leeson, and Russell S. Sobel, "Weathering Corruption," *Journal of Law and Economics* 51 (2008): 667–81.

21. Allison Plyer, Elaine Ortiz, Ben Horwitz, and George Hobor, *The New Orleans Index at Eight: Measuring Greater New Orleans' Progress toward Prosperity* (New Orleans: Greater New Orleans Community Data Center, 2013).

22. Haeyoun Park and Archie Tse, "Mapping the Recovery of New Orleans," *New York Times*, August 27, 2010, http://www.nytimes.com/interactive/2010/08/27/us/20100827-katrina-resettlement.html?_r=0.

23. Plyer et al., *New Orleans Index at Eight*.

24. Logan, "Impact of Katrina."

25. Michelle Krupa, "New Orleans' Official 2010 Census Population Is 343,829, Agency Reports," *Times Picayune*, February 3, 2011, http://www.nola.com/politics/index.ssf/2011/02/new_orleans_officials_2010_pop.html.

26. Elizabeth Fussell, Katherine J. Curtis, and Jack DeWaard, "Recovery Migration to the City of New Orleans after Hurricane Katrina: A Migration Systems Approach," *Population and Environment* 35, no. 3 (2014): 305–22.

27. Logan, "Impact of Katrina."

28. Lyndsey Layton, "In New Orleans, Major School District Closes Traditional Public Schools for Good," *Washington Post*, May 28, 2014, http://www.washingtonpost.com/local/education/in-new-orleans-traditional-public-schools-close-for-good/2014/05/28/ae4f5724-e5de-11e3-8f90-73e071f3d637_story.html.

29. Danielle Dreilinger, "John White: New Orleans Charter Civil Rights Complaint 'a Joke,'" *Times Picayune*, May 15, 2014, http://www.nola.com/education/index.ssf/2014/05/john_white_new_orleans_charter.html.

30. Plyer et al., *New Orleans Index at Eight*.

31. Ibid.

32. Ibid.

33. Richard Campanella, "Gentrification and Its Discontents: Notes from New Orleans," *NewGeography*, 2013, http://www.newgeography.com/content/003526-gentrification-and-its-discontents-notes-new-orleans.

34. Alberto Amore, "Regeneration from the Rubble. Culture and Creative Urban Renewal in Post-Earthquake Christchurch, New Zealand," n.d., Academia.edu, http://www.academia.edu/9057248/Regeneration_from_the_rubble._Culture_and_creative_urban_renewal_in_post-earthquake_Christchurch_New_Zealand.

35. Michelle W. Anderson, "The New Minimal Cities," *Yale Law Journal* 123, no. 5 (2014): 1118–1227.

36. Ben Austen, "The Post-Post-Apocalyptic Detroit," *New York Times*, July 11, 2014, http://www.nytimes.com/2014/07/13/magazine/the-post-post-apocalyptic-detroit.html.

37. Monica Davey, "A Private Boom amid Detroit's Public Blight," *New York Times*, March 14, 2013, http://www.nytimes.com/2013/03/05/us/a-private-boom-amid-detroits-public-blight.html.

38. T. S. Bernard, "Rebuilding After Sandy, but with Costly New Rules," *New York Times*, May 10, 2013, http://www.nytimes.com/2013/05/11/your-money/after-hurricane-sandy-rebuilding-under-higher-flood-insurance.html.

39. Definition from *Merriam-Webster*, http://www.merriam-webster.com/dictionary/profit.

CHAPTER 8. DISASTERS AS CASUS BELLI

1. Aaron Morrison, "Ferguson Police Racism Report: Full Text of Justice Department Probe after Michael Brown's Death," *International Business Times,* March 4, 2015, http://www.ibtimes.com/ferguson-police-racism-report-full-text-justice-department-probe-after-michael-browns-1835944.

2. Radley Balko, *Rise of the Warrior Cop: The Militarization of America's Police Forces* (New York: Public Affairs, 2013). See also "Radley Balko on the Militarization of America's Police Force," *Vice,* http://www.vice.com/video/radley-balko-on-the-militarization-of-americas-police-force. This equipment has comes from two sources: one is money in large amounts provided to local municipalities in the wake of 9/11, to be used to strengthen their ability to fight terrorism; the second is from the Obama administration, direct supply of equipment to the military.

3. Matt Apuzo, "War Gear Flows To Police Departments," *New York Times,* June 8, 2014, http://www.nytimes.com/2014/06/09/us/war-gear-flows-to-police-departments.html?_r=1.

4. Susan Sontag, "The Imagination of Disaster," *Commentary Magazine,* August 1965, https://www.commentarymagazine.com/article/the-imagination-of-disaster/; see also https://americanfuturesiup.files.wordpress.com/2013/01/sontag-the-imagination-of-disaster.pdf.

5. "Jury Convicts Blackwater Guards in 2007 Killings of Iraqi Civilians," *Guardian,* October 22, 2014, http://www.theguardian.com/us-news/2014/oct/22/us-jury-convicts-blackwater-security-guards-iraq.

6. Thomas Piketty, *Capital in the Twenty-First Century,* trans. Arthur Goldhammer (Cambridge, MA: Belknap Press, 2014).

7. Jim Salter and Jim Suhr, Associated Press, "Ferguson Election Triples Number of Blacks on City Council," *U.S. News & World Report,* April 8, 2015, http://www.usnews.com/news/us/articles/2015/04/07/ferguson-voters-go-to-polls-to-elect-3-to-council-members.

TECHNICAL APPENDIX I: SIMPLIFIED SOCIOECONOMICS OF NATURAL DISASTER SHOCKS AND THEIR CONSEQUENCES

1. All illustrations of this style are the author's original drawings.

2. Binyamin Appelbaum, "U.S. Economic Recovery Looks Distant as Growth Stalls," *New York Times,* June 11, 2014, http://www.nytimes.com/2014/06/12/business/economy/us-economic-recovery-looks-distant-as-growth-lingers.html.

3. The area is $L(T_i-T_e)/2$, where i is either 1 or 2. T_e can be made zero without loss of generality; then it is clear that the lower area is greater than the upper.

4. Jeremy Ashkenas and Alicia Parlapiano, "How the Recession Reshaped the Economy in 255 Charts," *New York Times,* June 6, 2014, http://

www.nytimes.com/interactive/2014/06/05/upshot/how-the-recession
-reshaped-the-economy-in-255-charts.html?_r=0.

5. This figure and the previous are similar to those presented by Stéphane
    Hallegate and Michael Ghil, "Natural Disasters Impacting a Macroeco-
    nomic Model with Endogenous Dynamics," *Ecological Economics* 68, nos.
    1–2 (2008): 582–92. Their work provided significant inspiration for the
    discussion in this section.

TECHNICAL APPENDIX II: DISASTERS IN NEOCLASSICAL GROWTH THEORY

1. Robert M. Solow, "A Contribution to the Theory of Economic Growth,"
    Quarterly Journal of Economics 70, no. 1 (1956): 65–94; doi:10.2307/188
    4513; Trevor W. Swan, "Economic Growth and Capital Accumulation,"
    Economic Record 32, no. 2 (1956): 334–361, doi:10.1111/j.1475-4932.1956.
    tb00434.x. Robert M. Solow, "Technical Change and the Aggregate
    Production Function," *Review of Economics and Statistics* 39, no. 3 (1957):
    312–320, doi:10.2307/1926047.
2. According to the *Encyclopaedia Britannica,* in economics, the production
    function is an equation that expresses the relationship between the quan-
    tities of productive factors (such as labor and capital) used and the amount
    of product obtained. It states the amount of product that can be obtained
    from every combination of factors, assuming that the most efficient avail-
    able methods of production are used.
3. Costas Azariadis and John Stachurski, "Poverty Traps," in *Handbook of
    Economic Growth,* Philippe Aghion & Steven Durlauf, eds. (ed. 1, vol. 1,
    no. 1, Elsevier, 2005), 326. The Wikipedia entry under "Poverty Traps" is
    useful and refers to Sachs's work. Also see Abhijit V. Banerjee and Ester
    Duflo, *Poor Economics: A Radical Rethinking of the Way to Fight Global Pov-
    erty* (New York: Public Affairs/Perseus Book Group, 2011).
4. Stéphane Hallegatte and Michael Ghil, "Natural Disasters Impacting a
    Macroeconomic Model with Endogenous Dynamics," *Ecological Econom-
    ics* 68 (2008): 582–92, doi:10.1016/j.ecolecon.2008.05.022.

INDEX